LEGENDARY LOCALS

OF

GREER
SOUTH CAROLINA

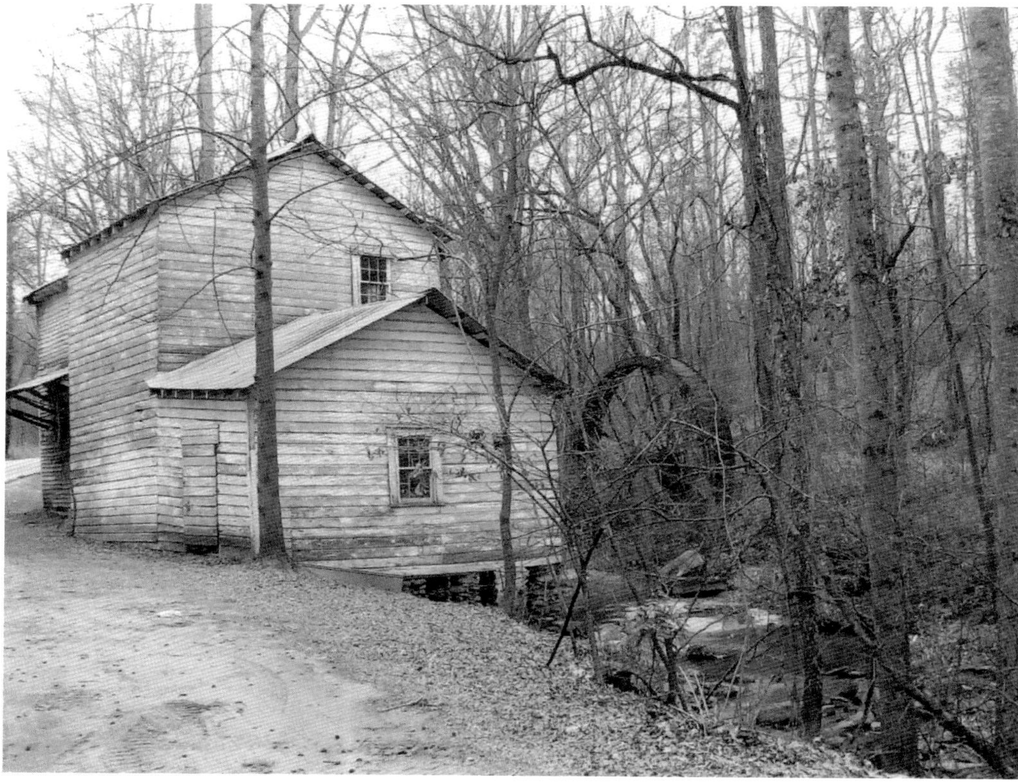

Page 1: Trade Street
Trade Street is the heart of Greer's historic district. (Courtesy of Greer Heritage Museum.)

Page 2: Gilreath Mill
P.D. Gilreath, high sheriff of Greenville County, owned and operated the gristmill. (Photograph by Ray Belcher.

LEGENDARY LOCALS

OF

GREER

SOUTH CAROLINA

RAY BELCHER AND JOADA P. HIATT

LEGENDARY LOCALS

ISBN 978-1-4671-0022-9

Published by Legendary Locals, an imprint of Arcadia Publishing
Charleston, South Carolina

Printed in the United States of America

Library of Congress Control Number: 2012930628

For all general information, please contact Arcadia Publishing:
Telephone 843-853-2070
Fax 843-853-0044
E-mail sales@arcadiapublishing.com
For customer service and orders:
Toll-Free 1-888-313-2665

Visit us on the Internet at www.arcadiapublishing.com

Dedication

For my family
—Ray

For my favorite local legend, Alan
—Joada

On the Cover: From left to right:
(TOP ROW) P.D. Gilreath, high sheriff of Greenville County (Courtesy of Carl Gibson; p. 15), J.W. Gregory, businessman (Courtesy of Martha and J.W. Gregory; p. 56), William Jordan, musician (Courtesy of William Jordan; p. 125), Phil Clark, Greer High School coach (Courtesy of Lynn D. Clark; p. 93), Central School teachers: from top Maggie Garlington, Leila Cunningham, Bess Owings, Lura Langston (Courtesy of Greer Heritage Museum; p. 75).
(MIDDLE ROW) Sam and Odell Davis, outdoorsmen (Courtesy of Tom Davis; p. 25), Victor Wildcats (left to right) Bobby Lemmons, Butch Miller, Bobby Spearman, Don Godfrey, Jimmy Jackson, Jack Gorman, and Millard Leonhardt (Courtesy of Butch Miller; p. 89), Callie and Alvin Berry (Courtesy of Carl Gibson; p. 113), John Good, handyman (Courtesy of Don Robinson; p. 34), D.D. Davenport, businessman, and wife Martha (Courtesy of Denby Davenport; p. 15).
(BOTTOM ROW) Massalena Durham, bride (Courtesy of Margaret Hill; p. 120), David Sheppard, Greer High School band director, second from left in picture (Courtesy of David Sheppard Jr.; p. 83), B.L. Fricke, principal of Greer High School (Courtesy of Greer Heritage Museum; p. 79), Leland Burch, former editor and owner of the *Greer Citizen* (Courtesy of Leland and Margaret Burch; p. 55), the Reverend Clinton Cox, minister (Courtesy of Nellie Williams; p. 75).

CONTENTS

ACKNOWLEDGMENTS

The authors wish to thank the many people in Greer who so kindly shared their pictures. They realize that asking people to search through family albums, trunks, and drawers to find these treasures was time-consuming. They also wish to thank all those who helped to identify subjects in the old pictures. The authors acknowledge that mistakes may have been made because of the large number of images.

These are the people who shared pictures: Carole Smith Olmert, Ann Dillard Withrow, Lem Dillard, Sonny Rhem, James Paget, Truman Henderson, Karl Beason, Leland and Margaret Burch, Bobby Howard, Ken Mullins, Carolinda Robison, Frankie Boling, Carey and Sue Werner, Martha and Doug Gregory, Nellie Williams, Margaret and James Hill, Don Wall, the Hughes family, David Duncan, Anne Dobson, Ellen Henson, Mary Greer, Richard and Karolyn Taylor, William and Rose Marie Jordan, David Sheppard Jr., Milda Walkley, Susan Walkley Topper, Don Robinson, Janie Cloninger, Dr. and Mrs. T.O. Walker, John Rollins Jr., Terry Dobson, Katherine Johnson, the King family, Azalea Garden Club, Tom and Chris Davis, Dr. Thomas McAbee, Carl Gibson, Jay Gibson, Denby Davenport, Allen Cullum, Nancy Welch, Susan Hiatt Maybin, Butch Miller, Lynn D. Clark, Wayne Farmer, Mary Ponder Vickery, Judy Ponder, Rosemary Bomar, Clint "Pepper" Greene Jr., Elaine Stokes Bishop, Bernard Price, Ruth Duckett, Dick Wood, Steve Owens, Allen Collins, F.E. Hendrix, Jody Carman, the Belcher family, Lou Herman, the Carman family, and the Pennington family.

Special thanks go to the Greer Heritage Museum and the City of Greer for sharing their archives.

Finally, the authors acknowledge the photographers known and unknown who captured moments in Greer. Known historical photographers are Charles Drace and the Solesbee Studio. The *Greer Citizen* photographers, especially Leland, Eddie, and Preston Burch, merit recognition for photographing the community. The authors appreciate Joe F. Jordan Photography for permitting the reprint of Joe Jordan's photographs.

In the search for images, the authors found many interesting pictures but could not use them all. There are many legends in Greer—all as important to the fabric of this community as the ones represented here.

INTRODUCTION

Greer, South Carolina, incorporated in 1876, began as the dream of Greenville investor William Shumate, who bought a fragment of the old Hugh Bailey cotton plantation that lay near the survey for a rail line between the county seats of Greenville and Spartanburg. Although Shumate may have envisioned masses flocking to the cheap residential and commercial lots into which his property had been subdivided, sales languished, in part, because of a general recession that had begun three years earlier.

Eventually, by the early 1880s, cotton buyers like the Burgess Brothers, Chaney Littlefield, and D.D. Davenport had begun to set up tiny offices near the depot during the autumn, and area farmers were attracted by the prices offered, which were often from a fraction of a cent to a cent above those offered by buyers in larger towns.

The cotton market enabled Greer to experience a lackluster but dependable growth for the next two decades, and virtually every storekeeper was active in the cotton trade. It was the cotton profit rather than the mercantile trade that fueled local prosperity. Every farmer had a cotton patch; those who had grown mostly grains, like William D. Ballenger, Cunningham Pennington, and Will Hudson, bought guano and planted cotton to take advantage of the local market.

An abundance of cotton meant declining prices. But cheap cotton created a new class of investors, post–Civil War merchants like David and Noah Cannon, William A. Hill, and others who prospered in the falling market. Following the logic of Henry W. Grady, the Atlanta journalist who maintained that the South's only hope after the Civil War was to rebuild on the foundations of industry, many locals began talking about bringing cotton manufacturing to Greer. It made sense to manufacture the goods where the raw materials were available and save the costs of drayage, storage, and insurance. In 1894, Henry V. Westmoreland, William Wesley Burgess, and John Robinson organized a movement to promote a modern mill for Greer. The idea caught on.

By 1910, Greer's capitalists had constructed their fourth area mill, bringing hundreds of new faces into the villages positioned just outside the town limits. Victor Manufacturing was the largest of the mills and the earliest; Franklin, the smallest operation, was constructed in 1900. Apalache, also located in Spartanburg County, was rebuilt on the site of Cedar Hill Factory, one of the small mills that had manufactured various textile products for some 80 years. Greer Manufacturing Company rounded out the textile industry in Greer and achieved full production on the eve of the First World War. By the end of the war, all except Franklin had been sold to the Victor-Monaghan Corporation and placed under the leadership of Greer native C. Rhett Ballenger.

With the influx of new business, the town thrived and expanded. Despite the boll weevil and the perennial industrial issue of overproduction of some classes of cotton goods, Greer's mill men avoided many of the industry's pitfalls by keeping informed of the latest technology, equipping the mills with the most efficient machines, and diversifying their production.

The commercial center along Trade and Poinsett Streets enjoyed booming business for much of the 20th century. The streets were alive with a variety of shops and stores. Gone were the dozen general stores that had supplied everything Greer residents needed during the town's first quarter century. In their place were millinery, shoe, and candy shops; bakeries; jewelers; butchers; grocery stores; and automobile dealerships. J.C. Cunningham established C & D Chevrolet, which became Paget Chevrolet and operated continuously for over a half century. Many professionals like doctors, dentists, lawyers, and of course, cotton brokers opened offices to meet public demand for services. Dr. Viola Kirkwood became the town's first female optometrist. Early doctors included Henry V. Westmoreland, Robert Marchant, and T.O. Walker. As long as the cotton textile business thrived, so did the commercial center of Greer.

Many of Greer's long-thriving businesses have been family operated. The Wood Mortuary dates its service to 1902 and has been managed by three generations of the Wood family beginning with the founder, John D. Wood. The Henderson family operated three stores at various times, operated by Charlie, Truman, and Troy.

Greer's community-wide commitment to providing education for its children has been an important factor in its success. Greer was four years old when the first board of education met. The board of education raised the funds for construction of a school, which was completed in March 1881. The graded school unified Greer. Greer High School was opened by November 1881 by Prof. Joseph W. Kennedy. It brought together citizens for performances, recitations, and town meetings. Under Professor Kennedy's guidance, the local school offered a public education commensurate in quality with that offered by any other municipality in the state as well as a private term for paying students. Products of Greer's schools were readily accepted by colleges and significant numbers of college-prepared young adults were returning to their hometown by 1900 to work in the growing business and professional community.

Greer's history was not all smooth sailing. Like all new towns, it experienced some growing pains. Nor was Greer spared its share of social ills. Diphtheria and smallpox epidemics in the area demonstrated the need for addressing public health. Several large fires miraculously contained by bucket brigades suggested more had to be done. Water and sewer lines were in place by the beginning of World War I. A volunteer fire department headed by Bill Pennington was established and by the end of the war, a continuing Board of Health was appointed with Dr. T.O. Walker serving as the chairman. Throughout its history, Greer's citizens have risen to meet the problems brought by growth and expansion.

Though the general crime rate in Greer remained low in the first few decades of its history, whiskey-related crime was a problem from Greer's earliest days. Try as they did, temperance and prohibition organizations made little headway in terms of a "persuasive" solution to the problem. A town astraddle the county line, Greer was a haven for bootleggers and a market for moonshiners for decades until law enforcement gained the upper hand by 1940. Before then, violence was not unknown on the streets of Greer.

When economic hardship arrived after the stock market failed in 1929, citizens less affected came together to provide relief and recovery for their neighbors and friends who lost jobs. Textile manager Claude Hemphill, superintendent of Greer Mill, allocated work in such a way that at least one occupant of each household in the villages worked enough to buy groceries when the mills were in operation. Businesses extended credit as long as possible to established customers. In 1933, after economic recovery had begun, Hemphill was honored by his employees with a barbecue that over 90 percent of the workers attended.

Most of the time Greer surmounted its problems in an orderly fashion. In the 1950s when the country righted itself after the Depression and World War II, Greer returned, briefly, to the life it knew much earlier. The mills operated on a regular basis; business was good despite increasing Japanese imports. Commercial Greer thrived once again as large crowds came to town on Friday nights and Saturdays to make purchases, eat at cafes and restaurants, and watch movies at one of Greer's theaters. Reggie Chesson and Bill Drace, managers at the Greer Theatre and the Grand Theatre, were two of the best known citizens in town when movies were the rage.

Textiles remained important to Greer well into the 1960s, although the cotton textile community had evolved. The mills had been sold to conglomerates; the village houses had been sold. Company stores were closed. Even production had changed; cotton goods were no longer the primary output, synthetic fibers having come of age. Even those changes to the industry could not forever protect it from foreign competition; by the 1980s, the cotton mills of Greer were out of business.

With the loss of traditional mill village life, Greer began to focus on its schools once again. The recreational facilities that had been built by the mills had been sold, but sports and recreation had always been important in Greer. When more responsibility in those areas was assumed by the public school system, it proved to have a unifying effect on the town. The mills had introduced the Young Men's and Young Women's Christian Associations (YMCA, YWCA) to village life and built facilities for housing the activities of these organizations. Here, basketball and baseball teams composed of mill workers were organized to compete with similar teams from other area mills. Over the years, as these textile league sports began to wane, greater public focus came to rest on public school sports, which were more representative of the larger community and offered other sports competitions including track and field and football. After the First World War and under the leadership of W.H. Ward, Greer athletic teams were consistently organized, uniformed, and competitive with other schools. Football, basketball, and track and field events were popular, but Greer became a football town. A new stadium was completed in 1938 when Dan Riggs coached the team. David Sheppard organized Greer's first marching band just before he left for service in the Army Air Corps in 1941.

After World War II, interest in sporting events grew. Little League baseball clubs were formed in and around the mill villages; the American Legion teams gained statewide respect. Greer High played respectable basketball and football. To the coaches of the era must go some credit, particularly Phil Clark, who divided his time for years between coaching and serving as assistant principal.

When the decline of the American textile industry began to be felt in Greer during the late 1960s, local leaders began to seek out a new industrial base for the city. Greer's strengths were promoted as far and wide as possible to attract notice. The South Carolina Peach Festival, which came to Greer in 1957, proved to be an effective vehicle for promoting the location, transportation facilities, and potential workforce the area offered. Laurens I. James was a principal organizer of the event, which offered beauty contests, golf tournaments, and a parade. Leaders extended invitations to national and regional celebrities to attend. During its 11-year run, the Peach Festivals helped put Greer on the map and in the forefront of similar towns competing for business.

By the 1980s, a few non-textile industries had found a home in Greer. New industries manufacturing chainsaws, batteries, and electric organs took up some of the slack in the job market. That the new manufacturers were more diverse and smaller in impact than the textile industry had been viewed as a strength, making the prospects of long-term economic stability much brighter. Area agriculture had also undergone considerable transformation. No longer were cotton cash crops the rule of the countryside. Many of the farmers had long since reduced or abandoned their fields for steady work in the mills and, later, other industrial settings. A few like Roy Chandler farmed and worked in industry. Others, like Henry Clark, diversified their farm operations. Much of the lands that once empowered the economy of Greer were simply abandoned for agricultural use in favor of real estate development.

Despite considerable long-range planning at the local level and the use of expert advice from state and federal sources, by the 1980s Greer was beginning to noticeably decline, especially in the eyes of those who had witnessed its remarkable rise over much of the century. Many of its once thriving small shops were becoming vacant; trade had migrated out of the central commercial district, in some cases, to other towns. Attempts to revive Greer made little headway toward that goal. Expansion of the city limits seemed to be a viable approach to increase the tax base and keep up with the demand for municipal services.

Dedicated public leadership was critical to Greer's success during this long period of change and uncertainty. A long line of mayors fiercely dedicated to keeping Greer intact and prominent helped make a difference. Lloyd Hunt, who actively sought to bring more business to Greer, had been a businessman since the 1920s, a partner in the Tire Exchange. Don Smith presided over a Greer seeking to revitalize itself and promoted various efforts to rekindle interest in commerce in the downtown center. Shirley Rollins made beautification of the community a priority. Don Wall crusaded on behalf of his hometown against a renewed threat of drug-related crime. At other levels of service, State Senator Verne Smith, Representative Lewis Vaughn, and others were influential in many ways that brought benefits to Greer. By the 1990s, Greer had begun to reinvent itself, helped by solid leadership as well as important physical assets such as the nearby airport and interstate highway.

Towns are more than the sums of their stores and shops and factories. It is the people who live there whose bonds are wrought from common heritage, common experience which gives life to a sense of community differing from that of any other settlement. This living personality, powerfully molded by tradition and deeply rooted like an ancient tree to the place it occupies, is what is noticed by non-natives. Visitors perceive a town's personality, its *élan vital*, through its physical appearance; the condition of its streets, residences, and stores; by the tone of its newspaper, the size and enthusiasm of turnouts at public events; the support given its athletic teams; the confidence of its spokespersons; the attitude of its public servants; the friendliness of its merchants; and the empathy demonstrated by its churches and charities.

Twenty-first-century Greer is a work in progress. It has experienced many incarnations, from railroad stop to cotton town to mill town to whatever new identity is presently being molded by circumstance and humanity. What is in store for the Greer of the future? It will depend on the actions and thoughts of the descendants of its founders and the inheritors of its rich past.

CHAPTER ONE

The Founders

Greer's founders include those earliest settlers who arrived shortly after the American Revolution seeking good land on which to farm. In the upcountry, well-watered, level land was at a premium; the large parcels originally sold for tiny sums mostly to soldiers of the recent war were rapidly subdivided and resold into smaller parcels. Henry Hughes kept his property intact until 1798 and sold to John McDade for $200. The property was further divided and came into the hands of James Vernon, Robert Greer, Phillip Lester, and Hugh Bailey. Bailey, an immigrant from Ireland, held onto the land the rest of his life after which his upland plantation was divided after yet another war, the War Between the States.

It was the northern end of the Bailey plantation that William Shumate bought on speculation shortly after the Atlanta-Richmond Airline Railway announced plans for a track across the upstate, passing through this parcel. The arrival of the railroad was welcome news, the first good news area residents had heard in a while. There had been many changes to their way of life over the past decade and a half. How this change would affect them remained to be seen. However, in the long course of events, the rails brought prosperity; the Shumate purchase brought a settlement, and the residents already living in the area helped to establish that settlement, Greer's Depot, with their trade and commerce.

One of the earliest families living north of the tracks was that of Elijah Ballenger. The Ballenger family came from Virginia, Elijah being at least a fourth-generation American when he was born in 1819. The Ballengers farmed lands about four miles north of Bailey's Crossroads for over a century. The third generation on that property was among the county's last self-sufficient farmers, producing all they required to live and much of what they wanted. Elijah did his own blacksmithing and made the furniture for the house, which he built on site. Son William D. Ballenger traded farm produce or his own labor for coffee and cane sugar from time to time to supplement the pork, corn, dried beans, and dried fruits that were staples of the family's diet. Once a cotton market developed at Greer's, the Ballengers, like their neighbors, planted a small cotton field that provided the little cash they needed.

Greer became the social and business focus of the Ballenger family. William D. Ballenger walked to Greer's Depot once or twice a week when he was caught up on his farm chores. He met friends and acquaintances, negotiated trades of goods and labor, and swapped news of the day that arrived by train and telegraph. He frequented William A. Hill's store on the corner of Emma and Mosteller Streets, one of the first general stores in Greer. In the fall, after cotton was picked, he hauled it by horse-drawn wagon to a ginnery in Greer where he sold it for cash. He was not known to have produced more than a few bales of cotton, spending most of his efforts raising feed grain and food crops. After his death, his children continued the family farm tradition well into the 20th century. When William's son J. Henry died, the farm passed down to siblings Tommy and Mamie, neither of whom ever married. After their deaths, the farm, reduced to some 26 acres, became residential property.

The Ballengers typify the farmers of the area who adopted Greer as their hometown. The farmers gave Greer their business; they elected to receive their mail there, handed over the counter at the tiny post office decades before rural delivery was available. The farmers gave Greer credibility and validated it as a legitimate town by selling their produce and cotton there and in so doing earned the right to be counted among its founders.

Greer has been described as a "New South" town, one which departed from the character of earlier towns founded before 1860 and relied on commerce and industry. The only problem was lack of any funding for such a resurrection. Henry W. Grady believed that Northern money would channel down to assist the South, and so some did. But in Greer, it was up to the entrepreneur to scratch out the best profits from the simplest enterprise and save long years before he could invest in industry.

D.D. Davenport, originally from North Carolina, best exemplifies this approach to the New South. He was a Confederate veteran, farmer, postal worker, astute businessman, Greer's first self-made millionaire, and was consummately generous with his wealth. He was a man of action and strong belief. Of his willingness to take a chance, the stories about him are numerous. As a Confederate soldier home on furlough, he was said to have surprised a pair of Yankee raiders in his father's house and engaged them in a gunfight, killing one on the stairway and driving the other away.

When Davenport came to Greer, he bought property and set up a business on Trade Street. He built a large home and for a time, provided rooms to traveling businessmen before local hotels were constructed. He traded with anyone who walked through his doors. He knew no enemies. He would as soon accept moonshine in trade from the Dark Corner as a bale of cotton from Oneal.

When other local businessmen invested much of their capital in Greer's first cotton mill, Davenport spent his on a cotton oil press and still made a profit. He progressed rapidly, making connections with bankers and merchants in Greenville, diversifying his investments into real estate and insurance. He amassed a fortune shortly after the turn of the century. With his money, he provided amply for his family and extended unmatched generosity to his many tenants and associates. He even presented toys to his renters' children at Christmastime. In his final years, he tithed his worth for a number of causes including a gift of $60,000 for construction of a modern high school for his adopted town.

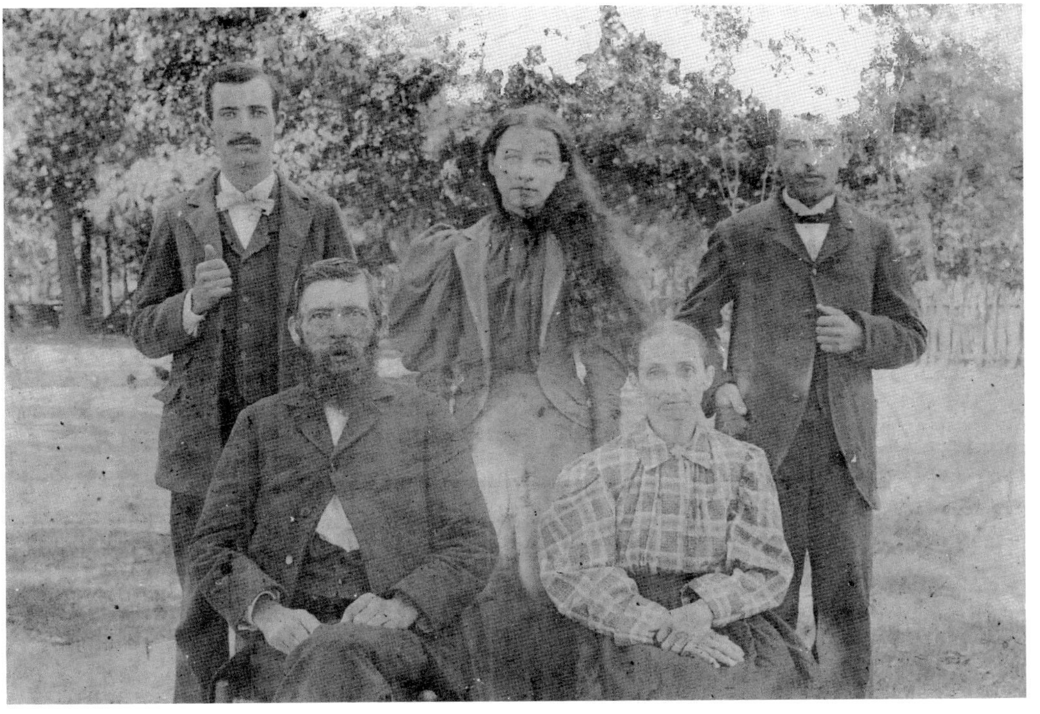

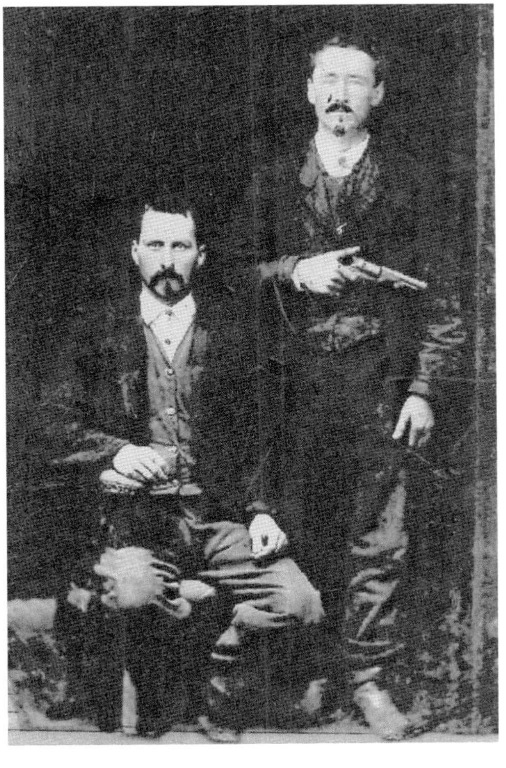

The Ballenger Family

The Ballenger family farmed lands north of Greer for over 125 years and managed to hold on to their lifestyle and farm despite a plunging cotton market and boll weevils. Mamie and Tommy farmed well into their old age, dying a week apart in 1970. Seated are William D. Ballenger (left) and Jane P. Ballenger. Standing (left to right) are James Henry, Mamie, and Thomas O. Ballenger. (Courtesy of the Belcher family.)

Capt. Alfred Marion Davis

Davis (1822–1910) served as a sergeant in the 16th Infantry of the Army of the Confederacy. After the war, he was awarded the honorary rank of captain. He married Helena Hastings of Greer. A master carpenter and farmer, he owned numerous acres in the Apalache area. His son Alfred (1866–1939) is standing beside his father in this 1864 tintype. Alfred Jr. married Martha Singleton and farmed. (Courtesy of Tom Davis.)

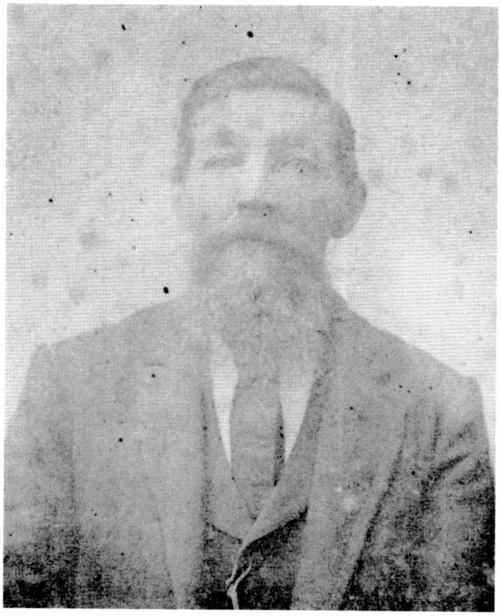

Cunningham Pennington

A sergeant in Hampton's Legion of the Army of the Confederate States of America, Pennington returned to his farm in the Oneal community after the war. He was one of the early purchasers of a lot on the Shumate tract, now the site of Victoria Arms Apartments. There he built a house and rented pasturage to drovers from the mountains. (Courtesy of the Carman family.)

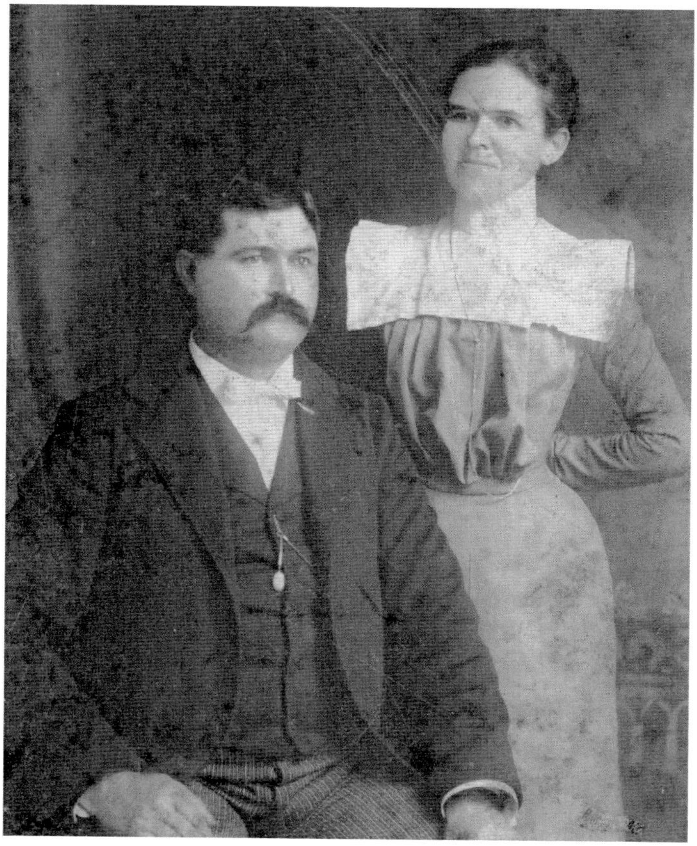

Chaney Littlefield

Littlefield, shown here with his wife Annie Cunningham Littlefield, was a cotton buyer and fertilizer dealer. He was instrumental in building Greer's first commercial cotton warehouse. The cotton market was an important part of the commercial development of Greer. (Courtesy of Carl Gibson.)

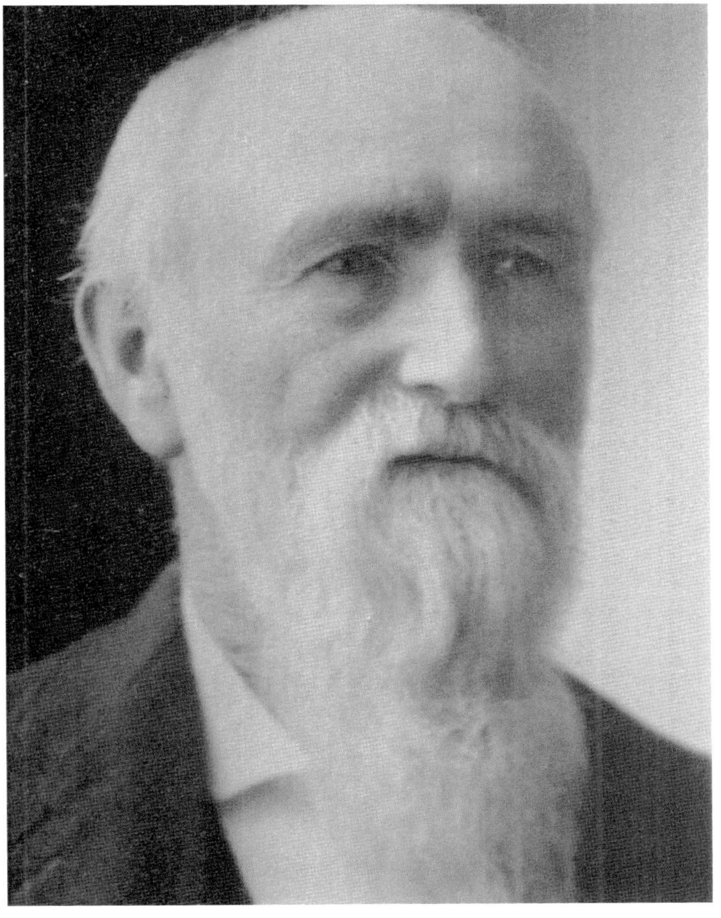

Perry Duncan (P.D.) Gilreath
Gilreath served in the 16th South Carolina Regiment of the Army of the Confederate States of America. After Reconstruction, he was elected sheriff, a post he held until the turn of the century. Well known for his courage and integrity, Gilreath rarely carried a gun, preferring instead to rely upon the public's respect for the law to carry out his duties. (Courtesy of Carl Gibson.)

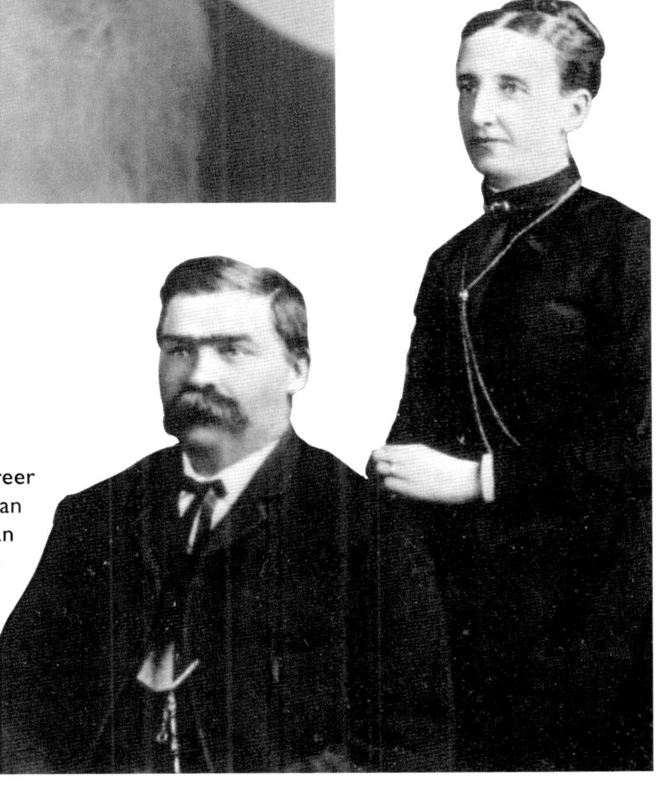

David D. Davenport
Davenport (1844–1918) moved to Greer in 1880. He was a leading businessman in the development of Greer. He began as a merchant and expanded into the cotton oil business, real estate, and insurance. D.D. is shown here with his wife Martha Ann West. They had two children, Mae who married John D. Wood, and Malcolm. (Courtesy of Denby Davenport.)

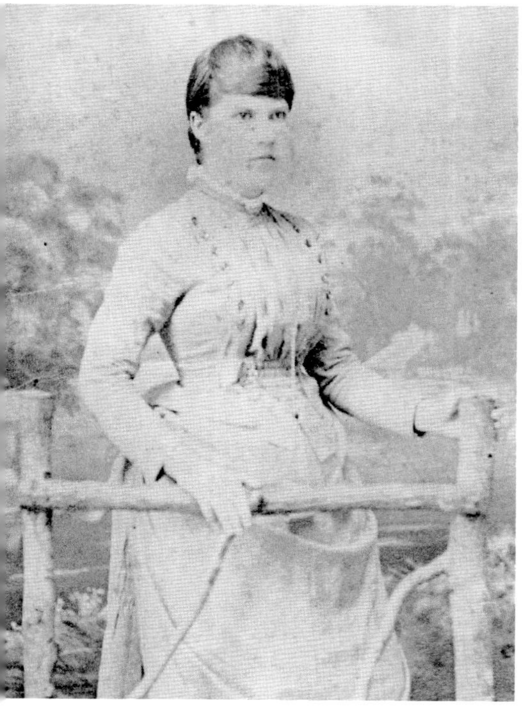

Eugenia "Eula" Gilreath (LEFT)
Eugenia Lipscomb married James F. Gilreath, the son of P.D. Gilreath. They had eight children and lived both on the farm and in Greer where he was mayor briefly from 1904 to 1905 and again in 1919. (Courtesy of Carl Gibson.)

Virginia Gilreath (BELOW LEFT)
Gilreath was the daughter of Eugenia Lipscomb and James Franklin Gilreath. In 1904 and 1905, he was mayor of Greer, giving up the office when he returned the family to the farm. Virginia married Wilton Gibson to merge two very old local families. (Courtesy of Carl Gibson.)

Annie Wilson
Annie Wilson married Claude Hemphill, who was superintendent of the Greer Mill. They reared a family in the mill village along the Southern Railroad tracks. (Courtesy of Ann Dillard Withrow.)

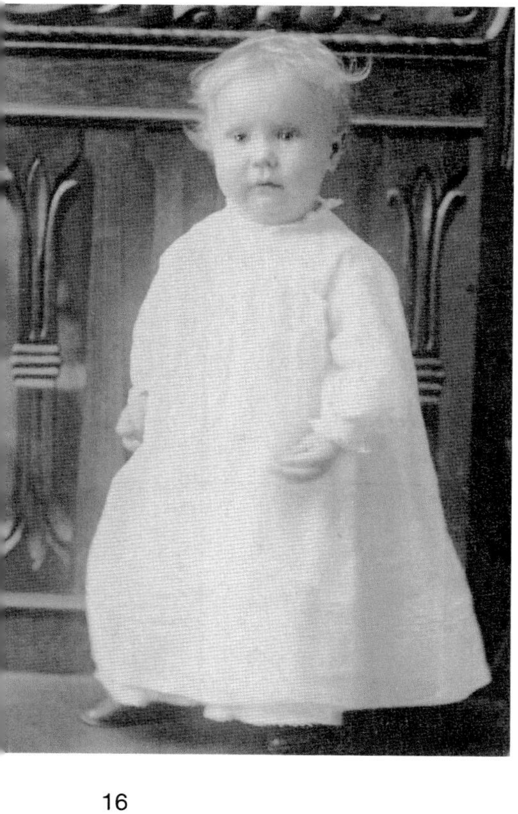

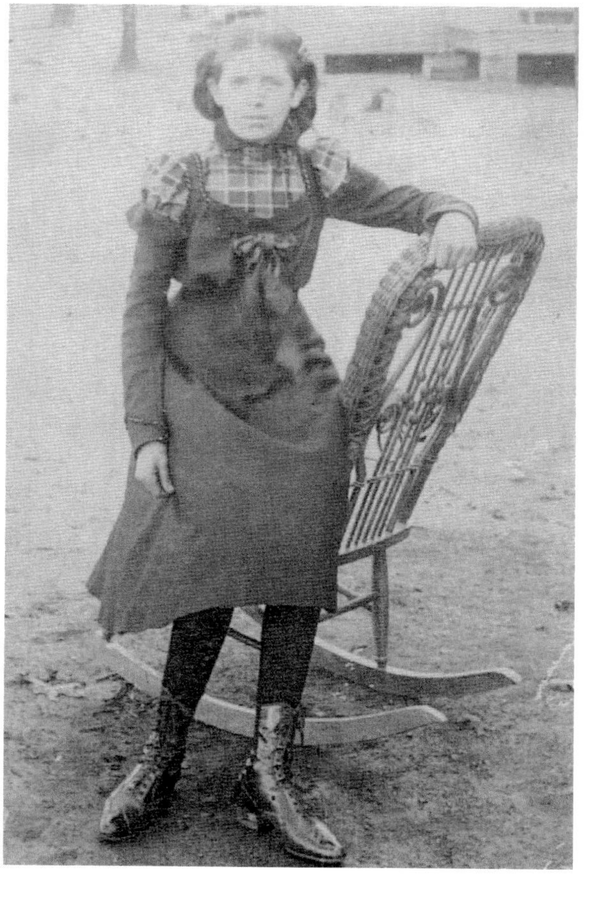

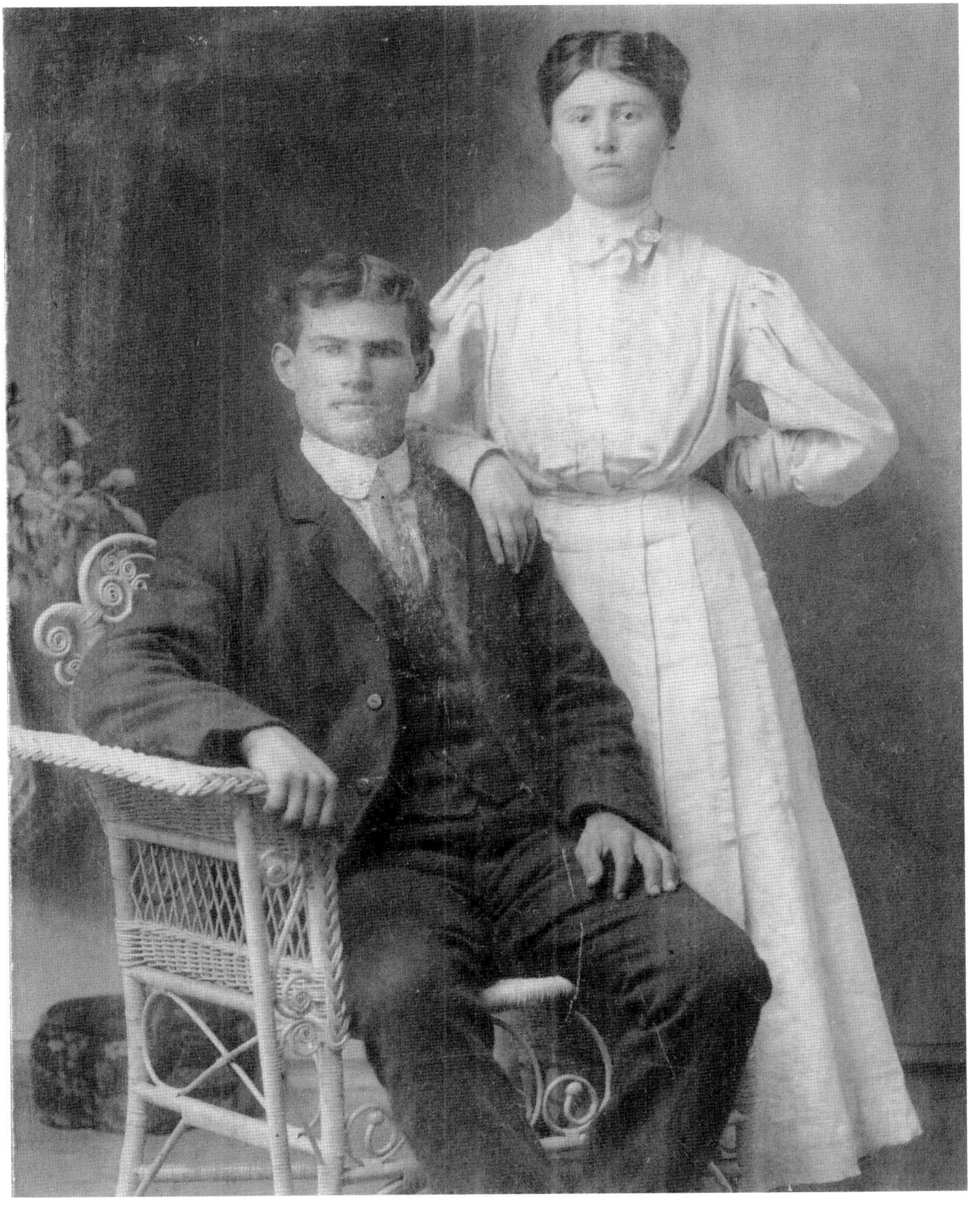

Vena and Bee Hayes
Vena Neves (1889–1983) married James Baxter "Bee" Hayes (1883–1950) on December 16, 1906, and came to Greer to have this wedding picture taken at Drace Studio. They were from the Mush Creek community, which was between Mountain View and Tigerville. When they came to Greer, they brought a bale of cotton in their wagon to sell to purchase housekeeping items for their new home. (Courtesy of Rosemary Bomar.)

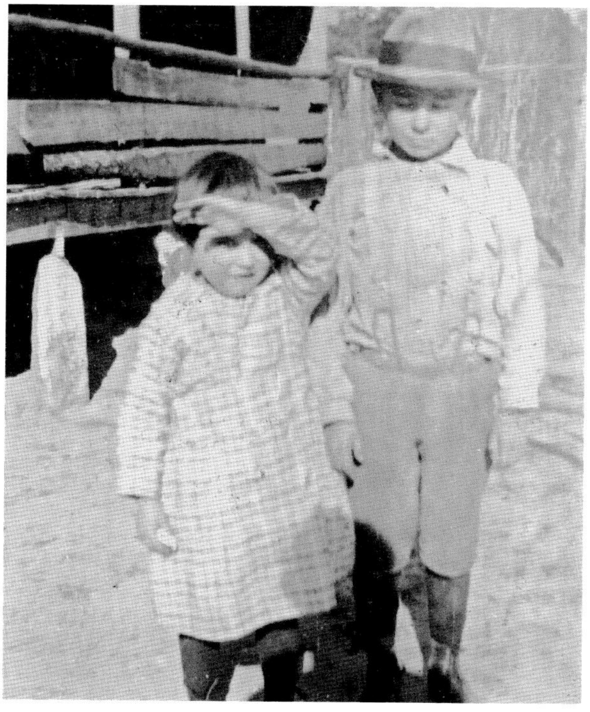

Lou Herman and David B. Stone
Herman and Stone, children of Lee Stone of the Oneal community, are shown here visiting the farm of their grandfather, William Hudson. (Courtesy of Lou Herman.)

George and Ellen Sudduth
George Sudduth and his wife Ellen pose with her sister Mag Wilson (standing) at the Wilson home in Batesville. The dog posed with them, but they are unaware that the cow has taken an inopportune time to look for better grass in the yard. (Courtesy of Ann Dillard Withrow.)

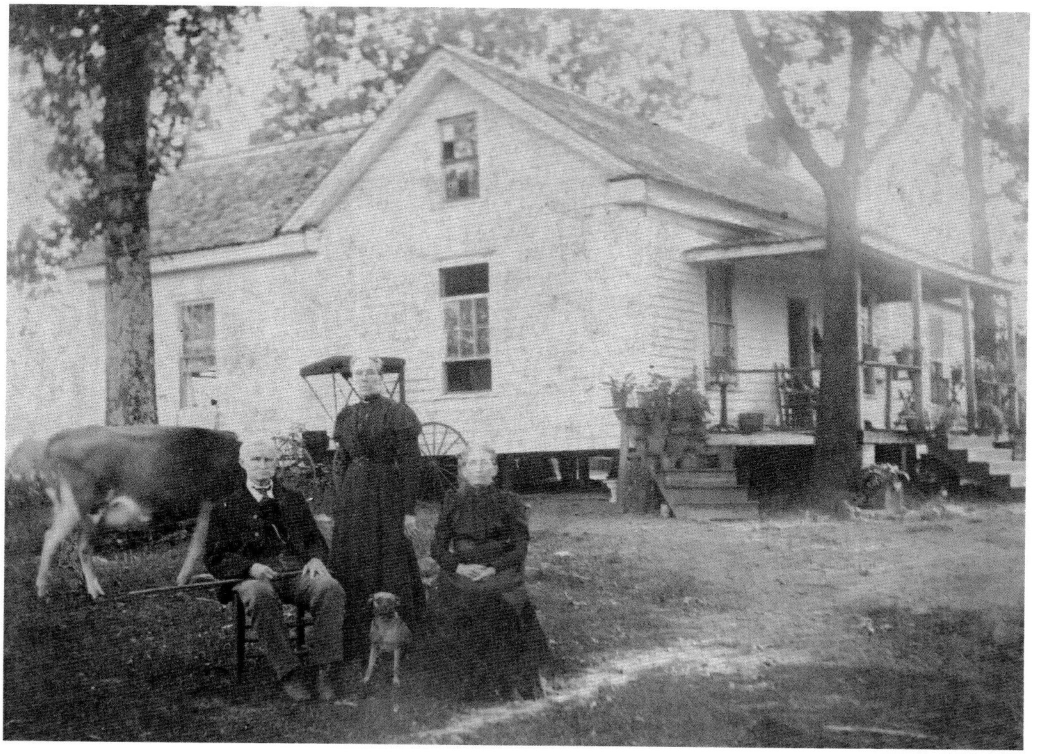

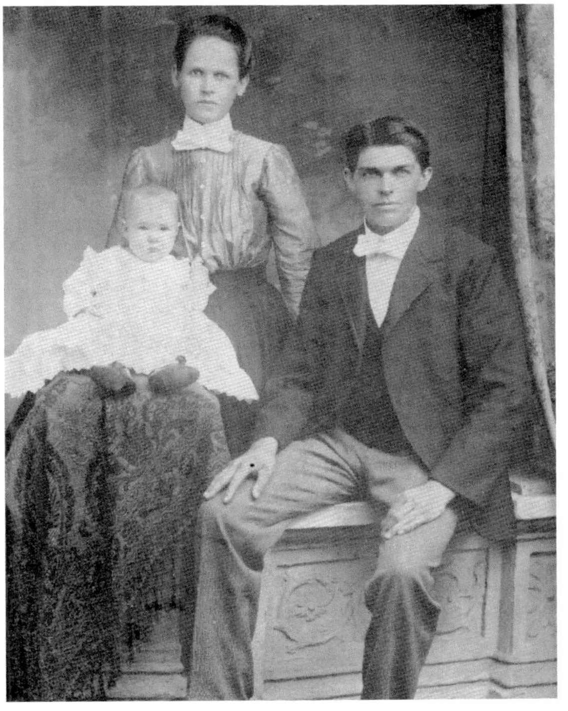

Bessie and Jason Gibson
Bessie Cunningham married Jason Hudson Gibson. Their first child was certainly an occasion to celebrate with a family picture. This Drace photograph shows their first son Estes, but this happy moment was later turned to sadness when Estes died. (Courtesy of Carl Gibson.)

Robert Murray Hughes
Hughes and his horse Belle pause in front of his family's home on South Main Street. The son of Simeon Hughes, Murray Hughes was the founder and president of Planters Savings Bank and president of Greer Oil Mill and Feed Company. (Courtesy of the Hughes family.)

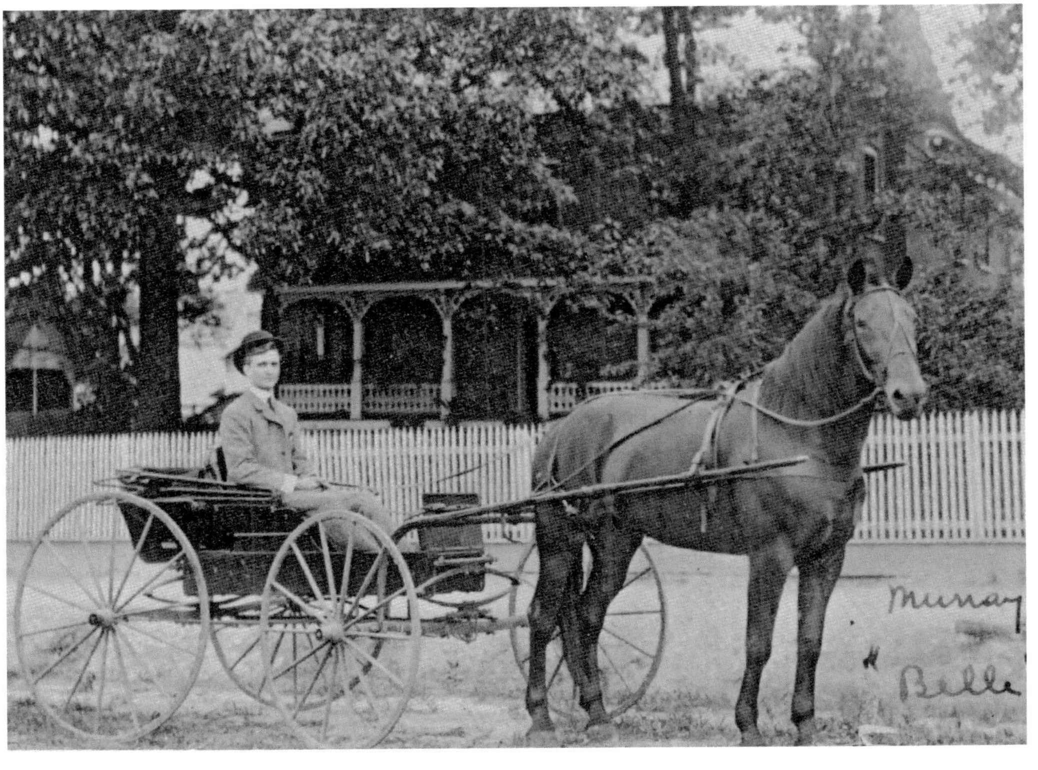

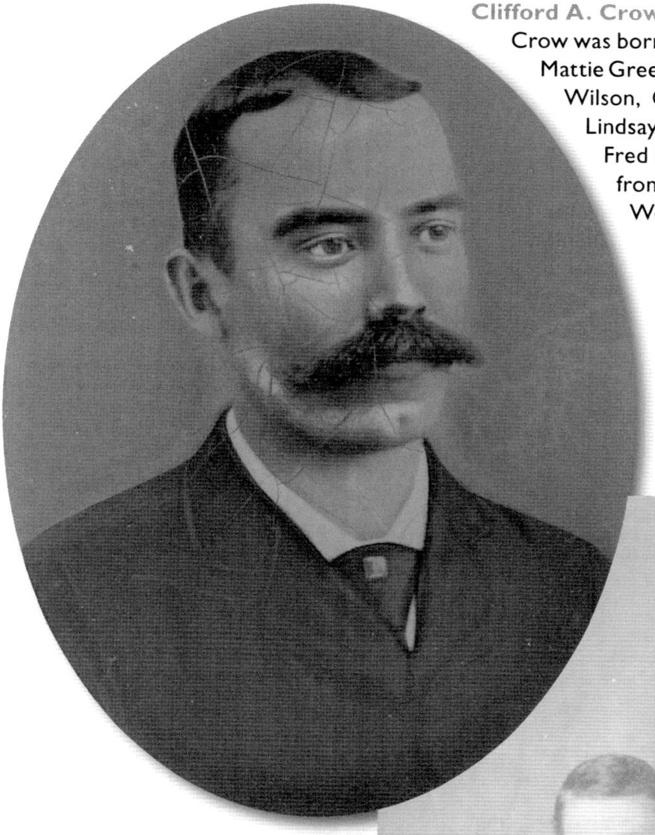

Clifford A. Crow

Crow was born in 1871 and died in 1921. He married Mattie Greer, and they were the parents of Marian Wilson, Grace Stuart, Nell Oglesby, Frances Lindsay, Virginia Garrett, Lois Wood, and Fred Crow, who served as mayor of Greer from 1945 to 1951. (Courtesy of Dick Wood.)

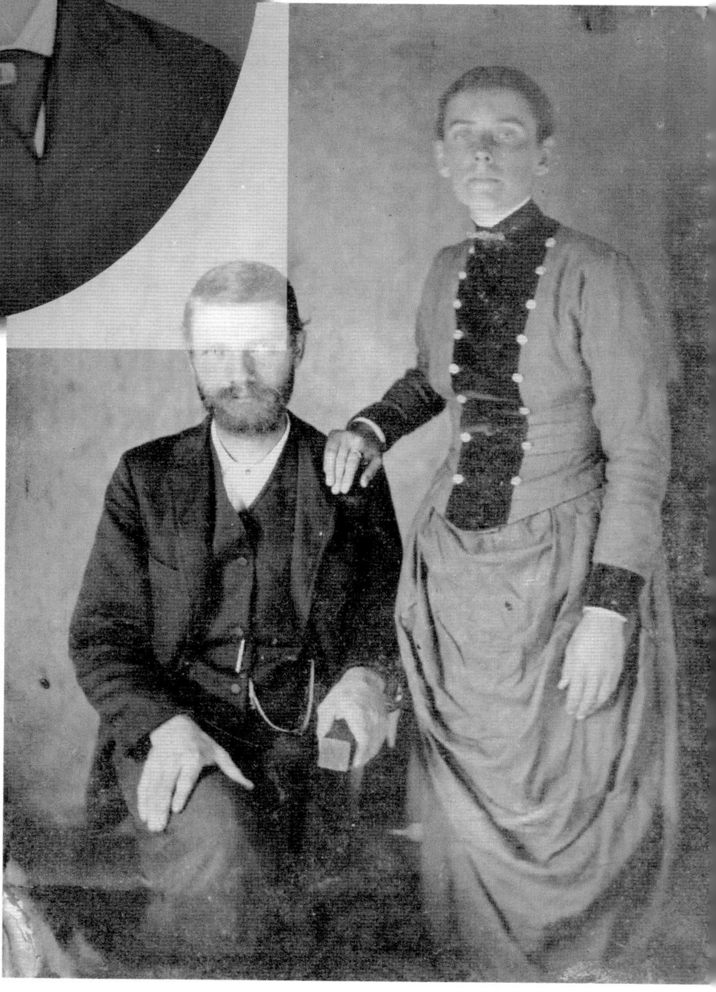

William and Frances Bright

William Bright (1838–1915) and his wife Frances Burnett (1843–1920) had six children. He owned the Bright-Wilson Country Store. They enjoyed two homes: one in Greer and a country home along Gap Creek Road where the Greer Country Club is today. (Courtesy of Greer Heritage Museum.)

CHAPTER TWO

The Farmers

Farming in Greer can best be understood by examining the different phases of Greer's development through the experience of the farmers. For the early farmers like the Ballengers and their neighbors, John Crane, Abraham Mayfield, and others, there was little choice before the arrival of the nearby rail line and depot except to produce all that was possible on the land one had.

When a railroad town grew up, seemingly overnight, opportunities abounded and farmers had more choices. Unfortunately, many of them borrowed money to buy the fertilizer needed to grow cotton and ended up losing their farms. Sometimes farmers fought change; other times they encouraged it as they did between 1875 and 1910 when local farmers joined the series of activist organizations—the Grange, Farmers Alliance, and finally the Farmers Union—that promised solutions to the plight of the farmer.

The organizations did not help much, leaving farmers where they started: hoping to keep their land and continue to farm and prosper all at the same time. It was a dilemma but not an insoluble one. Spartan Mosteller continued to raise grains as his ancestors before him had done, but he also continued to operate the gristmill his grandfather had built in 1814. This and similar strategies allowed other farmers to remain connected with the land. John Carman owned a farm in the country and a blacksmith shop in Greer that his sons, David and John Landrum, operated. Cunningham Pennington, for a time, also kept a farm and operated a business in town. Records of Leonard and Clyde Dobson, successors to R.A. and I.B. Dobson, show that this model of farming returned to popularity after World War II when millworkers who had enjoyed sufficient prosperity during the wartime economy bought modest tracts of land and continued to hold their industrial jobs while growing cotton in their spare time.

With the passage of time, it became clear that traditional farming was declining; the farmers who remained on their land and tried to continue found it difficult to find seasonal labor when the cotton mills were constantly expanding their workforce. Specialization in something other than cotton seemed to be the most viable alternative. Greer farmers made a number of attempts to diversify and find new niches. Dairying, peach farming, hog, poultry, and cattle operations were all small but valiant attempts to preserve tradition. J.A. Mahaffey operated one of the early dairies in Greer. Other farmers including James Taylor, J. Verne Smith, and W.W. Burgess planted peach orchards. Smith also tried the hog business briefly but apparently found peaches more to his liking.

By the 1950s, Greer was as well established as any town of similar size in the state. It boasted everything one could think of to meet public demand, from tires to jewelry to movies to specialty clothiers for men and women. Yet, in many ways Greer was still a farmers' town. D.C. Price, who succeeded J.B. Mendenhall

Jr. in the feed and seed business, observed horse- and mule-drawn cotton wagons negotiating red lights on Greer streets in the late 1950s en route to the gin house south of the railroad tracks. But farming had changed dramatically, and while no farmers remained entrenched in the traditions of early settlers like the Ballengers, there remained a few who found individual approaches to the perennial challenges of farm life. Through the 1960s, subsequent generations of Ballengers continued to farm their lands in the same way as had their earliest 19th-century ancestor.

Henry K. Clark was one of the last remaining local full-time farmers in Greer. He lived in the same house his father built and farmed family land as well as some rented parcels, from before he graduated from Greer High in 1918 until he produced his last commercial crop in 1991 with help from friends. During his long life as a tiller of the soil, he embraced the changes that came to farming.

Trained to plow with a horse or mule, he bought his first tractor during the late 1930s and kept it for a quarter of a century before he updated to one with a hydraulic lift. Until that time, he had to drag his heaviest implement, a set of disk harrows, up and down the tiny tar and gravel roads between his fields north of Greer. Observers at twilight during plowing weather could see the sparks kicked up as the steel bit into the stone while Henry Clark made his way to the next field or back home.

He never earned a great deal of money as a solitary and independent farmer, but he invested his profits in more land and better technology, especially after 1960. Eventually, he made the transition from cotton farmer to peach farmer and finally raised cattle before his semi-retirement. Pushing 80, Clark sold his hundred-head herd of beef cattle and devoted his remaining active years to raising produce crops for the local market.

An avid reader, he consumed everything he could about modern farming techniques. He corresponded with Clemson authorities about problems he found in his fields and took courses to learn how to administer agricultural chemicals.

A lifelong bachelor, he cared for his ailing mother until he was past middle age. During the layby seasons and the rainy winters, Clark studied his other passion: local history. He collected a small library on that and genealogy, often spending Sunday afternoons talking to the older generation and taking notes on things that interested him.

He formed a friendship with Spartanburg journalist Carl May and together they explored some of the sites of local historical importance, with Clark explaining and guiding May through the history and May, in turn, using their adventures as the bases for feature stories that appeared in the Spartanburg newspapers.

By the time that Henry Clark died, or shortly thereafter, farming in the greater Greer area was a thing of the past. Cotton had made Greer a successful investment for generations, but it had run its course. So too had the business of growing peaches on a vast scale. Greer's commercial cannery had moved; the school cannery also closed. Fields once dedicated to cotton stalks or peach trees sprouted new housing starts. Greer is no longer a cotton town or a farmers' town, but without that foundation, there would be no Greer.

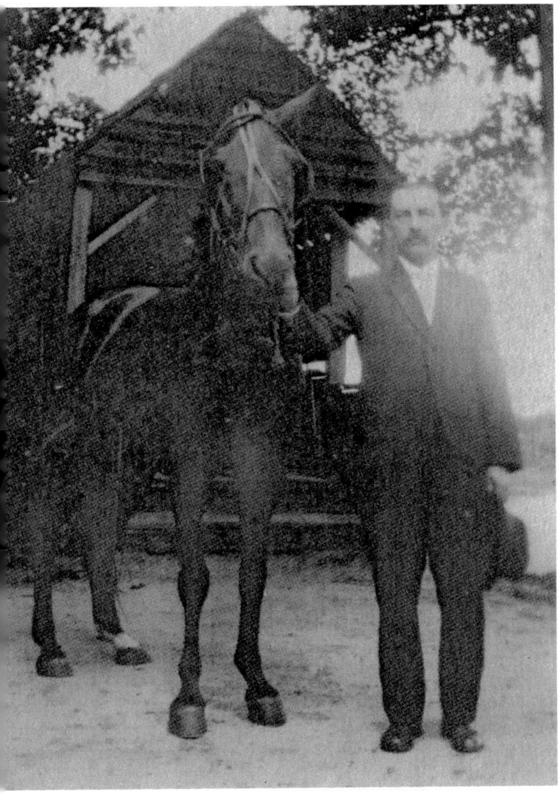

Tommy Ballenger

Ballenger was the third generation of his family to farm lands north of Greer first acquired during the 1830s. Thomas, known as Uncle Tommy in his later years, was active in the Farmers Union, which promoted cooperative buying and selling and the establishment of a state department of agriculture. (Courtesy of the Belcher family.)

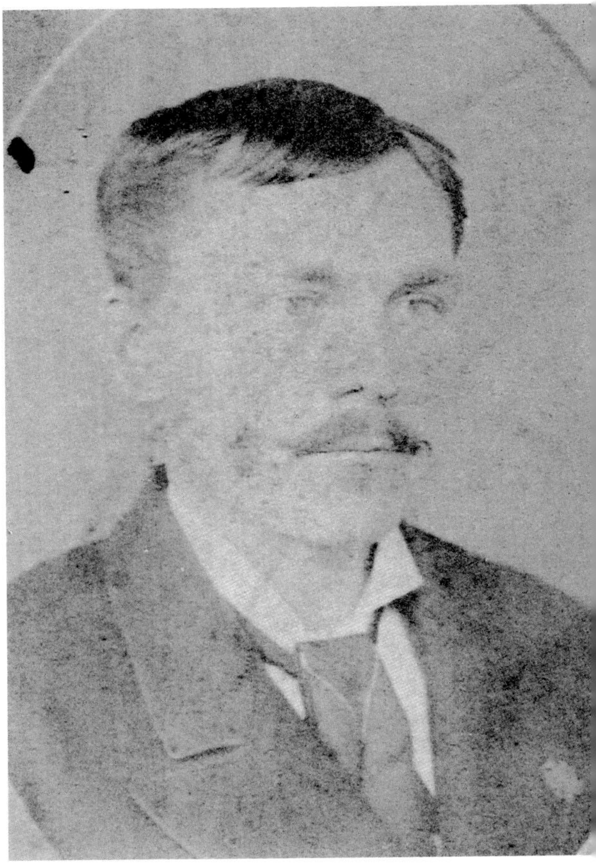

Will Hudson

Hudson planted a cotton field yearly and sold his crop at the cotton market in Greer. He continued to work his fields with the help of unmarried daughter Belle until he died at his work at the age of 81. (Courtesy of the Carman family.)

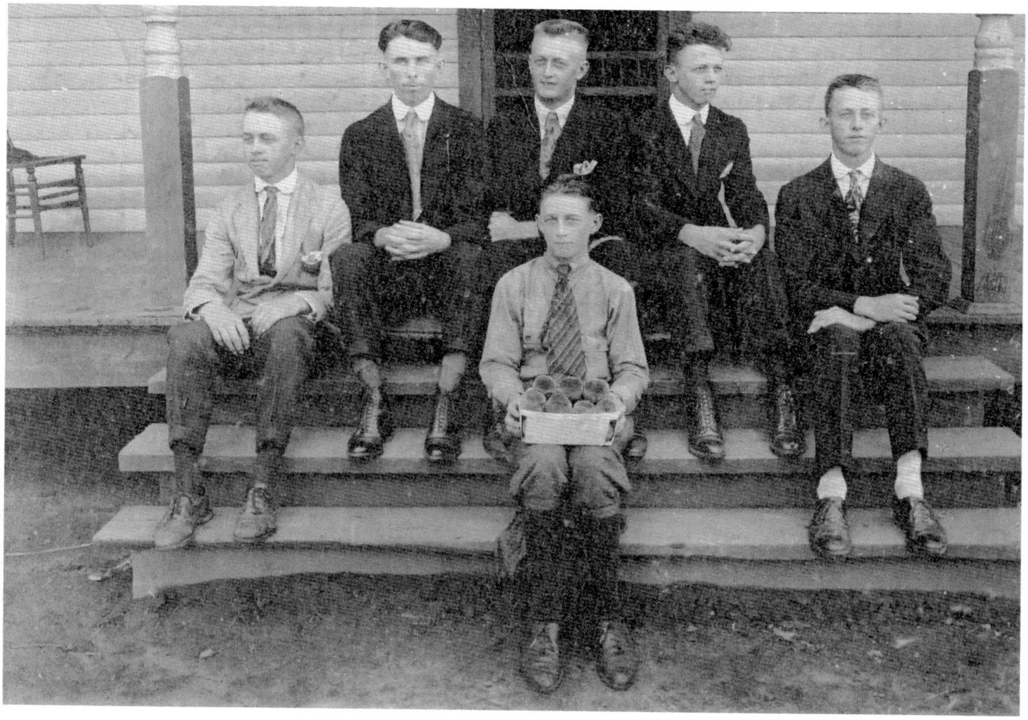

James Paschal Taylor

Taylor was blessed with sons to help him in the peach orchards. Shown here (left to right) are Spartan, Homer, Becco, Earle, Perry, and Albert, holding the basket of peaches. Taylor, who is called the "father of peach growing in South Carolina," was growing peaches as early as 1898. (Courtesy of Karolyn and Richard Taylor.)

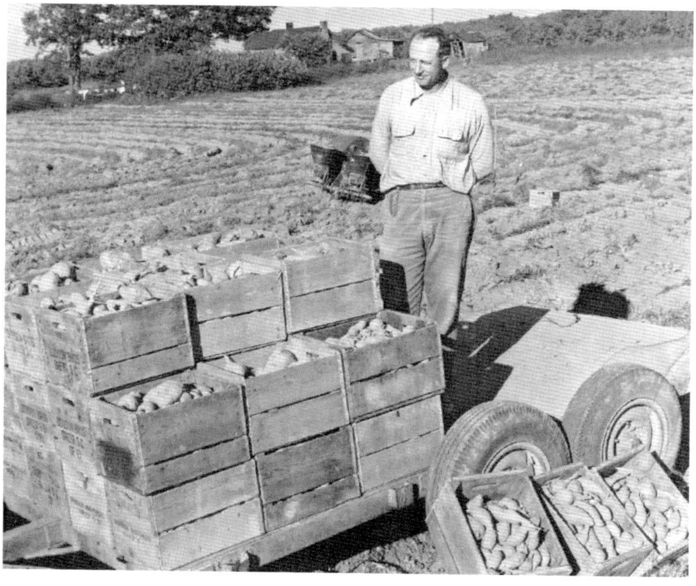

Clyde Dobson

Brothers Robert and I.B. Dobson began a large agribusiness with 100 acres each given to them by their father. The Dobson brothers also owned a fertilizer company and operated a cotton gin. The next generation—Leonard, Roy, Clyde, Connie, and Lawrence—continued the operation, increasing its size. Clyde Dobson, shown here surveying his sweet potato crop, was well known for his peach orchards near Greer. (Courtesy of Anne Dobson.)

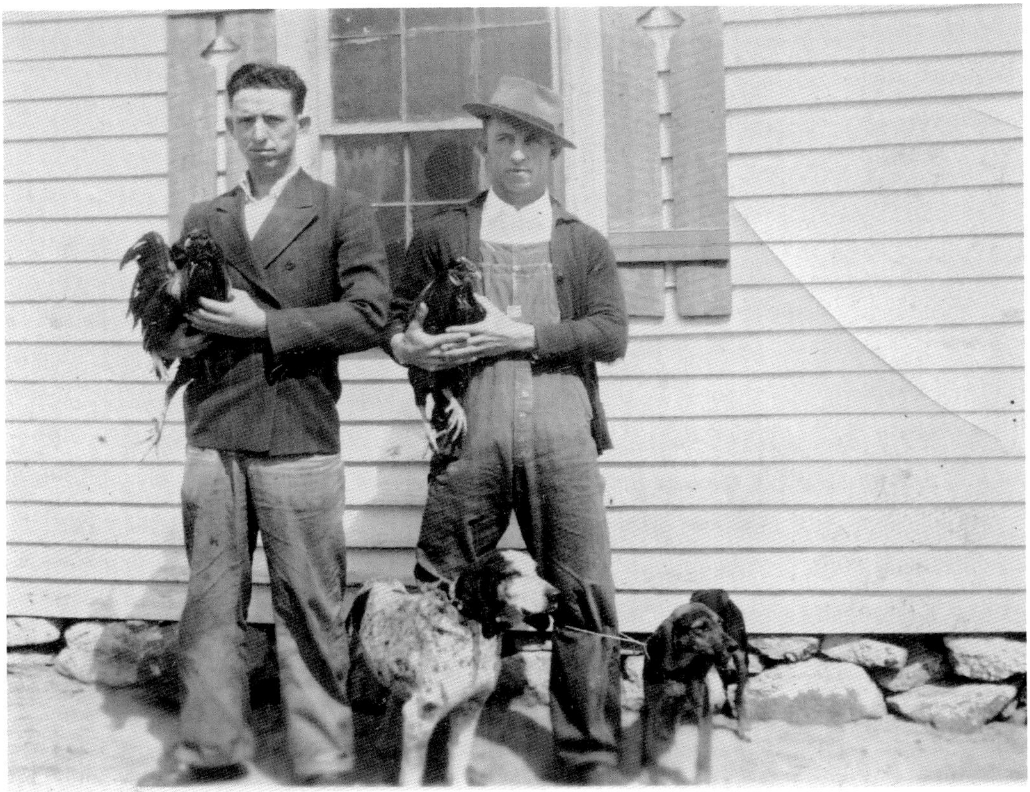

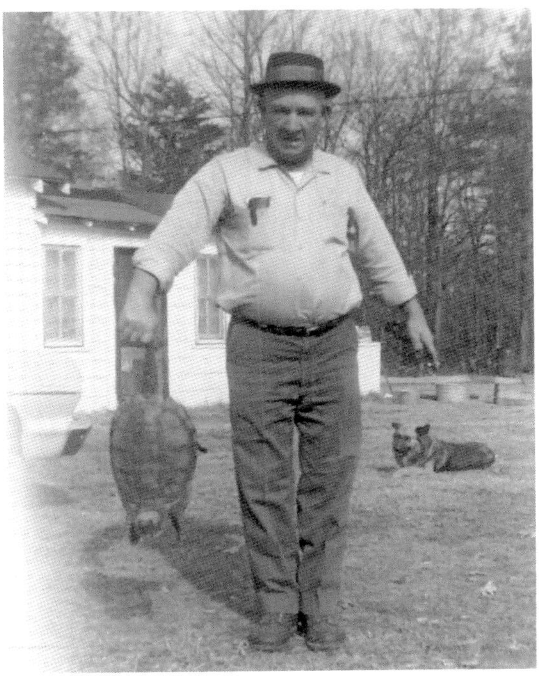

Nathaniel Greene "Sam" Davis

Sam Davis (1912–1939) and his brother Odell (right) show off prize game cocks. Minnie the blue tic hound is at their feet. In their youth, they enjoyed cockfighting and moonshine runs from Glassy Mountain. Sam was awarded five Bronze Stars in World War II. After the war, he farmed and worked as shift foreman for Southern Bleachery and Printworks. (Courtesy of Tom Davis.)

Ollie Davis

Davis is proud of the turtle he caught. The many creeks of the area provided a variety of wildlife for outdoorsmen such as the Davis brothers. (Courtesy of Tom Davis.)

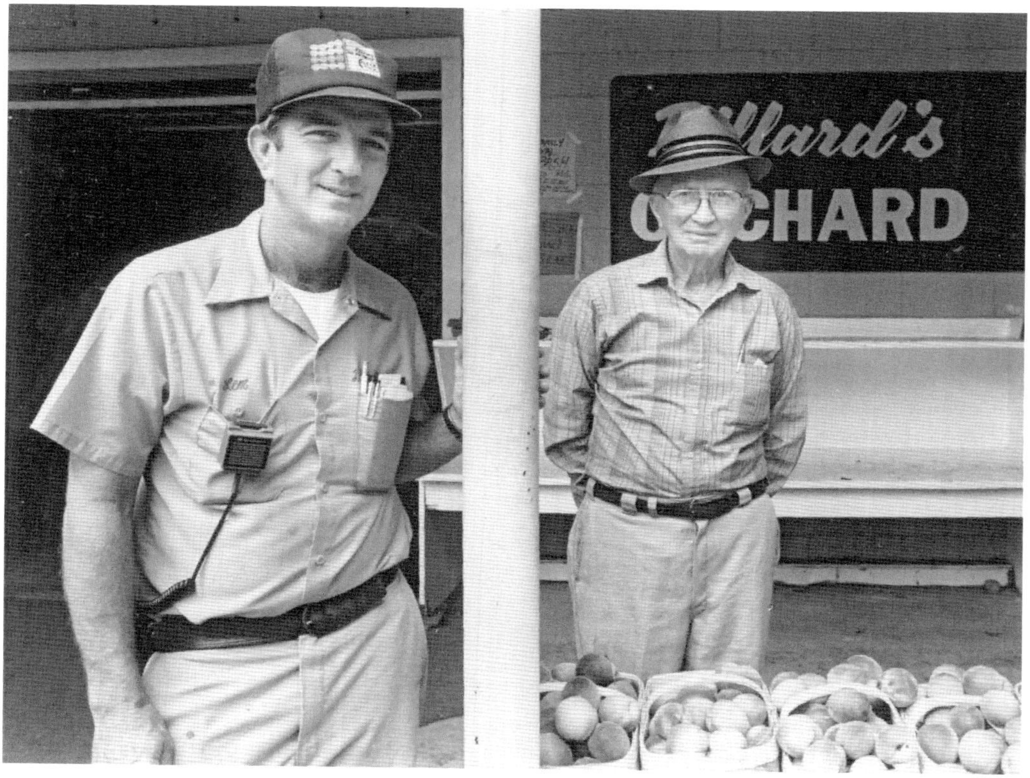

Lemuel and Palmer Dillard

The most popular summer stops in Greer are the peach sheds where local residents buy fresh, tree-ripened peaches. Shown here in their peach shed are Lem Dillard (left) and his late father Palmer, longtime peach growers. Lem closed Dillard Orchards in 2007 and leased the shed to Fisher Orchards, which continues to sell peaches to local residents. (Courtesy of Ann Dillard Withrow.)

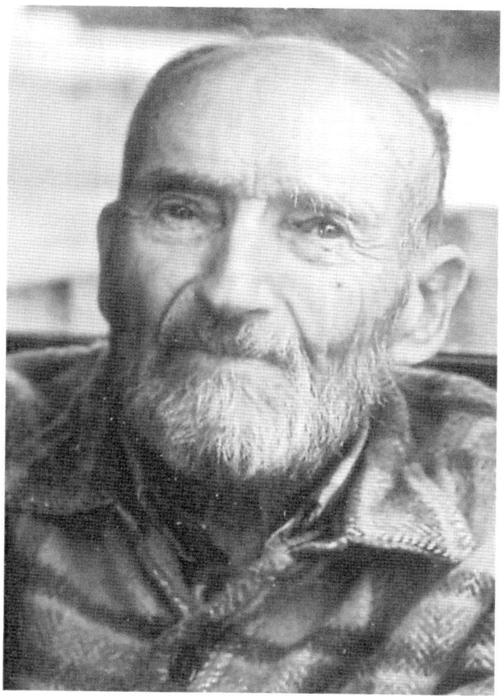

Henry Clark

Clark adjusted to changing agricultural conditions by transforming his father's cotton farm to a peach orchard, and later to a cattle operation. Sometime during the 1950s, his doctor ordered him to get more rest. Henry bought a Buick automobile and for several years vacationed at Myrtle Beach once a year, leaving on Monday and returning on Friday until his doctor died. Henry lived another 30 years. (Courtesy of Chris Davis.)

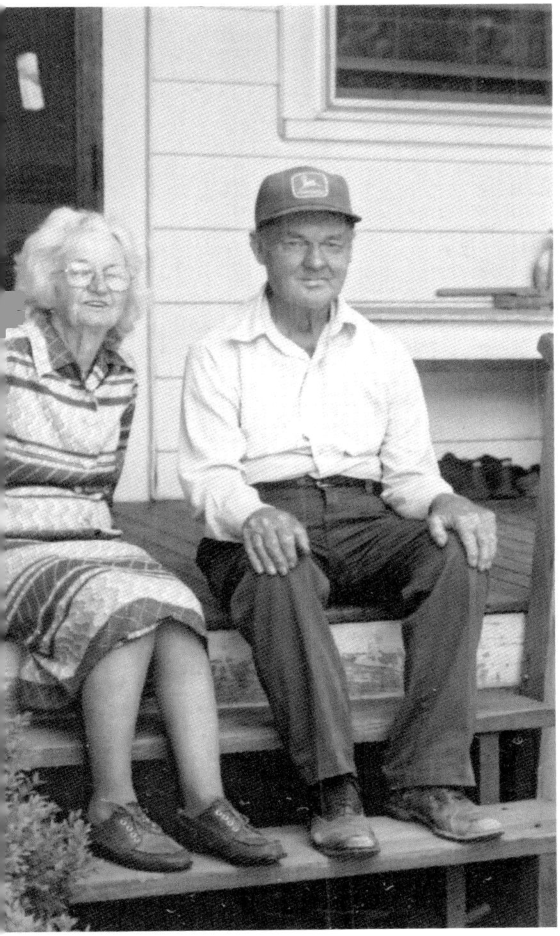

Roy Chandler
Originally from Gastonia, North Carolina, Chandler moved to Greer for a better job opportunity. He combined an industrial job at the Homelite plant with farming in the Ansel community. He is shown here with his wife, Sara Finley Chandler. (Courtesy of Chris Davis.)

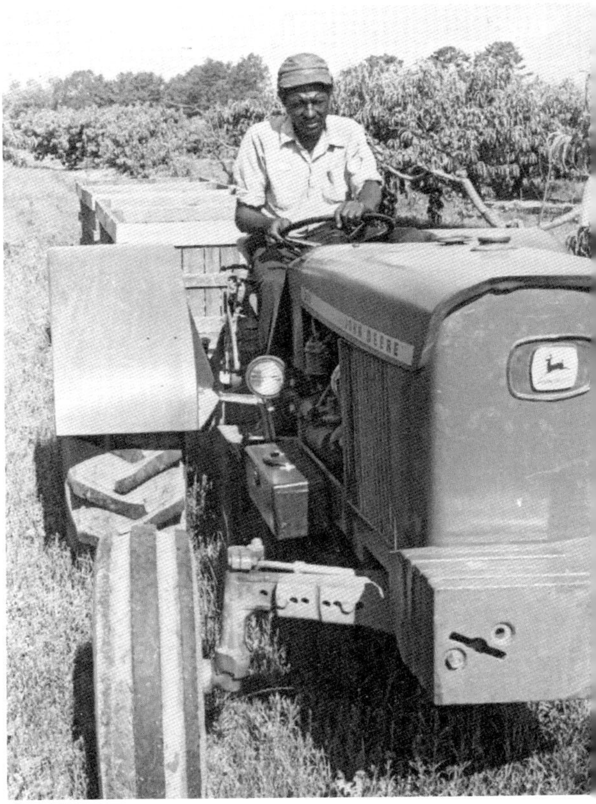

Tom Higgins
Peaches were a major part of the economy of Greer in the early and mid-20th century. Dillard Orchards employed workers such as Tom Higgins in the planting and maintenance of fields. In the summertime, the orchards provided seasonal jobs for teenagers. (Courtesy of Ann Dillard Withrow.)

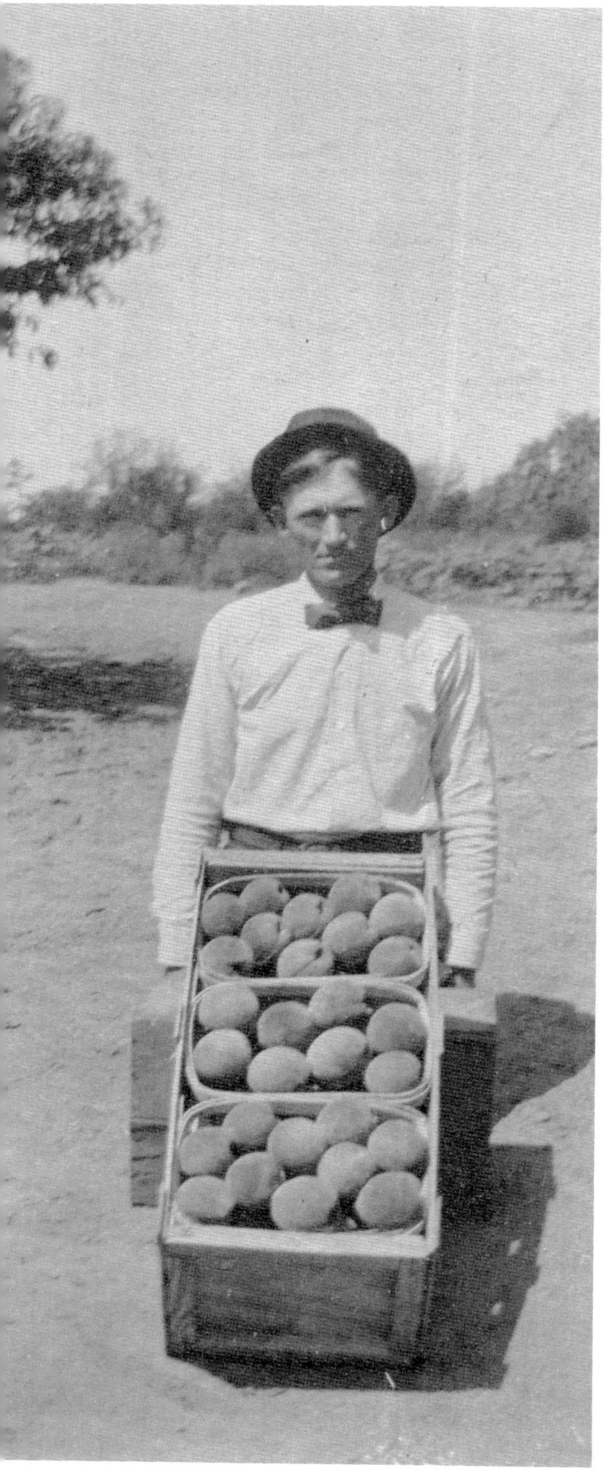

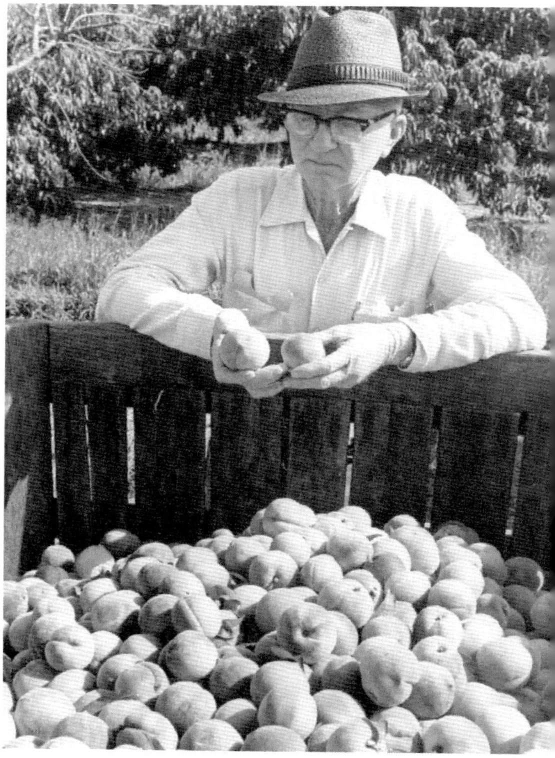

Palmer Dillard

Dillard surveys his successful peach crop. Weather was always a factor in the success of any season. Dillard left Clemson University to run the family farm as a young man. His operation along Buncombe Road produced many varieties of peaches. (Courtesy of Ann Dillard Withrow.)

Jefferson Verne Smith Sr.

Smith, who had worked for the Bank of Greers, planted peach orchards in the Mt. Vernon area around 1898 and became one of the foremost promoters of commercial peach production. His operation became a model for area growers. He died in 1933 leaving his widow to continue the operation. (Courtesy of Carole Smith Olmert.)

CHAPTER THREE

Textiles and Working Folks

Greer was founded with the hope that farmers would come to a new center of commerce. The founders' dreams began to come true when the first freight delivered to Greer's Depot was a load of fertilizer. The building of the town fell to the carpenters, masons, and their apprentices, helpers, and laborers. At first there was a lot of dust or mud depending on the season; the structures were small and made of wood. Twenty years would pass before the first cotton mill would or could be built.

All the while Greer was attracting increasing interest because of its cotton prices and the reputation of its school, which offered both a public and private session. The skyline profile of the infant town was shaping up. Jesse Cannon operated a sawmill and provided much of the first lumber for the frame structures that were the early town. He also made brick from the red clay found in abundance in the area and sold it to early settlers such as D.D. Davenport, who wanted his house and office to be more substantial structures. Jackson Green and Spartan Berry also operated sawmills as demand for building materials soared during the cotton mill era. When the first local mill was constructed, thousands of board feet of area lumber went into the construction, and Edward Mosely and his crew of masons laid an estimated two million bricks.

But before the mills went up, there had to be visionaries with almost unlimited optimism to see the potential of such a crude settlement as Greer in the 1880s. One of those individuals was a young man from just outside of the new town.

Eighteen-year-old John A. Robinson replaced D.T. Lane as depot agent in October 1888, becoming Greer's fourth depot agent in a dozen years. Robinson grew up with the town and became an instrument of its progress. He became associated with Lewis Parker when the new mills were being planned. Parker, a lawyer by profession and attorney for several textile clients, became Robinson's mentor when the young man demonstrated acuity and interest in the growing industry. Robinson was a fast learner and extremely energetic.

During the remaining 76 years of his life, he was involved in all four of Greer's cotton mill starts including being the principal founder and corporate president of Greer's final cotton mill. Robinson also was a principal in a batting mill set up in the old Farmer's Alliance warehouse and was corporate president of Greer Bonded Warehouse Company. Robinson had other interests, including real estate, and was a family man and promoter of his hometown. His civic involvements almost matched his business interests in terms of energy and devotion. He promoted education, served on a citizens' committee on school building, and chaired the third Liberty Loan Drive during the First World War.

Robinson became involved with the Victor Manufacturing project in his early 20s, a corporate co-founder at age 30, a corporate officer in a third mill before he was 40, and by that milestone age, the head of Greer Manufacturing Company. He did not manage a mill nor engage in the day-to-day operation; rather he was the planner and executive power responsible for the successful launching of Greer into the textile world.

Cotton had always been a presence, but the mills that Robinson and others built made all the difference in the world. It was an "up by the bootstraps" kind of struggle; the mills of Greer were modest affairs by comparison to some others in the state, but they were homegrown. Local merchants provided much of the funding for the mills, and they did it in a timely manner although they lacked any expertise in the industry. Expertise was imported from other mill towns and other states.

The mills of Greer gave life to the dusty little town and forced it to meet the increasing list of needs of an increasing population. They provided alternative opportunities for the next generation in Greer. Frank Carman learned the art of the blacksmith in his father's shop. David H. Carman, widower, made an adequate living for his five children, but son Frank also witnessed his father in physical decline from years of toil exposed to heat and cold. There were occasional accidents caused by animals; burns were a common hazard. He found the cotton mill to be so much preferable to the blacksmith shop that he was eventually able to persuade his father to quit the shop for the mill in 1918.

The textile industry also gave hope of regular work to many farmers displaced from their lands or those who farmed marginal lands. Elsie Belcher's family came to Greer in 1913 from the Dark Corner section. For them, the mills represented certainty to farming's uncertainty. Elsie was the oldest of seven children and one of the four hands the family agreed to provide in order to rent a village house. She was 16.

While John A. Robinson represented the visionaries who first planned the textile mills in Greer, the hundreds of laborers who came from the Piedmont, the mountains, even a few from foreign countries, made the dream reality as they provided the labor for the mills. The hours were long, and the work ranged from tedious to boring. The pay was low, but it was regular and the work was indoors. There was the convenience of a company-operated general store where credit was extended. There were recreational facilities, a union church, and virtually all village houses were new construction with nearby wells. The company supplied coal and wood at cost, hauled garbage, and cleaned the privies. For most of the operatives who spooled, spun, wove, or did other various and sundry specialty work defined by the mill operations, life in the village was an improvement over that which they previously had known.

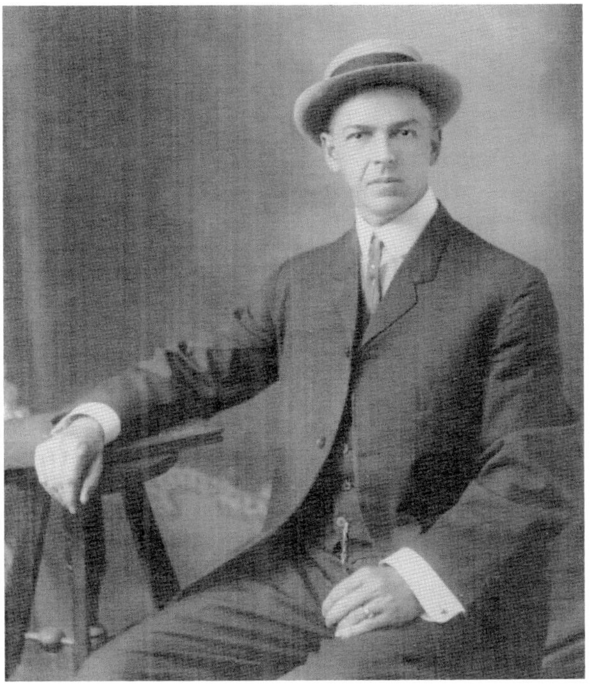

John A. Robinson
Robinson (1869–1964) is the American success story. From teenage telegraph operator, he rose to become a leading citizen and businessman in Greer. He was one of the organizers of the Franklin Mill in 1900 and the Greer Manufacturing Company in 1909. In 1913, he was chosen as the first chairman of the newly formed Commission of Public Works. Lake Robinson is named for him. (Courtesy of Don Robinson.)

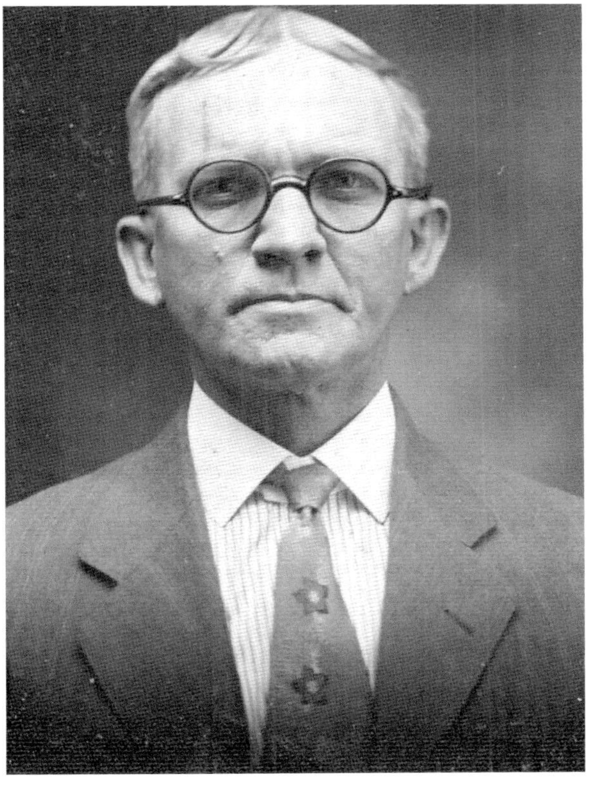

Claudius Milton Hemphill
Hemphill was superintendent of Greer Mill and Monaghan Mill. He also served as a local magistrate from 1940 to 1946. (Courtesy of Ann Dillard Withrow.)

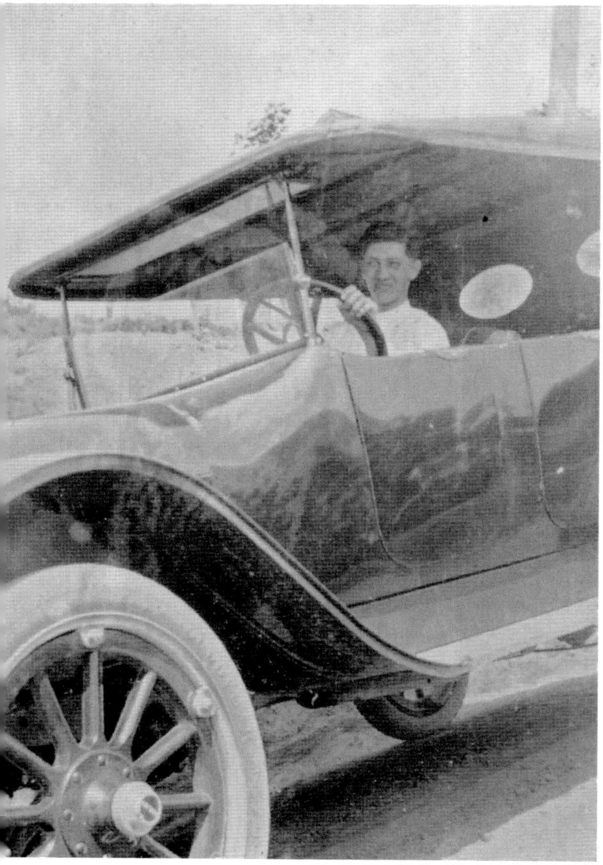

Frank Carman

Carman was the first in four generations of Carman sons who did not work as a blacksmith. His knowledge of the trade, thanks to his father, prepared him for related work. When he found work at Greer Mill, he was put on the maintenance crew where he specialized in boiler operations. He remained in the mill, a fixture himself, for a half century. (Courtesy of the Carman family.)

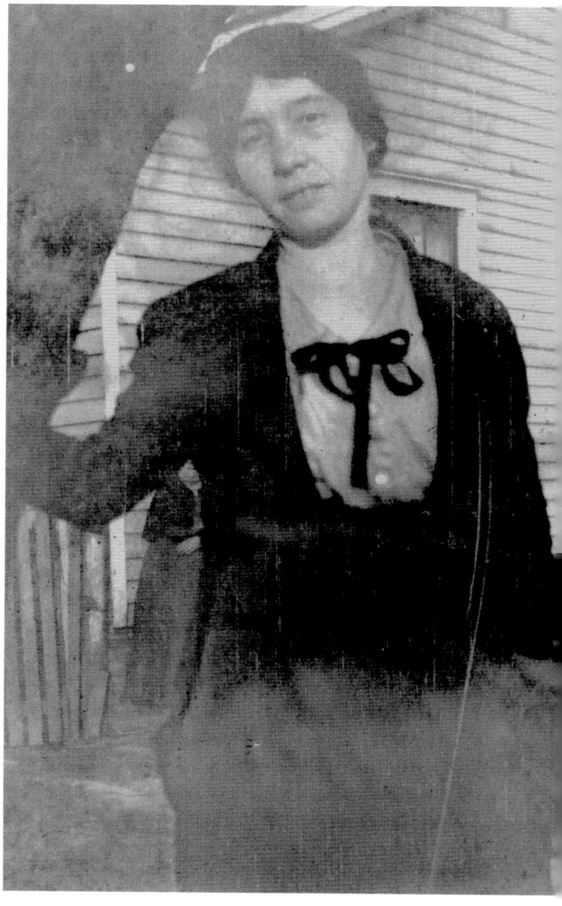

Elsie Pauline Belcher

Belcher moved from the Dark Corner with her family in 1913 to work in a cotton mill. She was stricken with a form of paralysis that required her to walk with crutches the remaining 70 years of her life. Nevertheless, she was employed as a drawing-in hand in the weave room, work which she continued until retirement. (Courtesy of the Belcher family.)

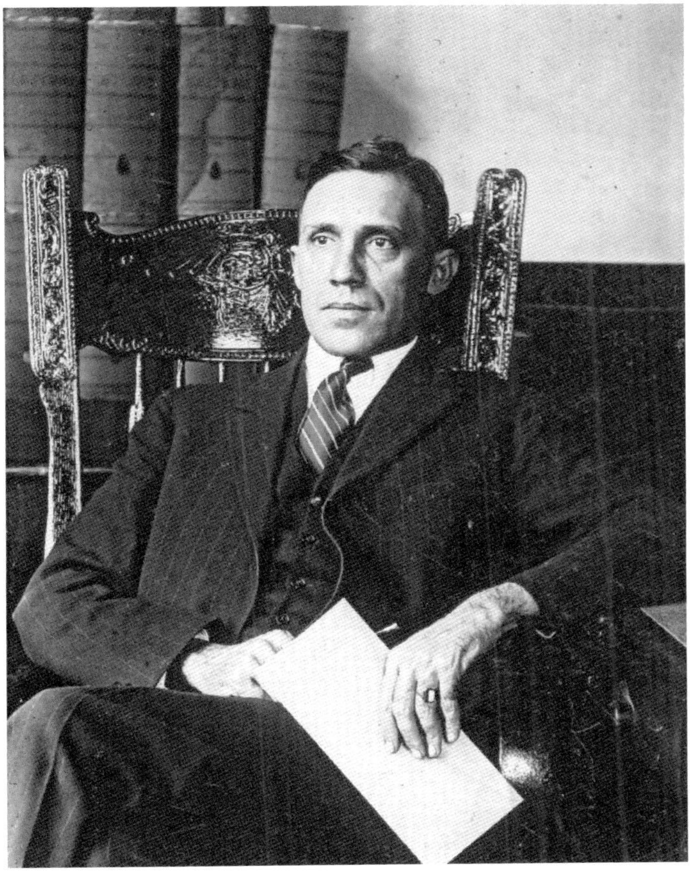

C. Rhett Ballenger

Ballenger, a native of Greer, came from a farming background. He acquired an education and entered the cotton mill industry as an office clerk at Apalache Mill. His knowledge and drive secured him the superintendent's job at Victor Mill. At 35, he became the general manager of all three of Greer's Victor-Monaghan Mills in 1919. (Courtesy of the Greer Heritage Museum.)

Alliene Carman

Snowball fight or snowman? Carman (far right) and other young people from the Greer Mill village prepare for action in the winter of 1918. (Courtesy of the Carman family.)

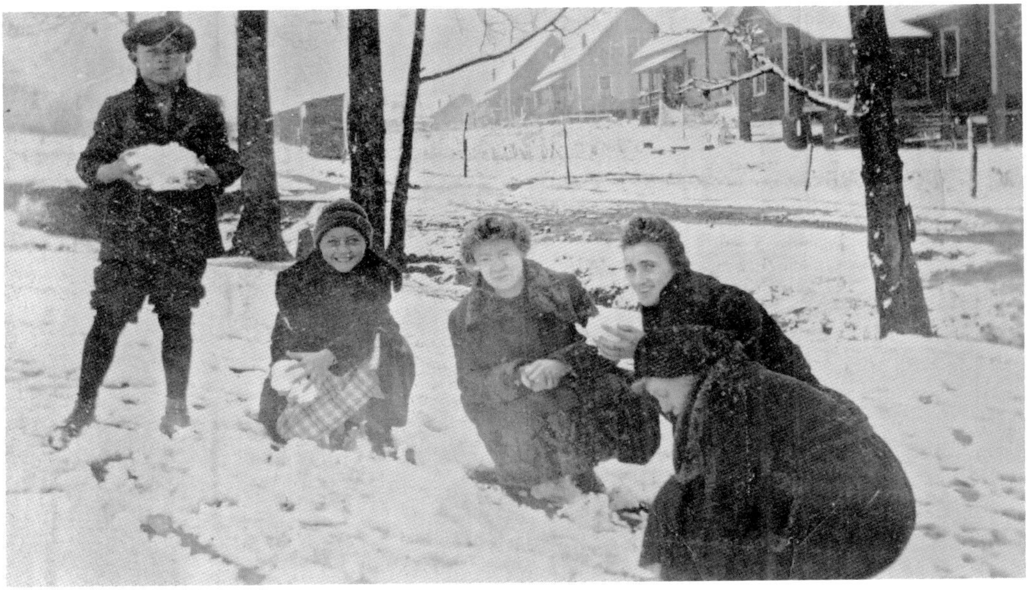

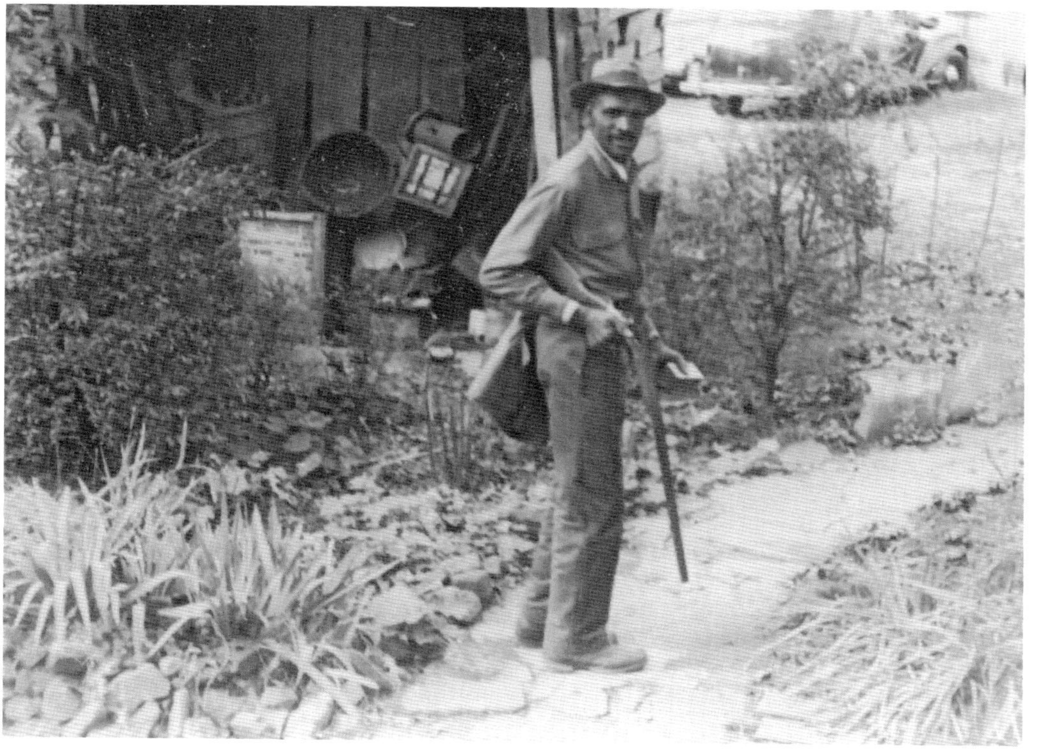

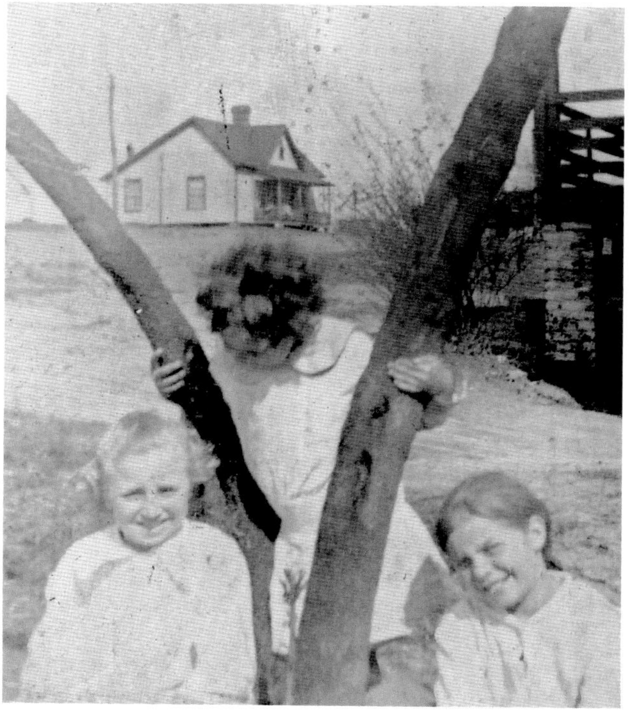

John Good
Good was a jack-of-all-trades who lived in a small three-room house behind the Robinson family home on South Main Street. He worked for the Robinsons and their neighbors as a handyman. When Highway 29 was paved in the early 1940s, Good appeared in Greer and stayed. Carpentry and shoe repair were his specialties. On this day, it appears that he has planned some hunting. (Courtesy of Don Robinson.)

Louise Hester
Hester was born on the village at Greer to Dollie and Luther Hester. Like many children of her generation, she enjoyed the community around her as if it were part of a giant extended family. She left the village to be the wife of a soldier during the last days of World War II. (Courtesy of the Carman family.)

CHAPTER FOUR

The Business and Professional Community

Greer has always enjoyed steady business as a commercial center. The volume, of course, slowed during times of recession, depression, and doubt, but the town, even in bleakest times, never withered. It managed to attract sufficient doctors, lawyers, and educators to meet the needs of its citizens during its early years, even though Greer was not the ideal environment for many to hang out a professional shingle and await growth. When times were hard, there was always some recourse to action or a collective willingness to retrench and wait out crises. There were business failures and transience among the professional class, but the overall outlook remained positive among Greer's business and professional community, who remained here and persisted. Most business owners acknowledged the fact that business is like a roller coaster; there are always going to be ups and downs. One succeeds if he just doesn't stand still.

J. Bratton Mendenhall did not stand still. He passionately pursued a good living first as a farmer, then ultimately as a shrewd businessman. Mendenhall was a native of York County, South Carolina. The son of Mill and Sarah Mendenhall, he was only eight years old when Greer was chartered; by the time he was 12, he was working as a farmhand on his father's farm. He and his wife Minnie migrated to Greer at the turn of the century where he opened a hardware store with J. Terry Wood in 1904. He managed the operation for over a decade as his interests drifted to other business. He eventually left the hardware business for cotton-related enterprises, becoming a fertilizer and cotton seed dealer and, later, a cotton broker.

He and William E. James became partners in a cotton brokerage in 1914. By 1916, his business was buying as much as 6,000 bales per year. He traded in the cotton market and invested profits earned from the postwar bull market in a new bank in 1920, Farmers Bank and Trust. Greer's fourth bank, it was managed by Rock Hill native C.L. Cobb. The founders besides Mendenhall included his business partner W.E. James, W.L. James, W.T. Brockman, and Allen R. Hawkins. The name suggests the clientele to whom its services were marketed. Catering to small depositors, it was popular among farmers and the millworkers. He then became the driving force behind the construction of Greer's largest cotton warehouse, Farmer's Bonded Warehouse, which had an estimated capacity of 2,000 bales.

Mendenhall was, in many ways, typical of the Greer businessman at the turn of the century. He was progressive in outlook, involved in civic affairs as well as his business interests. He served on the Commission of Public Works at a time when the town was taking on the responsibility of providing utilities for the public. He was a large man who stood firmly on his principles and at least in one case defended them with fisticuffs.

His children became well known in their own right, J. Bratton Jr. as the proprietor of a feed and seed company and Mattie Belle, who remained unmarried, as one of Greer's longtime and most beloved public school teachers.

Another longtime familiar face among the business community in Greer was that of Roy Collins. A World War I veteran, he was financed into business by George Bailes at the beginning of the Depression in 1930. The Bailes & Collins store specialized in dry goods and shoes. After Collins bought out his partner, it became a family affair with three generations of Collinses eventually owning and operating the business to the turn of another century. Despite what seemed to be bad timing for a business start-up, Collins not only ran his business but bought and sold cotton like so many before him in Greer. He accepted local farmers' cotton in trade at a higher price than the farmers could get on the market, stored it in a private warehouse until the price improved, and sold it. It required discipline and the willingness to take a risk, but it worked and his business prospered. Just after World War II, he followed in the footsteps of other Greer businessmen by entering the banking world as a director of Greer Federal Savings and Loan Association.

Bratton Mendenhall and many others who were involved in cotton had offices near the depots for convenience. That part of Greer was the active center of trade and commerce during the first half of the 20th century. Fertilizer dealers and others found it convenient to locate near the tracks as well. Among the next generation of business owners who found the location a good one was J.L. Jones, who operated Jones Coal Company for many years between the P & N and Southern tracks.

Jones's operation was small but critical for Greer for a while; he was one of only two coal dealers in town. He diversified into the moving and storage business when the demand for coal diminished by the early 1960s. The business remained a family affair with his wife, son, and brother-in-law actively participating in the business. "J.L.," as he preferred to be called, was active in public affairs and charity work. He served on the city council and held memberships in fraternal organizations and civic clubs.

During the 1950s, J.L. became interested in numismatics (coin collecting). Jones was a principal organizer of the Greer Coin Club which, at one time, boasted a membership of over a hundred. He was also instrumental in organizing the Blue Ridge Numismatic Association. In his later years, his interests expanded to railroading and antique bottles. He organized the Greer Bottle Club, and as he eased into retirement, operated a coin and bottle shop in part of his office space, catering to hobbyists who came to visit from all over the upstate. He left a lasting contribution to the bottle collecting hobby by writing a general catalogue, *Soda and Mineral Water Bottles,* in 1972.

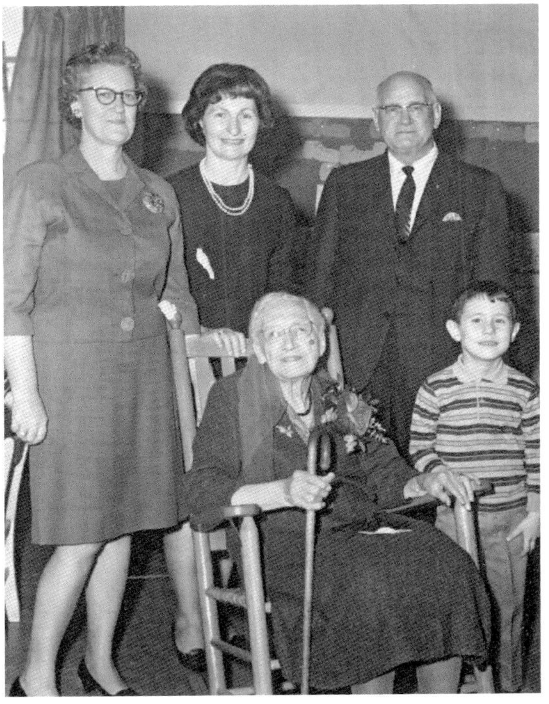

Dr. Viola Kirkwood

Kirkwood, indeed a legend, came from Mississippi in the early 20th century. Her husband was a jeweler and she was an optometrist, a rare achievement for her time. Besides her practice, she was a photographer and artist. She is shown here celebrating her 100th birthday with (left to right) Helen Holladay, Iree Wilson, Lewis L. Holladay (former Greer area school superintendent), and Mark Wilson. (Courtesy of Greer Heritage Museum.)

John B. and Minnie Mendenhall

John Bratton Mendenhall and his wife Minnie Cooley Mendenhall moved to Greer from McConnells, South Carolina, around 1900. They had five children. Mendenhall partnered with J. Terry Wood in establishing the Wood-Mendenhall Hardware on Trade Street in downtown Greer. He partnered with other businessmen to organize the Farmers Bank and Trust that operated from 1920 to 1923. (Courtesy of Karolyn and Richard Taylor.)

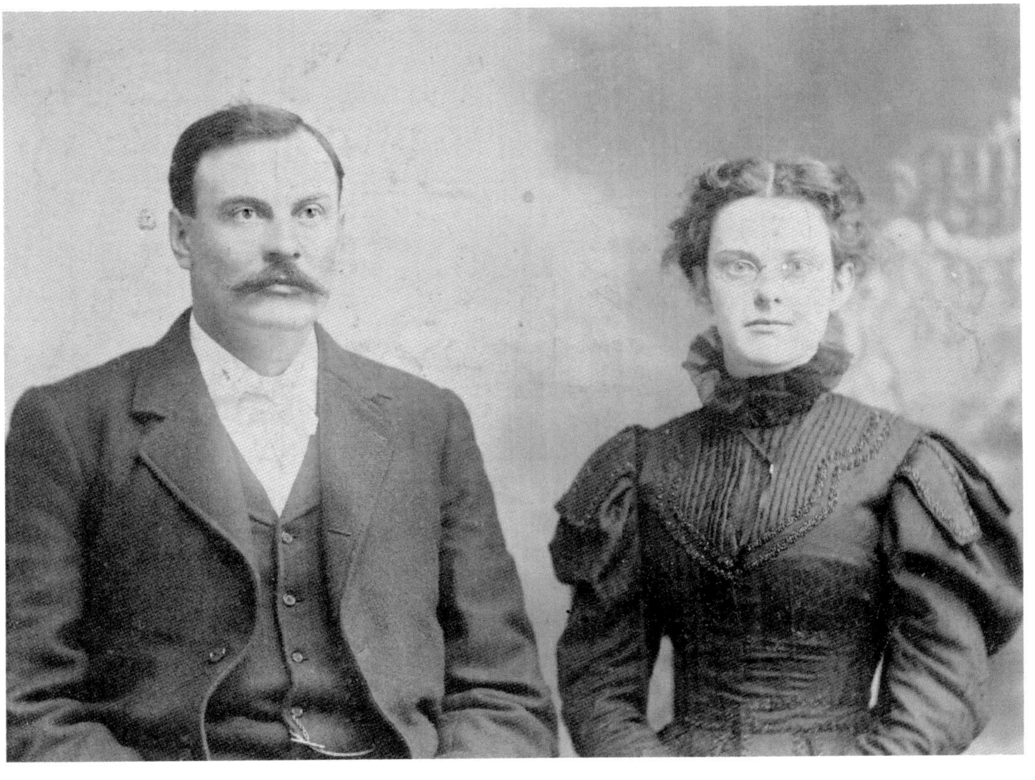

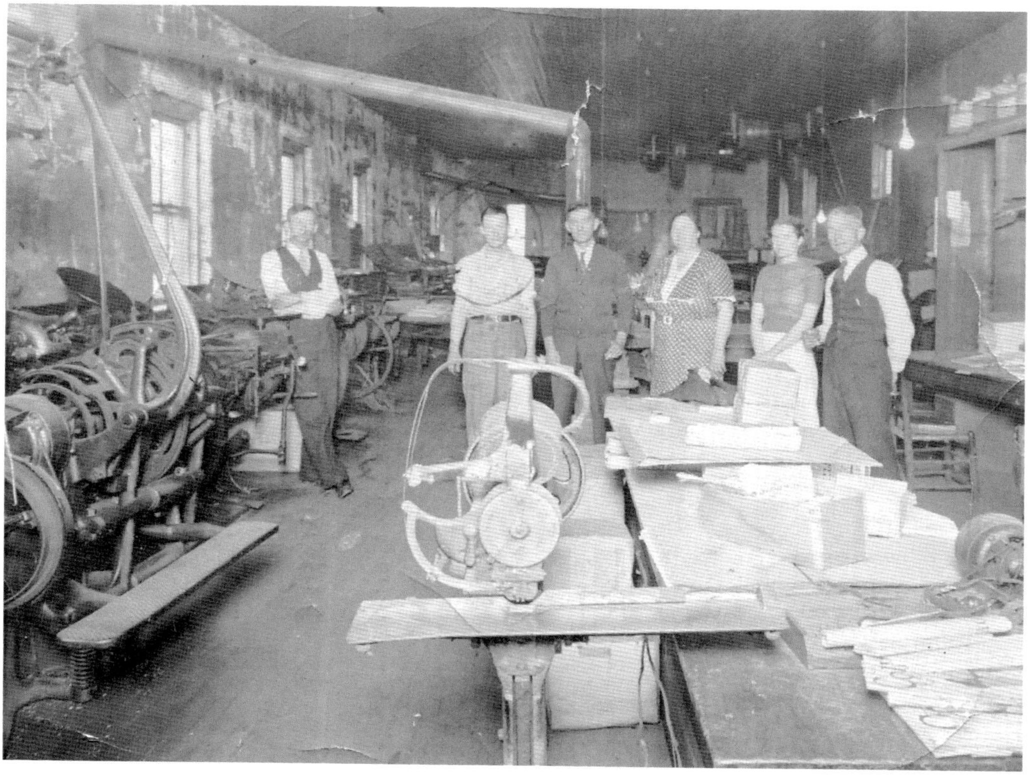

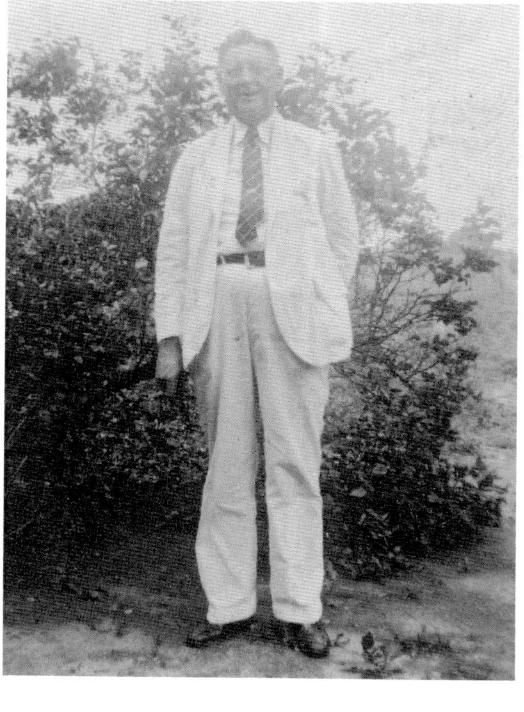

P.W. Smith, Editor

The *Greer Citizen* printing office in 1936 shows owner P.W. Smith and his wife Lula, the linotype operator. Also shown are Thomas Loftis, pressman; W.H. Burchmore, printer; Mr. ? Darby, linotype operator; and Nell Cannon. (The order is unknown.) Smith founded the *Greer Citizen* in 1918 and sold the weekly newspaper to E.A. Burch in 1942. It is still published today. (Courtesy of the Greer Heritage Museum.)

Carl M. Ponder

Ponder was born in the Washington community and came to Greer in 1903 to open a grocery store. His home-churned ice cream was so popular that he organized Ponder's Ice Cream Company in 1905 and operated it until the early 1960s. Ponder delivered ice cream in the immediate upstate area. In the early days he also did some bottling of soft drinks. (Courtesy of Mary Ponder Vickery.)

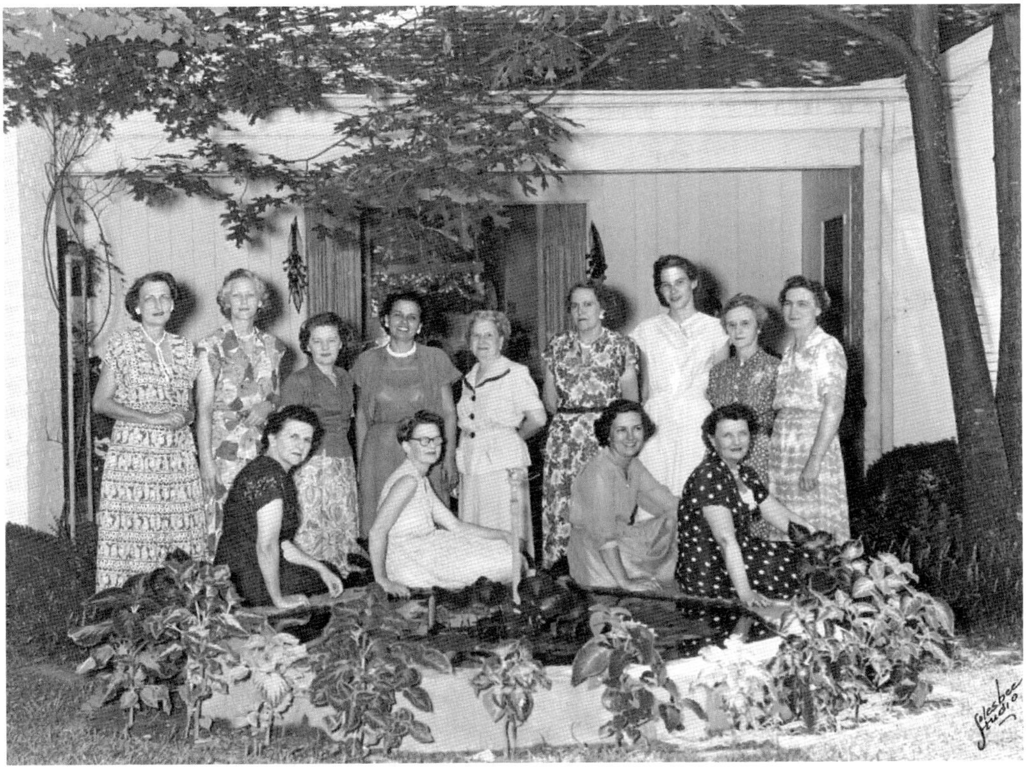

W.K. Hill Ladies Store

An early 1930s picture shows the employees of the W.K. Hill Ladies Store. Seated (left to right) are Earline Lanford, Elsie Dillard Fleming, Vera Edwards Burnett, and Virginia McAbee Baswell; standing (left to right) are Beatrice Black, Matilee Meares Hunt, Edith Allen Carver, Mary Henderson Wood, Mrs. W.K. Hill, Gladys Addy, Sallie Vaughn, Cora Howell, and Martha Howell Too ey. Fleming later opened a dress shop. (Courtesy of Greer Heritage Museum.)

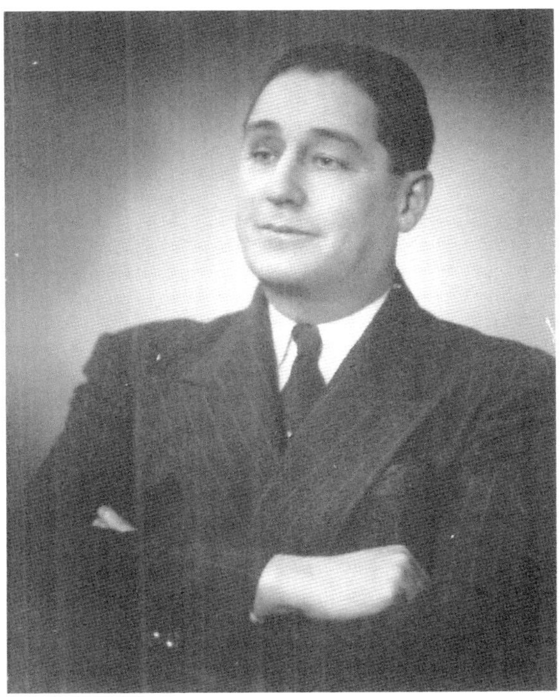

Jim Fleming

Jim Fleming and his wife Elsie were part of the business community for many years. Jim was with Greer Lumber Company while Elsie ran a popular ladies' dress shop, first by the Wayside Inn and later on Trade Street. (Courtesy of Jody Carman.)

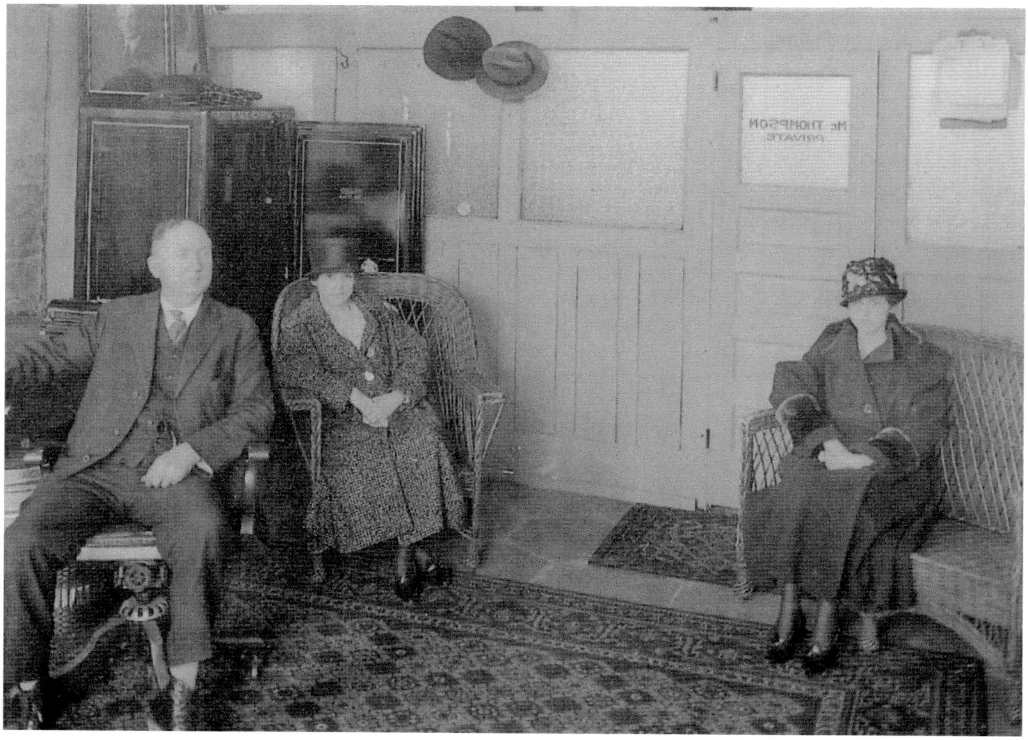

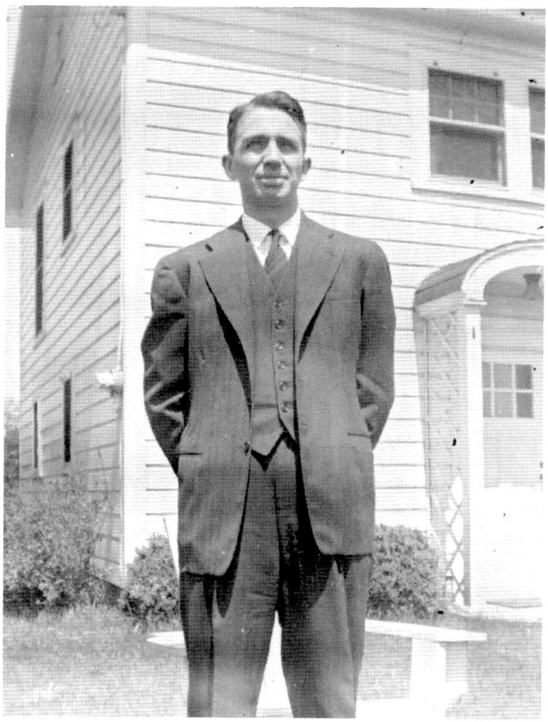

W.M. Thompson
William Morgan Thompson (1866–1942) opened a hardware store in Greer in 1906. Three years later he became Greer's first automobile dealer, selling Fords. He also opened an agency in Greenville. This picture inside the Greenville store shows Thompson with his daughters (left) Gertrude T. Marchant and Mildred T. Marchant. Mildred's husband John managed the Greenville agency. Thompson sold the Greer store to Dan Davenport, who renamed it D&D Motors. (Courtesy of Karl Beason.)

W.R. "Bill" Dobson
Dobson first worked at Sullivan-Eskew Hardware on Trade Street. In 1945, he started his own store in the old Howell grocery store. In 1963, he moved to the old Community Cash Grocery Store. Dobson's Hardware represented fine service and was a fixture in downtown Greer for many years. The site of the old store is now a city parking lot. (Courtesy of Terry Dobson.)

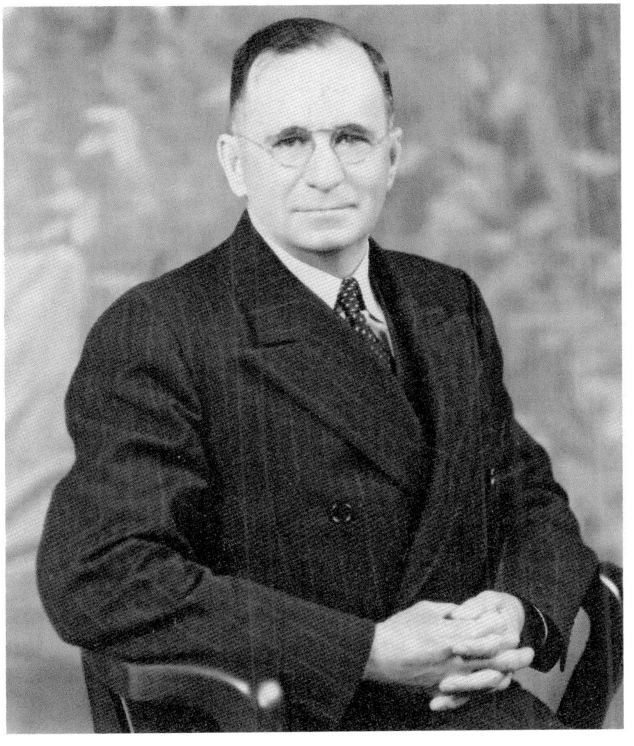

Dr. Theron Otis Walker
After graduating from Charleston Medical College in 1914 and serving in World War I in the Army Medical Corps, Walker started practice in Greer in 1918. He married Janie Hughes and they had two children. He died in 1943. (Courtesy of Dr. T.O. Walker.)

First Day of School
The first day of school was a momentous occasion for T.O. Walker Jr., as he poses with his father Dr. Theron Walker beside the family car in 1931. (Courtesy of Dr. T.O. Walker.)

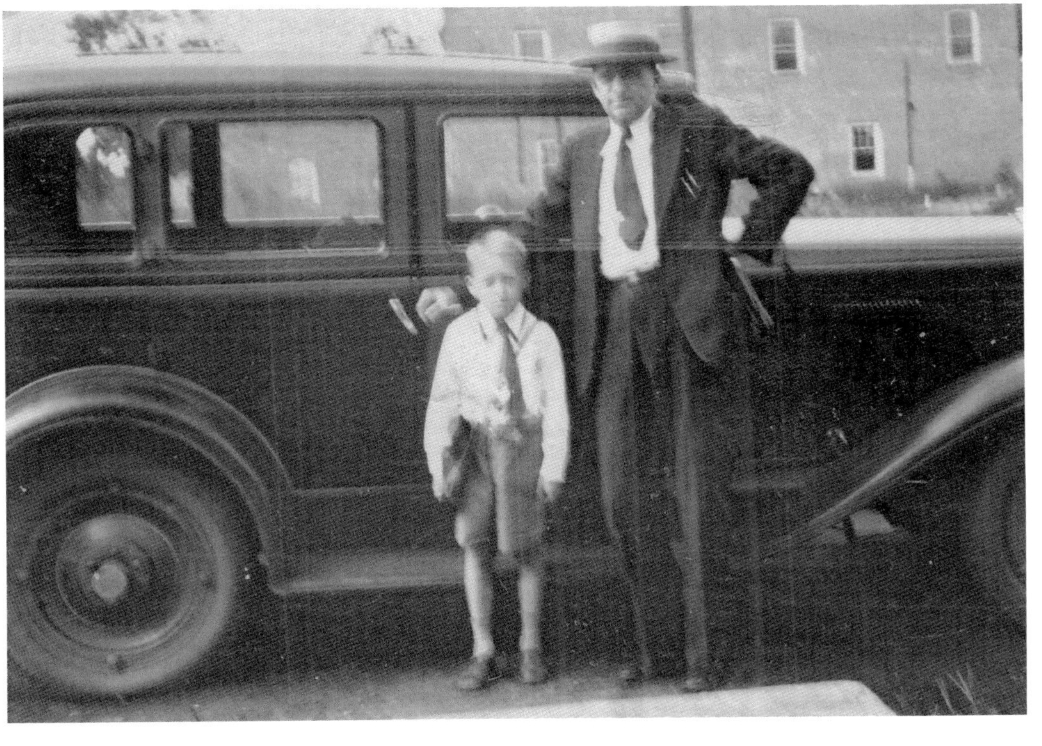

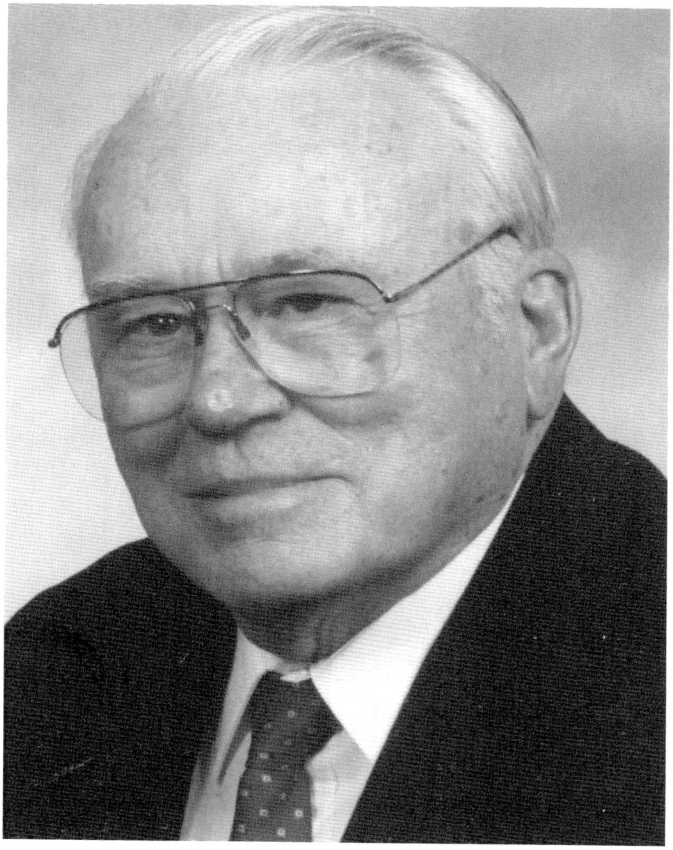

Dr. T.O. Walker Jr.
The younger Walker had planned to enter practice with his father, but T.O. Sr. died before T.O. Jr. finished medical school in 1948. He went into practice with Dr. James Hughes. Two months after he started his internship, he married teacher Sara Milford. He also practiced with Dr. D.C. Owens, and in 1973 moved to the Doctor's Clinic. He retired in 1996. (Courtesy of Dr. T.O. Walker.)

Smith & James
Smith & James, the oldest retail store in Greer, opened November 13, 1916, as Smith & Vaughn. In 1919, Vaughn sold his share to Don James. In 1934, Paul Smith joined his uncle, eventually buying the business. Paul Jr. started in 1963. Bernard Price, who joined in 1961, owns the store today. Shown here are (left to right) Paul Smith Jr., Bernard Price, and Paul Smith Sr. (Courtesy of Bernard Price.)

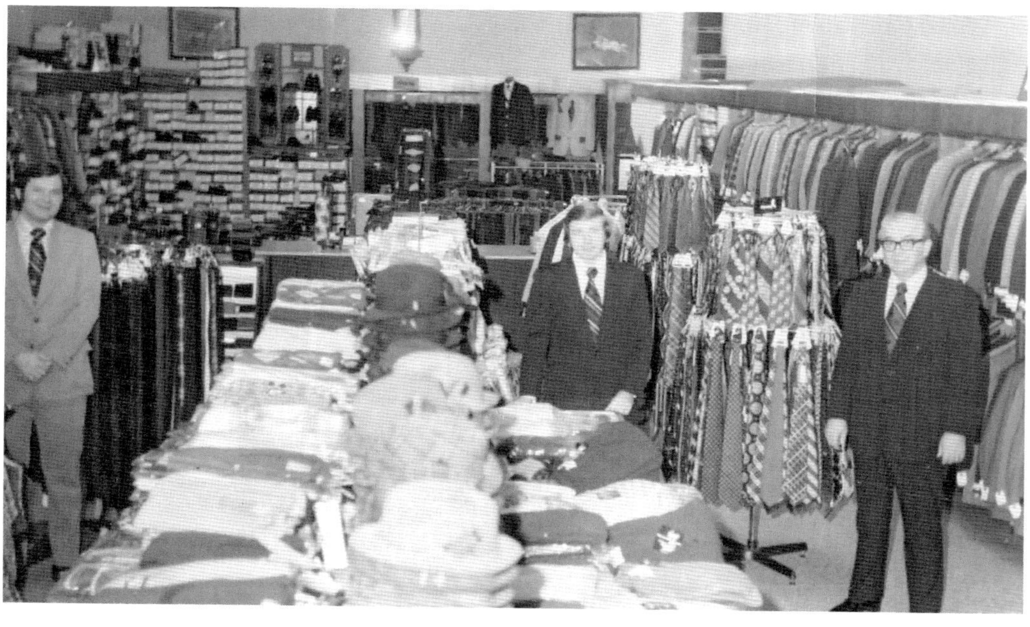

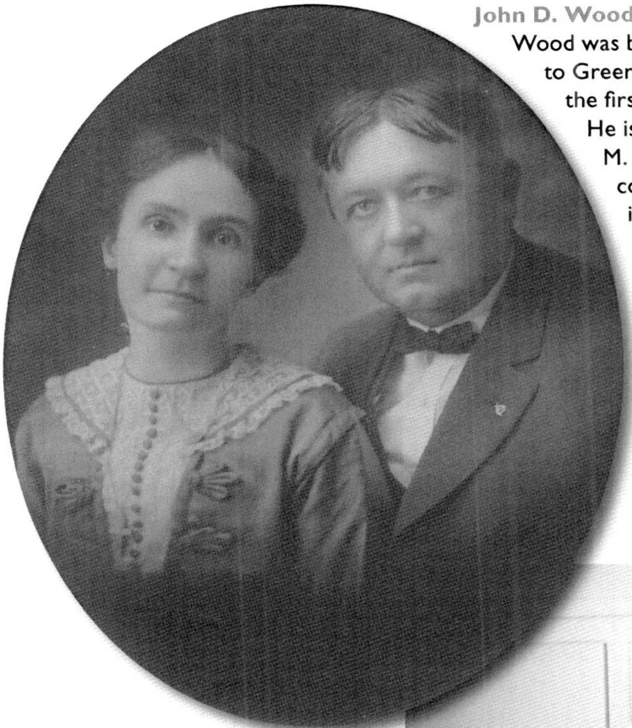

John D. Wood
Wood was born near Reidville in 1867 and came to Greer in 1890. He began Wood Mortuary, the first funeral business in Greer in 1902. He is shown here with wife Pearl Haynes M. Wood (1881–1961). Wood Mortuary continues today as the oldest business in Greer. He died in 1935. (Courtesy of Dick Wood.)

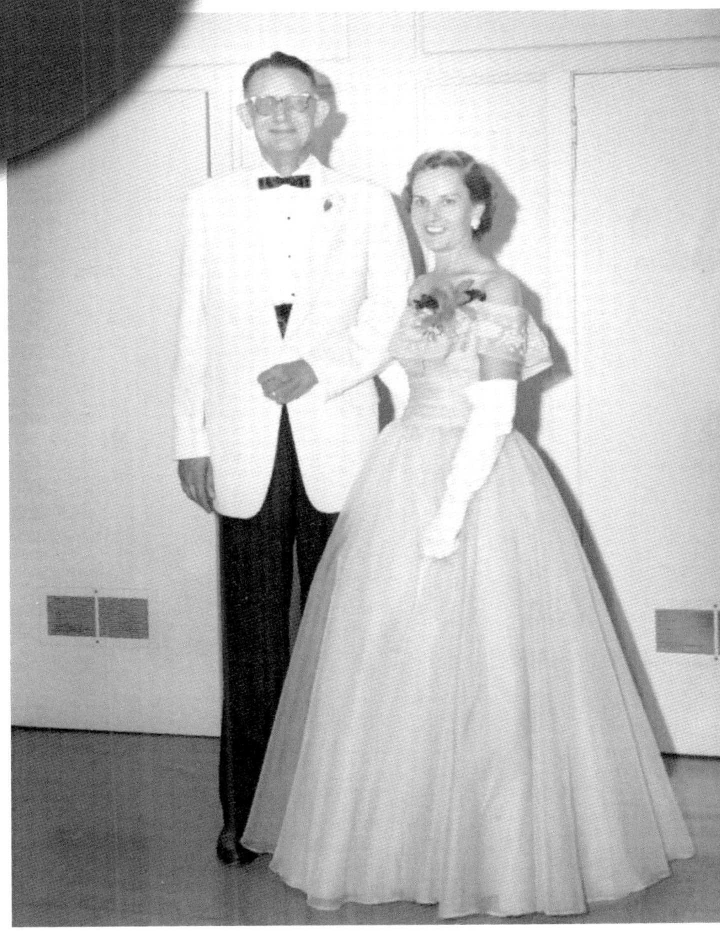

Richard H. Wood
Wood left Clemson University to return to Greer to help his father run the Wood Mortuary. When his father died in 1935, he found himself director at age 21. Incorporating the business with John O. Kendrick and T. Walter Glenn, he moved the business from Randall Street to its present location on W. Poinsett Street. He is shown here in 1960 with wife Lois. (Courtesy of Dick Wood.)

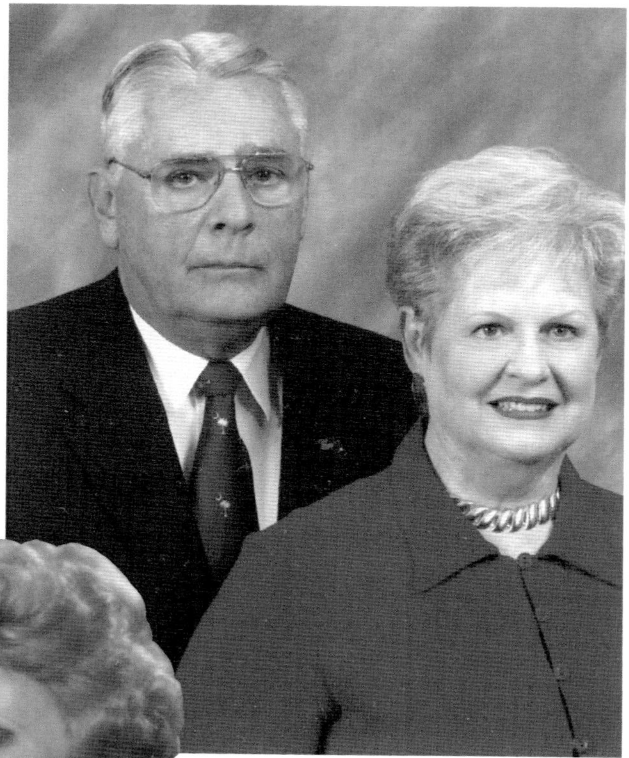

Richard and Sharone Wood
Richard Haynes Wood Jr. and his wife Sharone have been active in business, church, school, and community for many years. Dick began his career at age 17 riding in the flower truck for his father's mortuary. After college and the US Army, he joined his father at the Wood Mortuary. He retired from daily operations in 2003, but still owns one of the few family-owned mortuaries. (Courtesy of Dick Wood.)

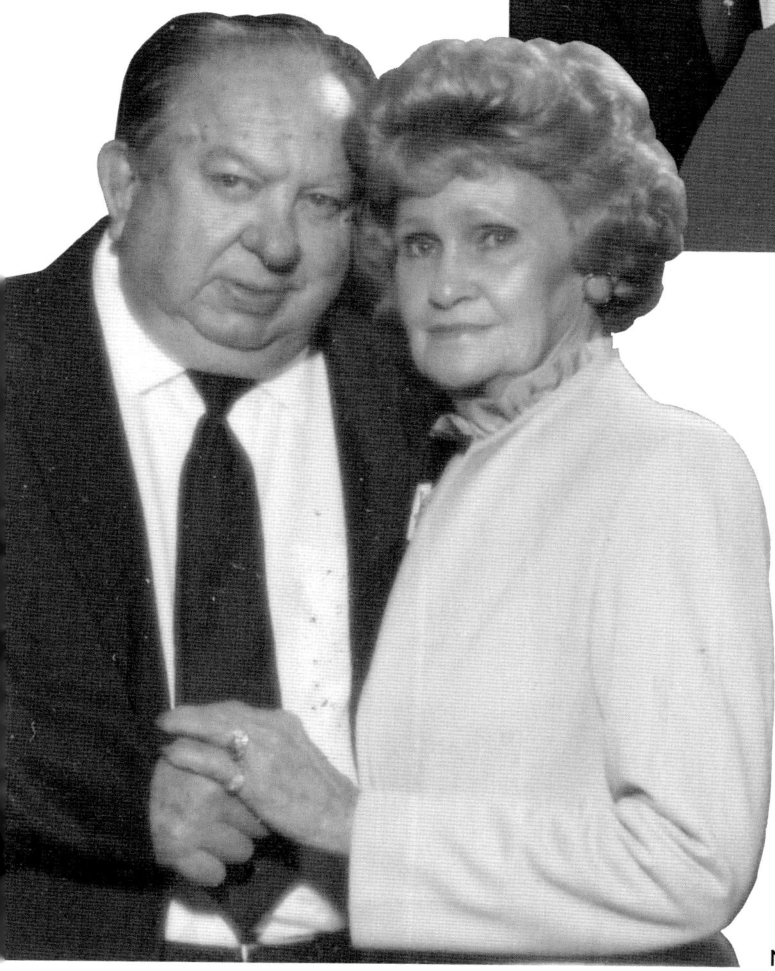

Lewis and Carrine Gosnell
The Gosnells ran Lewis Drive-In, "Greer's Fast-Food Landmark," on the corner of E. Poinsett Street and Littlefield Street. Opened in 1952, the restaurant was a favorite hangout for local teens. After 43 years, their sons Bucky and Davis Gosnell managed the restaurant until it closed. When the Drive-In opened, a hamburger was 40 cents and a Coca-Cola 15 cents. (Courtesy of Greer Heritage Museum.)

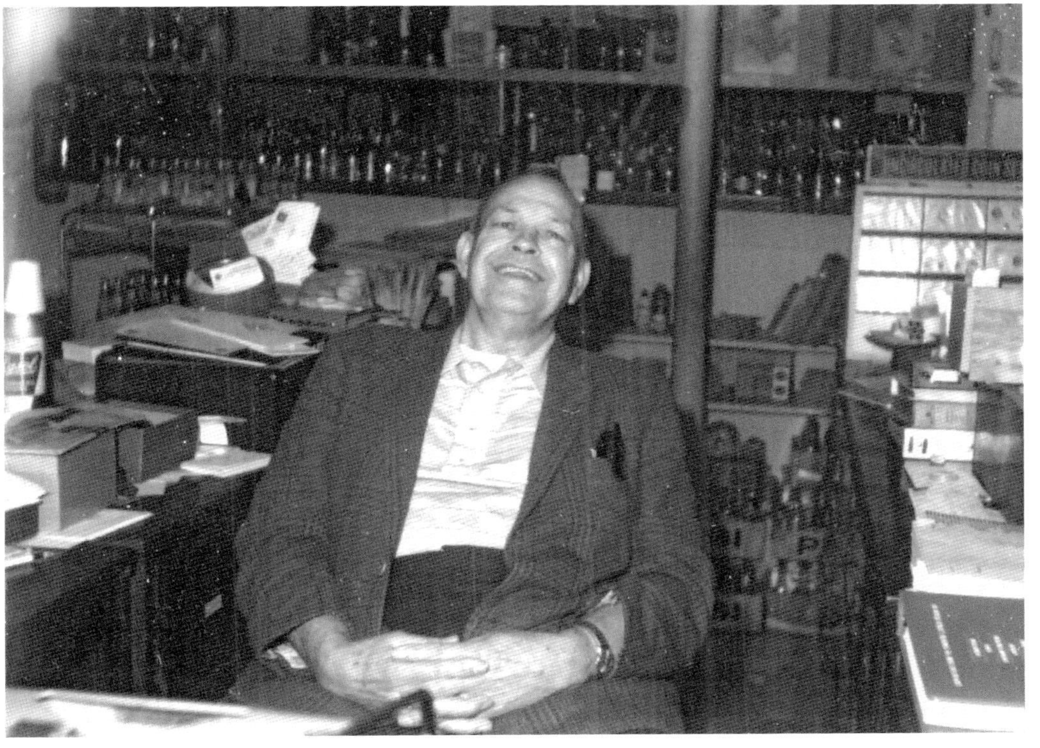

J.L. Jones
"What's on your mind—money, marbles, or chalk?" That was J.L. Jones's typical greeting to customers who came into his coin, stamp, and bottle shop. An avid collector of stamps, he assembled a collection of over 100,000 different varieties, specializing in pre-cancels and becoming regionally known for his expertise in the field. (Courtesy of the Pennington family.)

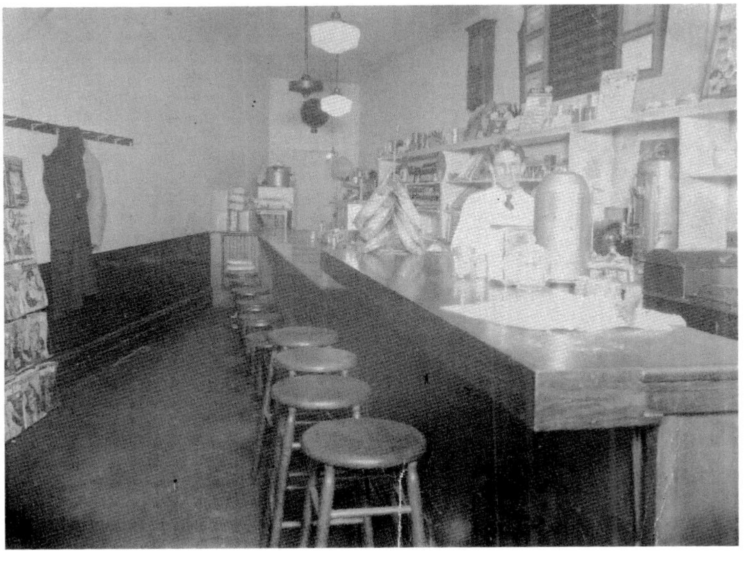

Praelo Howell
Praelo Howell worked for a while at the Dixie Café, a longtime landmark in Greer culinary history. The Dixie underwent several changes in ownership, and business sagged for local cafes when national fast food chains arrived. By then, Praelo had left the food business and joined his brother in the roofing business in which he remained active into his 60s. (Courtesy of Greer Heritage Museum.)

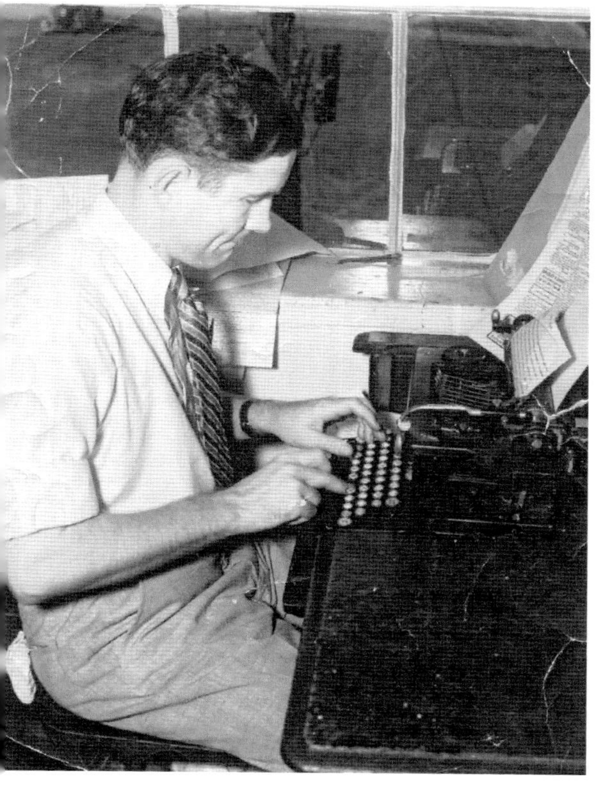

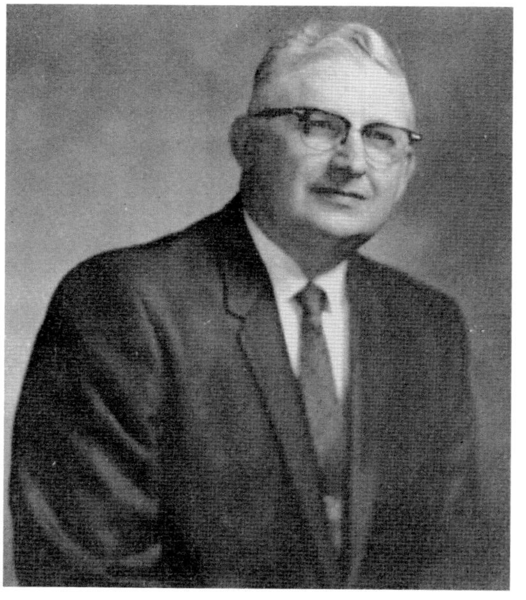

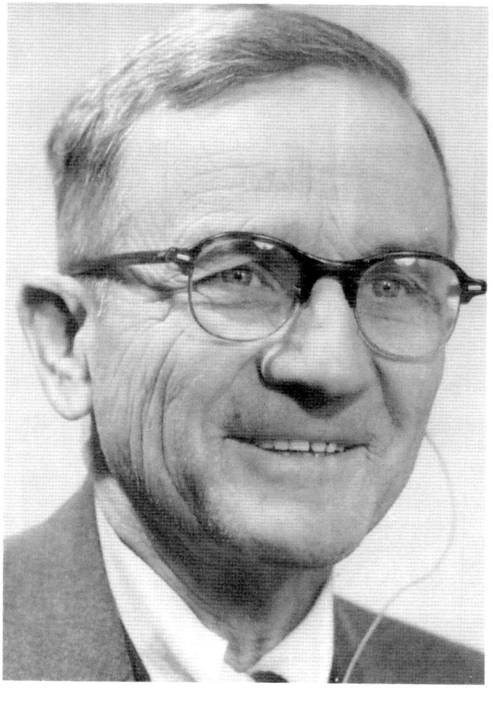

Dr. James Langston Hughes (ABOVE)
Son of R.M. Hughes, Dr. Hughes was a 1931 graduate of Furman University and a 1935 graduate of Emory University Medical School. He and Dr. T.O. Walker had a medical office on South Main Street. After some years in private practice, he became the medical director for Springs Industries in Lancaster but returned to Greer for his retirement years. (Courtesy of Hughes family.)

E.A. Burch (ABOVE LEFT)
Burch began his newspaper career as a young reporter in Georgia. In 1942, he bought the *Greer Citizen* and was editor until 1985 when he died. Edd Burch probably had more influence on Greer than any other citizen. According to son Leland, he was the champion of the common man and never backed away from a cause in which he believed. (Courtesy of Leland and Margaret Burch.)

Fred Cox
Fred Cox (1892–1971) was the circulation manager at the *Greer Citizen*. He had retired from working in the circulation department of other daily papers, but retirement wasn't for him. He started with the *Greer Citizen* part-time and found a family. When he died, the newspaper editor wrote: "He would go a mile out of his way (walking) to see that some person got his *Greer Citizen* on time." (Courtesy of Greer Heritage Museum.)

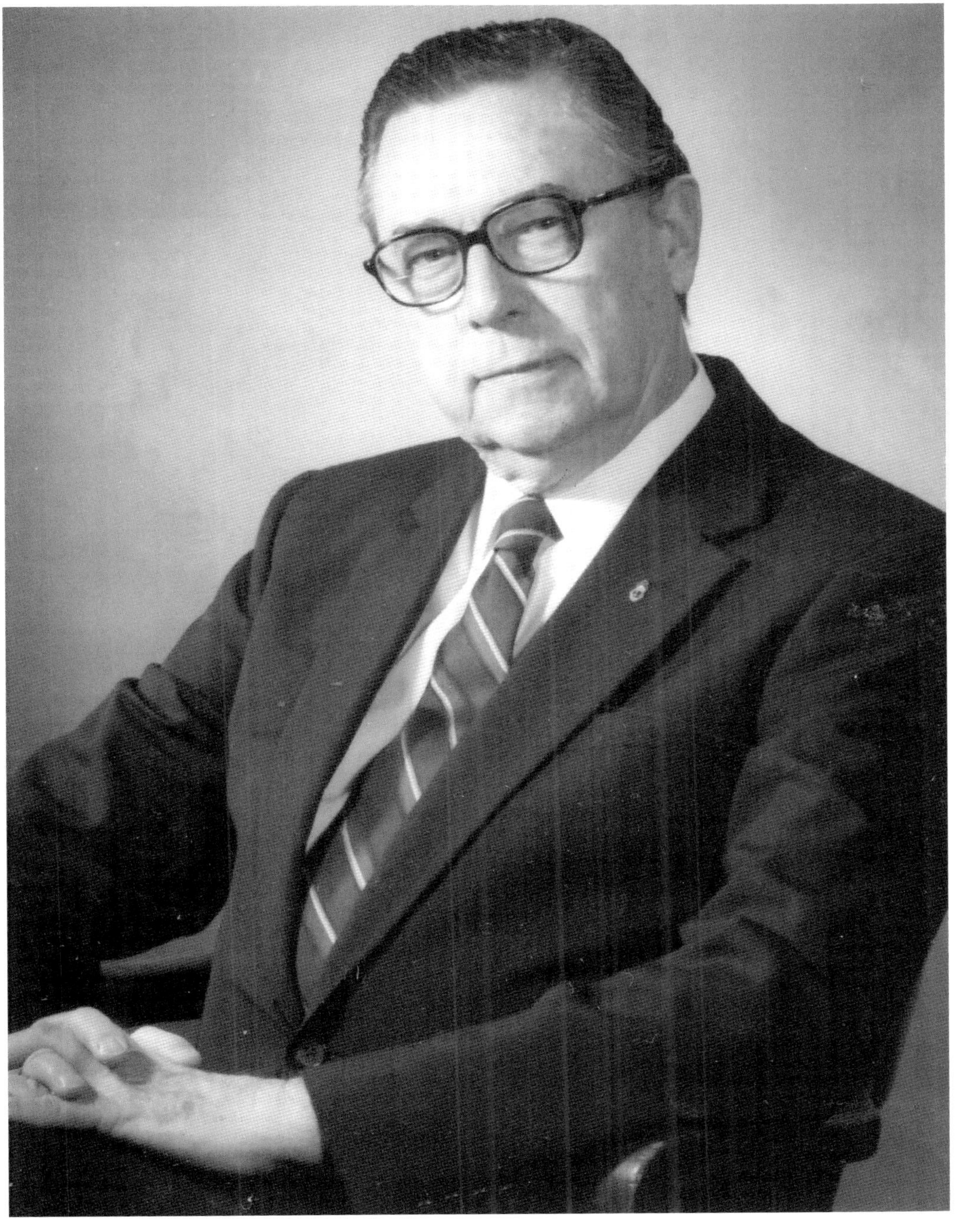

Hayne Preston Griffin
Griffin was a self-made man. During World War II, he worked as a comptroller for a Greenville company that made bandages for the Army. This led to his opening four cloth shops, including one in Greer. Later he expanded the Mutual Home Stores to furniture. He was active in church and community. (Courtesy of Leland and Margaret Burch.)

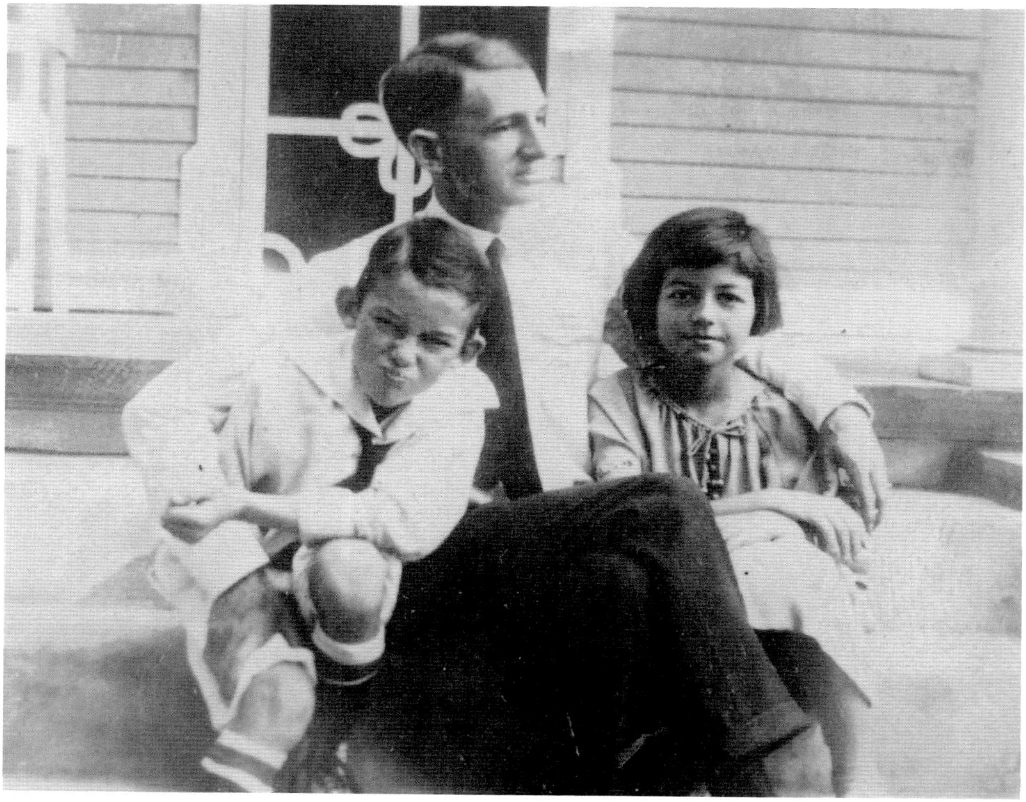

B.A. Bennett

Bennett enjoys a family moment with son Allen and daughter Margaret, affectionately known as Bobbie. A native of Reidville, Bennett was a business and civic leader who headed the Bank of Greer and Citizens Building and Loan Association. In 1928, Bennett organized B. A. Bennett and Co., a successful insurance company. From 1923 to 1933, he served as mayor of Greer. (Courtesy of Allen Cullum.)

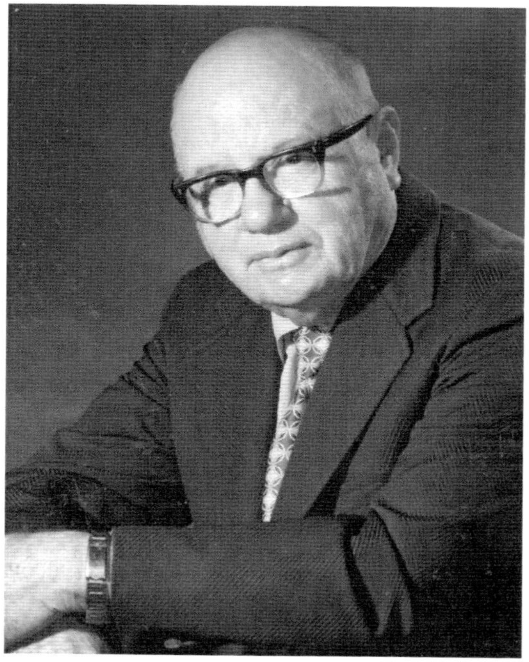

James Suddath Paget

Paget, known as Sud, was born in 1901 in Anderson, South Carolina. He moved to Greer in 1926 and began working as a bookkeeper for his father-in-law J.C. Cunningham at C&D Chevrolet in 1928. He became a partner in 1937 and eventually acquired the agency in 1961. In 1963, he sold to his sons James and Ben, changing the name to Paget Chevrolet. (Courtesy of Greer Heritage Museum.)

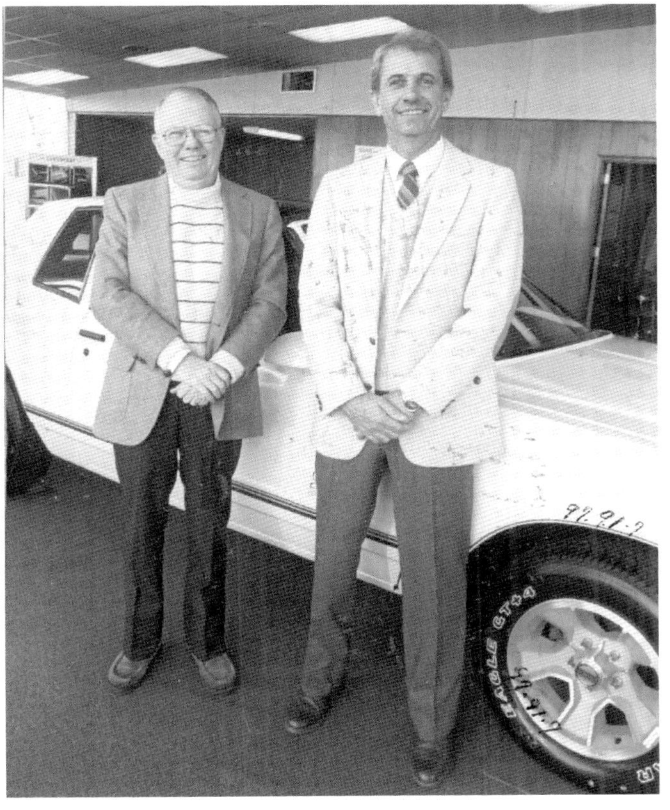

James and Ben Paget
Brothers James S. Paget Jr. (left) and Benjamin Lee Paget became partners with their father on January 1, 1963. In 1968, they moved the agency from downtown Greer to Wade Hampton Boulevard. They sold the business in 1988 to William Bradshaw. (Courtesy of Greer Heritage Museum.)

D.C. and Velmah Price
Growing up on a Cherokee County farm, D.C. Price knew a lot about farmers' needs. After Clemson University and the Korean War, he bought a Greer feed store in 1955. His wife Velmah taught school for 34 years and then joined him in the store. D.C. died in 1998 and Velmah operated Price's Feed and Seed until 2005. (Courtesy of Greer Heritage Museum.)

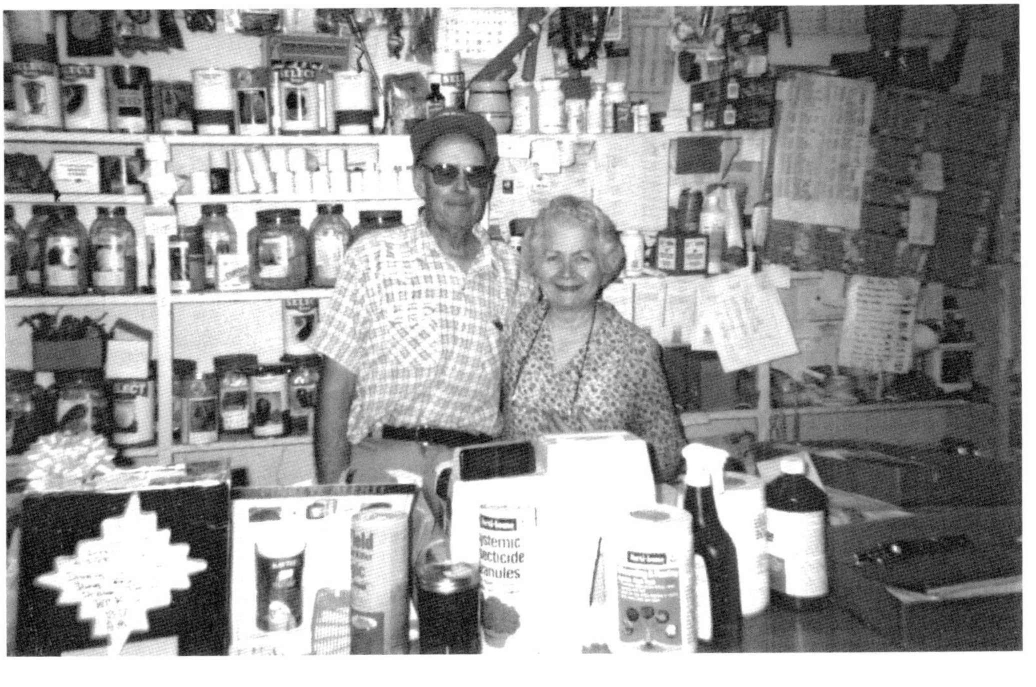

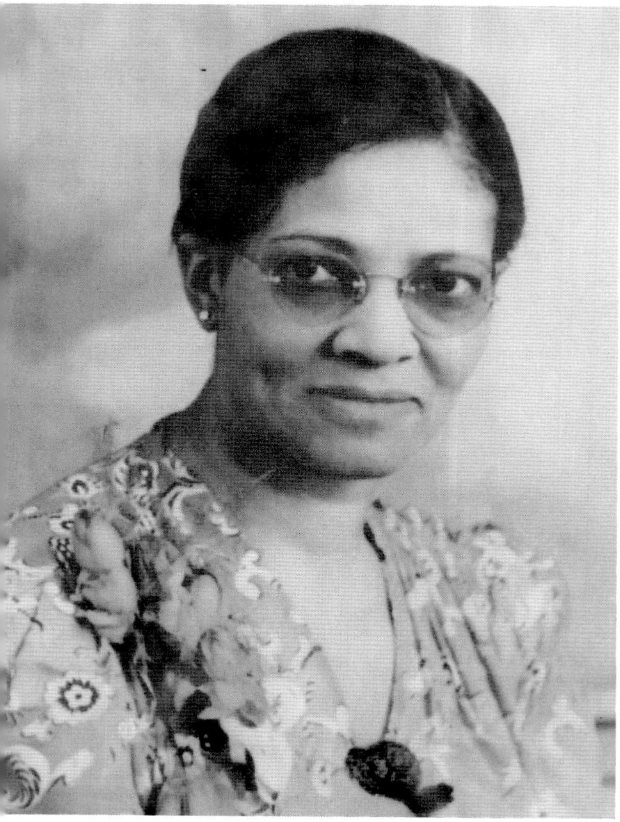

Blanche E. Thompson
Thompson owned and directed the Thompson Funeral Home at 122 Forest Street in the Needmore community. She began the business in 1932 and was a civic-minded businesswoman who cared deeply for the welfare of her community. She was born in 1890 and died in 1954. (Courtesy of Greer Heritage Museum.)

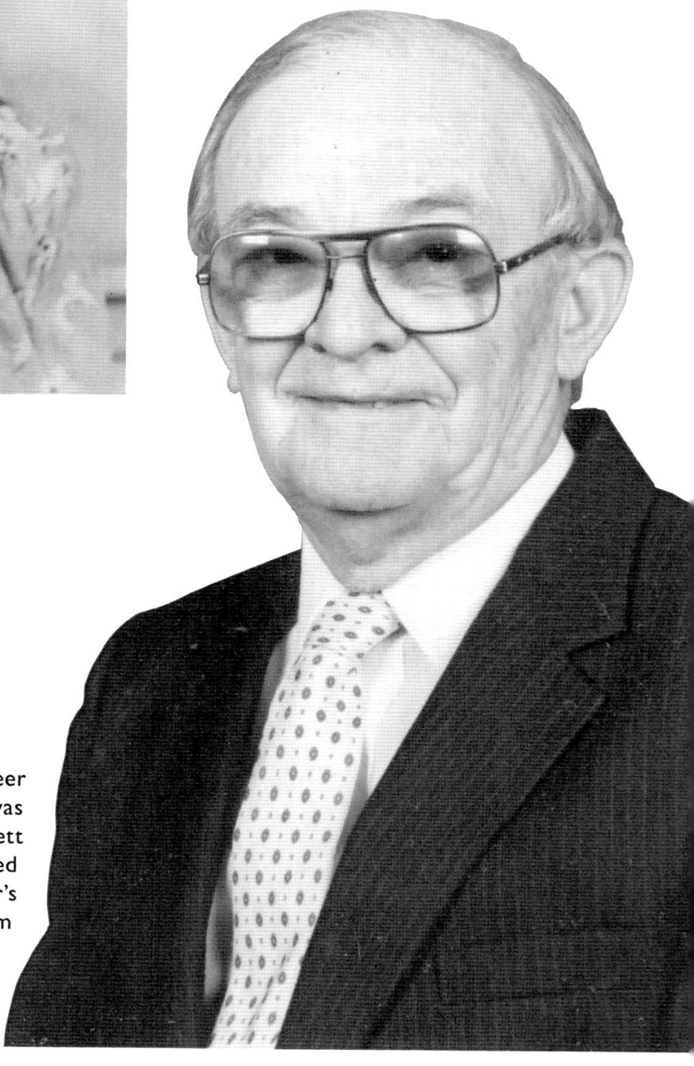

Dr. Lewis M. Davis, Surgeon
Davis began his practice in Greer downtown on Victoria Street. He was instrumental in establishing Allen Bennett Hospital in Greer. In the 1950s, he moved with other physicians to the new Doctor's Clinic on Memorial Drive across from the new hospital. After retiring, he served on the Greer Commission of Public Works. (Courtesy of Greer Heritage Museum.)

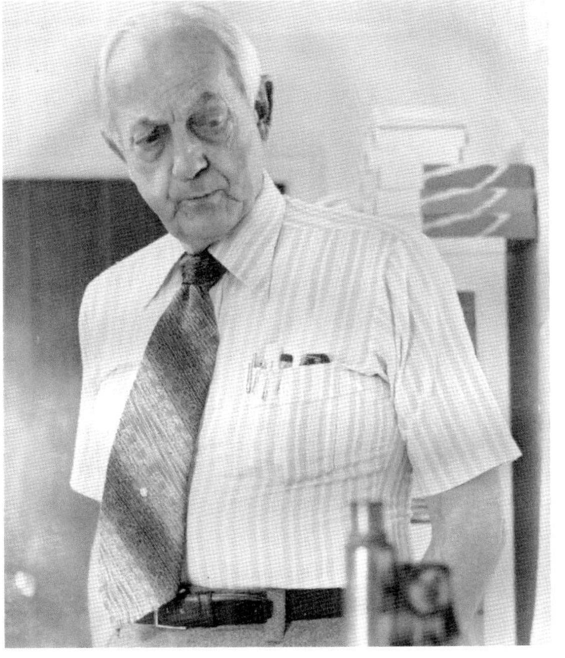

Dr. R.C. Alverson

Alverson first practiced medicine at the Chick Springs Hospital in Taylors. When the hospital closed in 1932, he began a practice in Greer. When his son W.E. "Bill" finished medical school, he joined his father. Both were popular doctors in Greer. (Courtesy of Greer Museum.)

Lloyd Hunt

Hunt (shown on the left) started the Tire Exchange in downtown Greer in 1931. Hunt, who served as mayor of Greer from 1955 to 1965, sold the business in 1955 to J. Verne Smith (center). An unidentified representative from Goodyear is presenting an award to the business. The motto for the business was "The best is yet to come." (Courtesy of Greer Heritage Museum.)

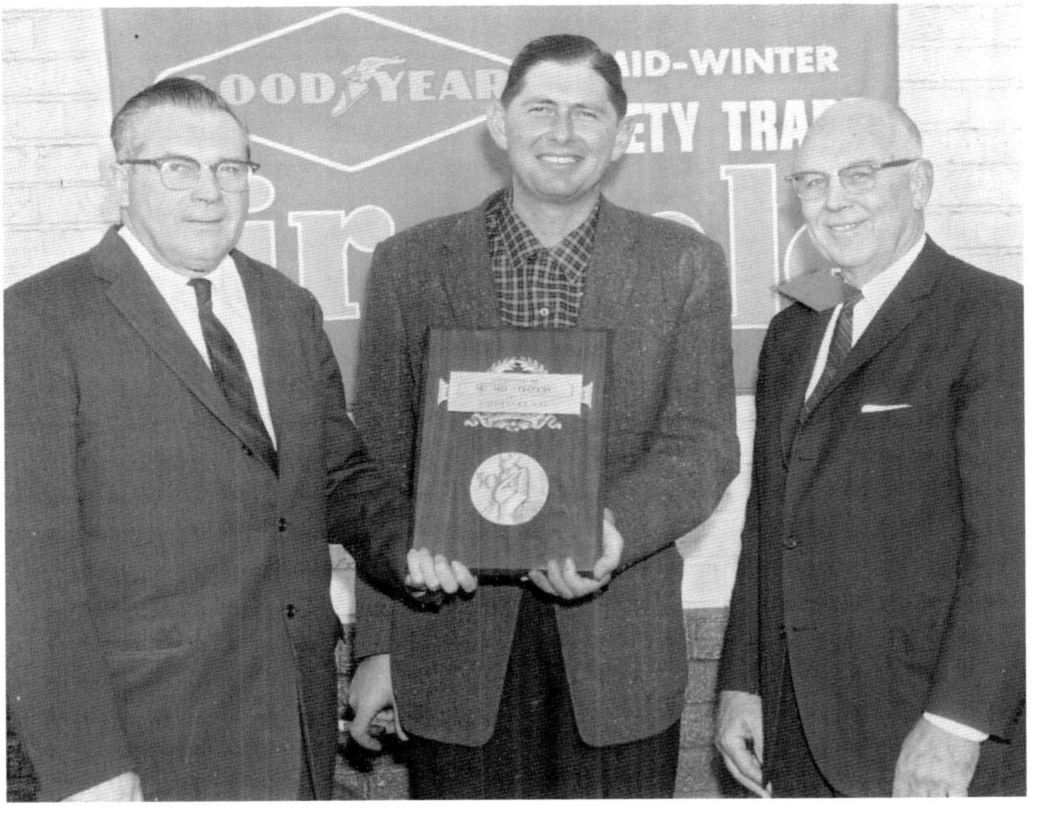

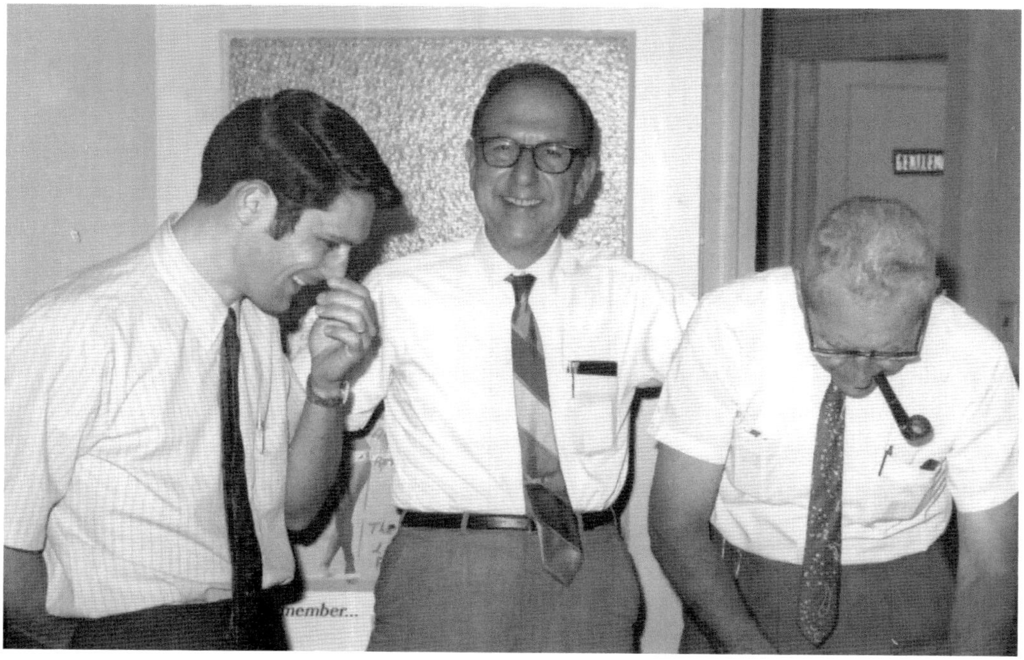

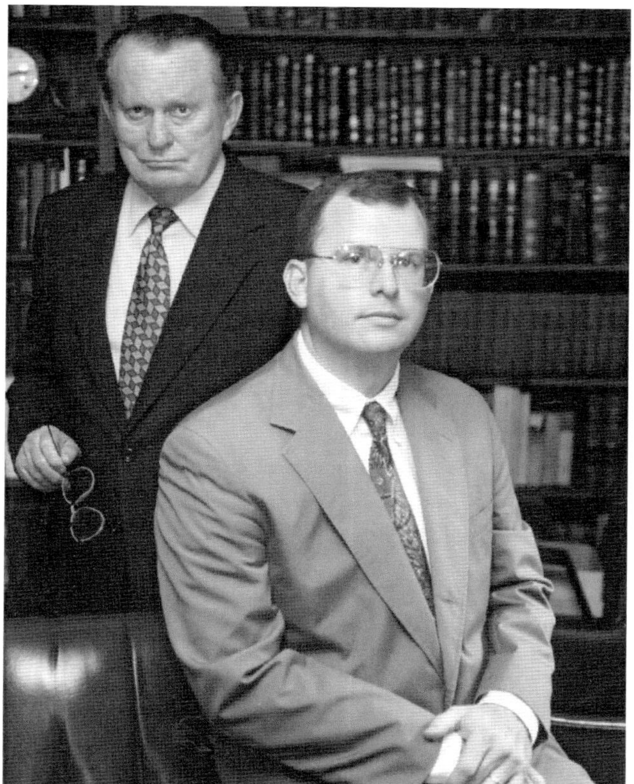

Lanford & Gibson Inc.
Marion Lanford founded Lanford & Gibson Inc. in 1945 to provide personal and professional insurance. Later Carl Gibson joined the agency and became sole owner. Gibson (left) joins Lanford (center) and E.C. Bailey in a relaxed moment away from business concerns. Today, Carl's son Jay directs the business. (Courtesy of Carl Gibson.)

John M. Rollins
The Rollins family has a long history in law. The first John Rollins, a justice of the peace, settled at O'Neal. His son C.B. Rollins was a Spartanburg County magistrate judge. John M. Rollins (1926–2000), shown here with his son, practiced in Greer from 1955 to 1999. Besides a practice in Greer, John Rollins Jr. is a Spartanburg County magistrate and the municipal judge for Landrum. (Courtesy of John M. Rollins Jr.)

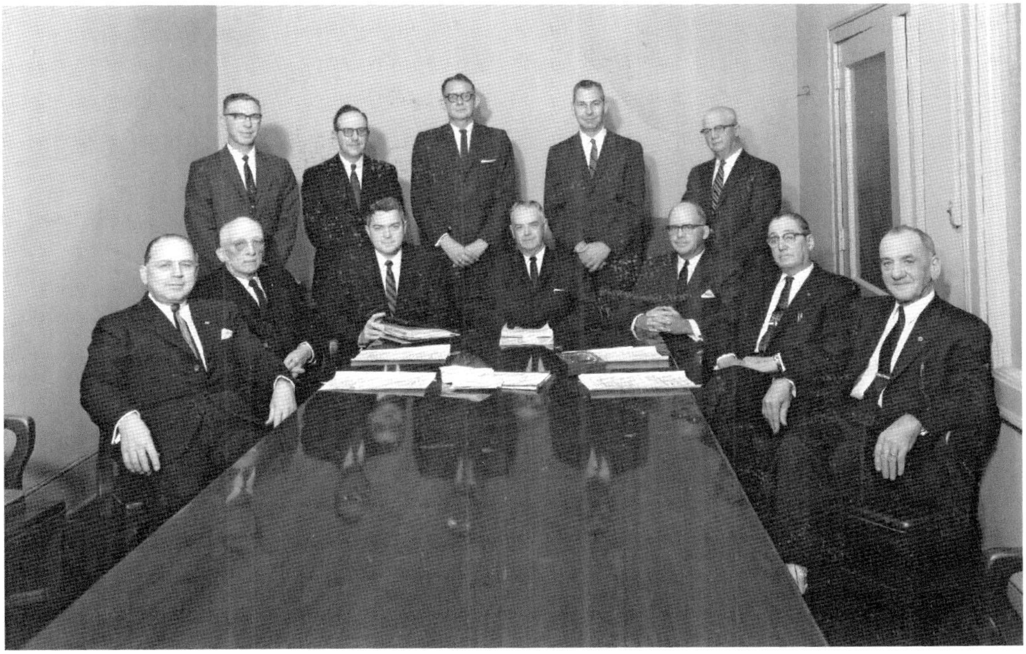

Greer Federal

Greer Federal was established on November 15, 1948. The early 1950s board of directors are (shown seated left to right) M.C. "Preach" Vaughn, Buford "B.B." Waters, Don Robinson, Fred Crow, Dan Davenport, Jim Fleming, and Roy Collins; (standing left to right) John McMurray, Marion Lanford, R.H. Wood, Dennis Dobson, and Earle Taylor. In 1982, it was acquired by the First Savings Bank. (Courtesy of Greer Heritage Museum.)

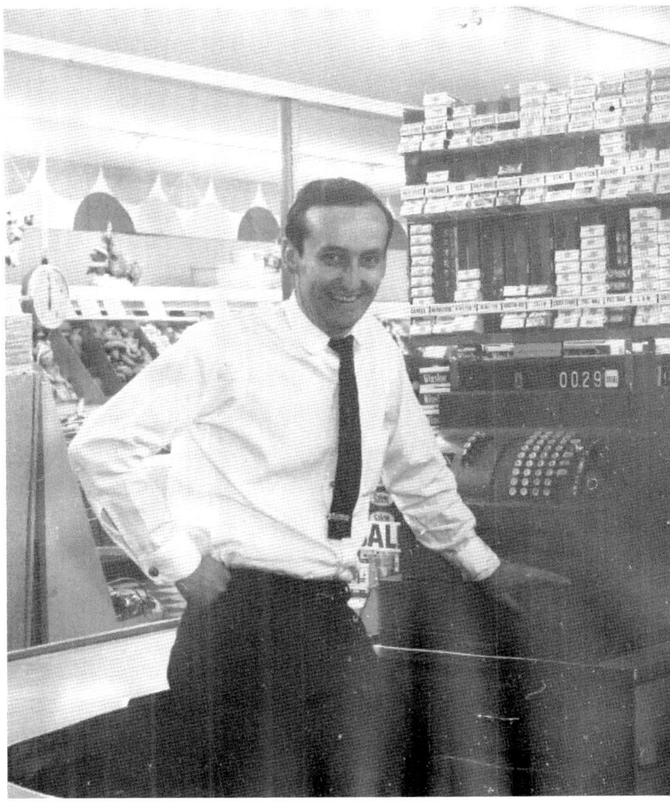

Verner King

Verner King, shown here in his second grocery store, opened his first store in 1955 with $700 saved from his service in the US Navy. This South Main Street store was called Southside Food Center. In 1980, when the new railroad overpass took his property, he moved to Pennsylvania Avenue, renaming the store Food King. The store closed in 1985. (Courtesy of the King family.)

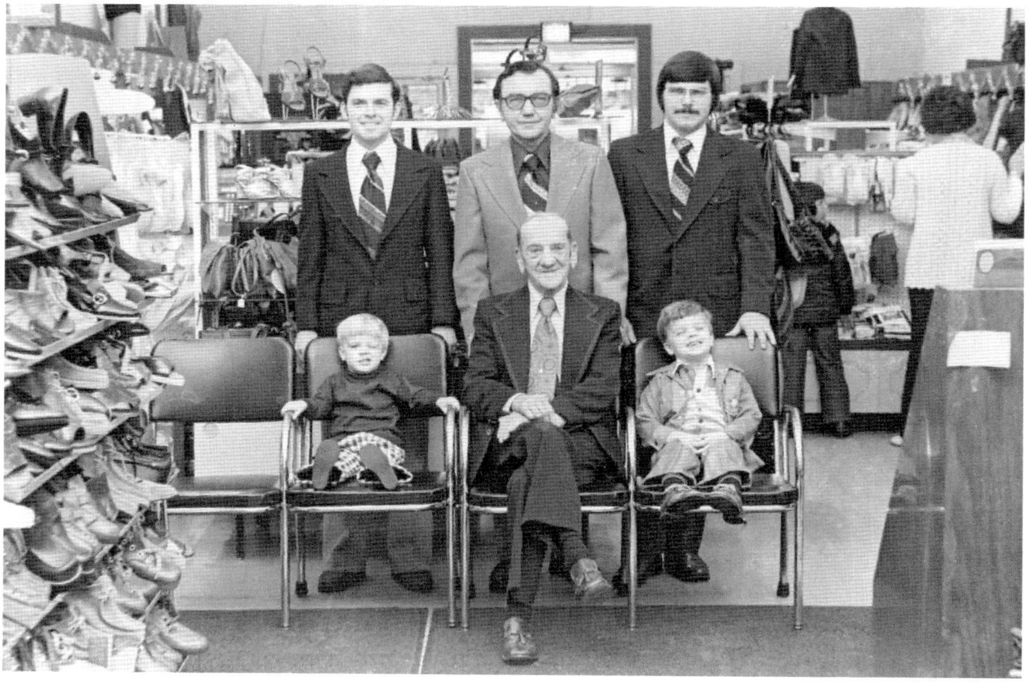

Bailes Collins Store
George Bailes and Roy E. Collins opened the Bailes Collins Store in 1928. Around 1938, Collins became sole owner. Three generations worked in the store. Shown here left to right are (front row) Timothy Collins, Roy E. Collins Sr., and Greg Collins; (back row) Allen G. Collins, Roy E. Collins Jr., and Roy E. (Gene) Collins III. (Courtesy of Allen Collins.)

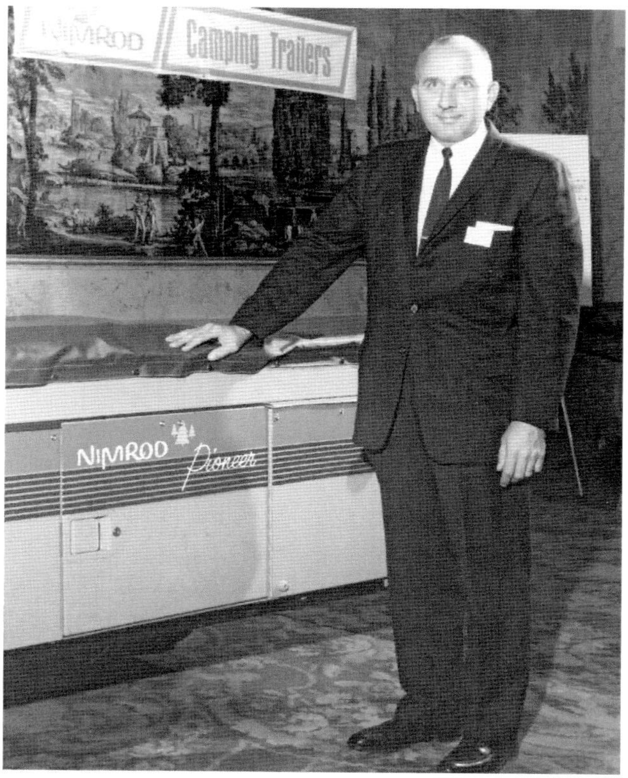

Leo Cloninger
Cloninger opened Cloninger's Motors, a Buick dealership, in 1956 on East Wade Hampton Boulevard. Mr. Cloninger is shown here in the showroom with a camping trailer. A decade after World War II, Americans were hitting the road with campers, which offered a new way for the family to vacation. (Courtesy of Janie Cloninger.)

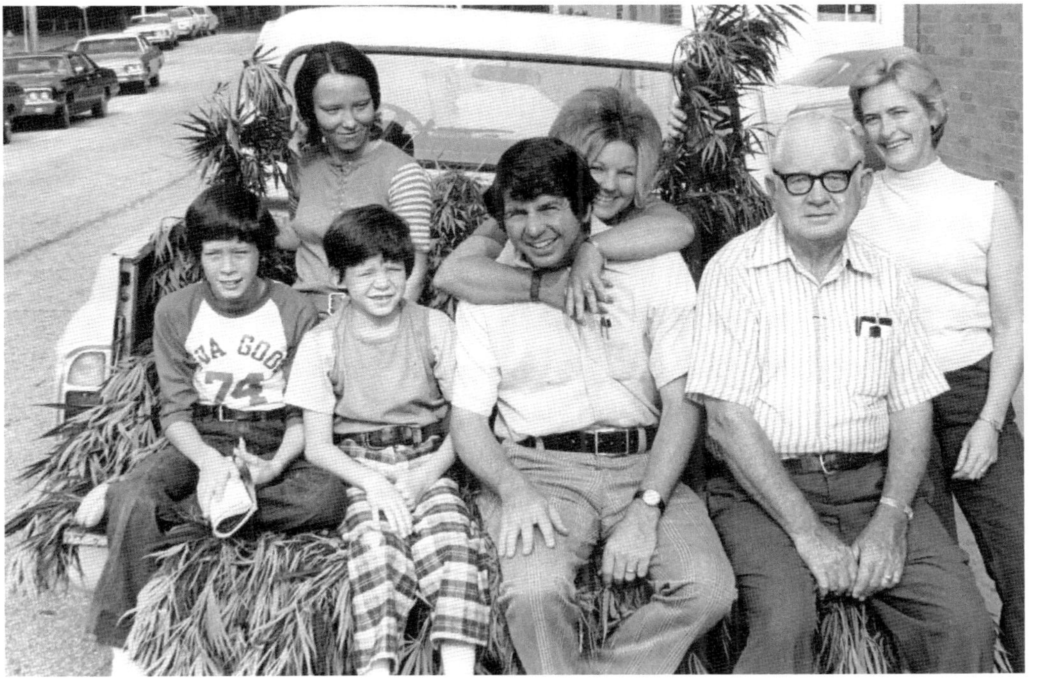

The *Greer Citizen*
Was the staff of the *Greer Citizen* covering news or making it? After a marijuana bust by the Greer Police Department, the staff posed with the haul. Shown here (front left to right) are Eddie Burch, Joey Burch, Walter Burch, Edd Burch, and Wilma Woodward. Debbie Tollison is hugging Walter. The other two females are unidentified. (Courtesy of Leland and Margaret Burch.)

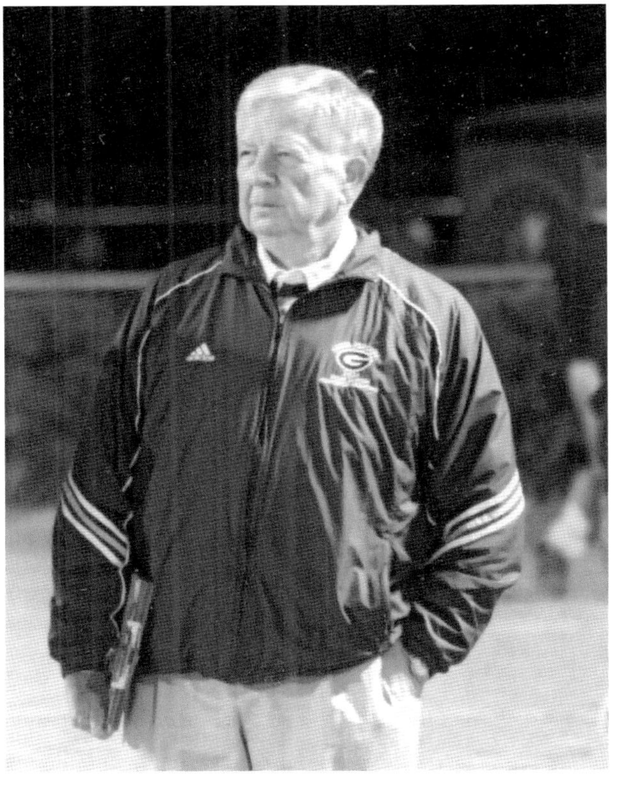

Leland Burch, Editor
In 1961, Burch joined his father at the *Greer Citizen*, covering Greer High football games, both in the paper and on the family-owned radio station WEAB. In 1985, he was named editor and continued until the newspaper was sold to Hometown News in 2006. A "rose" is presented to this legend for making all of Greer's residents legends in the paper. (Courtesy of Leland and Margaret Burch.)

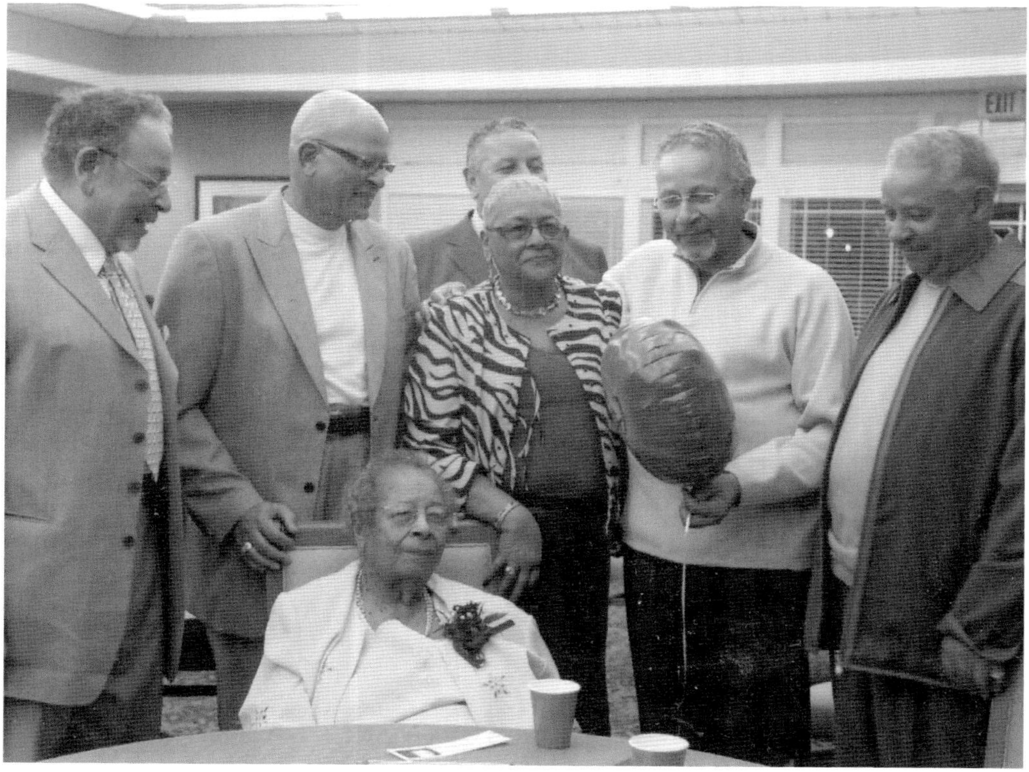

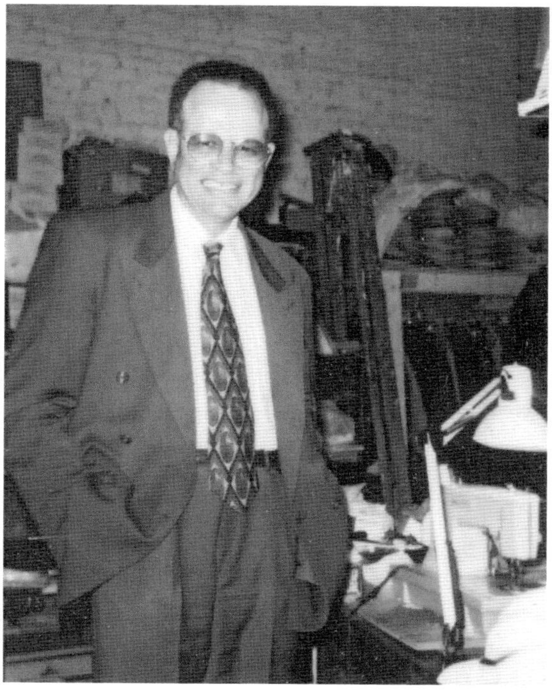

The Gregory Family
The Gregory family grew up in the Sunnyside community. Here they celebrated their mother Grace's 90th birthday in 2008. Shown left to right are Alvin, J.W., Johnny behind Lillie, Robert, and Everett. The only one missing is Everett's twin Margarett. J.W. started the Gregory's Boutique in Greer. Robert managed the Gaffney store. (Courtesy of J.W. Gregory.)

J.W. "Doug" Gregory
Gregory has been a part of the Greer business community since he opened his first store in 1968. After graduating from Lincoln High School, Gregory received his degree from Benedict College and began a teaching career. He entered retail part-time while still teaching and realized that this was what he wanted to do. Gregory's Boutique has been a fixture in downtown since. (Courtesy of J.W. Gregory.)

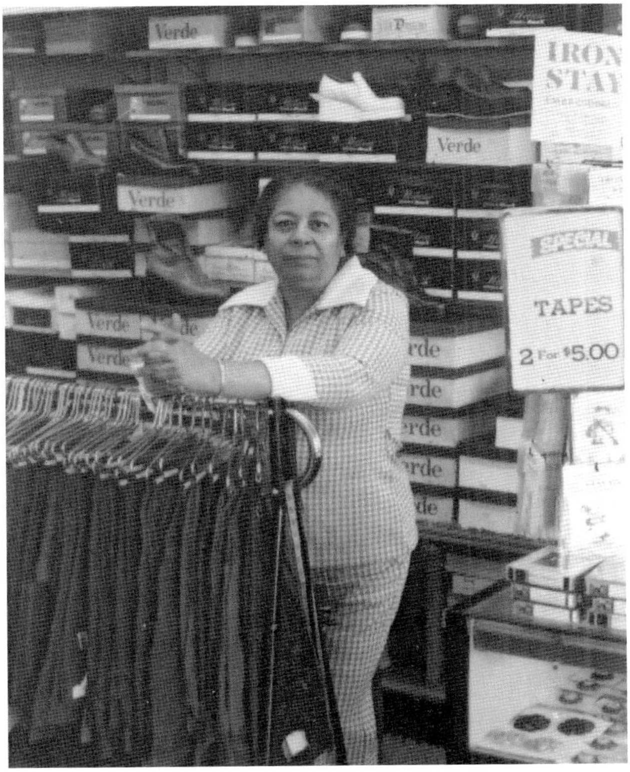

Grace Gregory
Mrs. Gregory was more than glad to help her son in his business. She is shown here in the store where she took an active role in the early years of operation. Gregory's Boutique is a family business that epitomizes small hometown business in America. (Courtesy of J.W. Gregory.)

James Herbert Carroll
Carroll was born in 1908 in York County. After working for Colonial Stores for 20 years, he moved to Greer in 1950 to start his own store on St. Mark's Road. During his retirement years, he was called the "Jelly Man," because of the jellies and preserves (shown here) he sold at Tab's Flea Market. He died in 1997. (Courtesy of Wayne Farmer.)

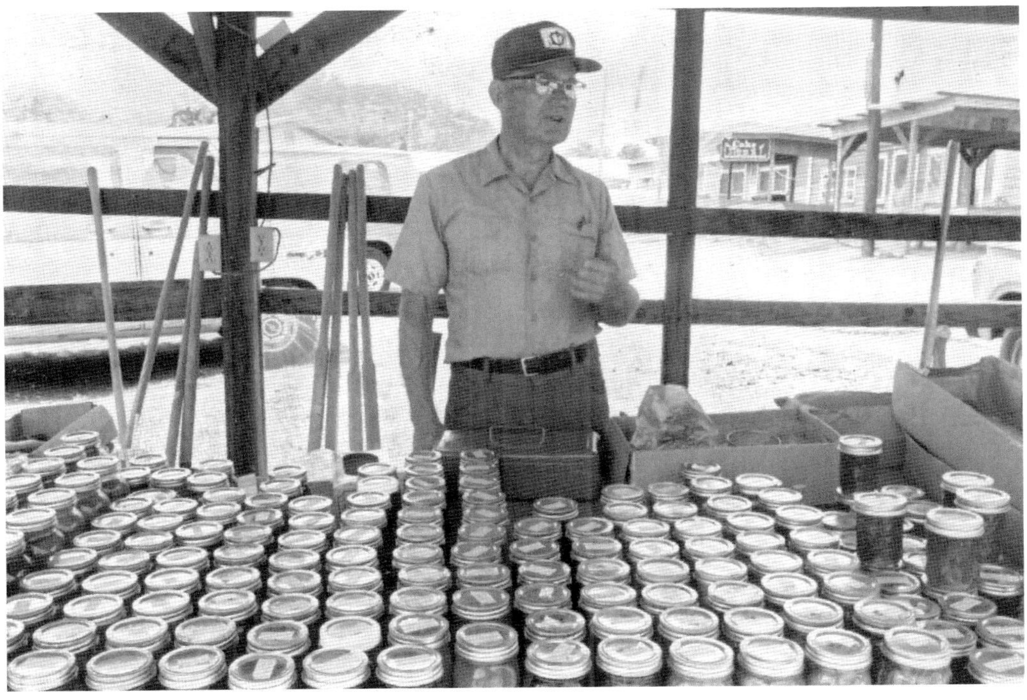

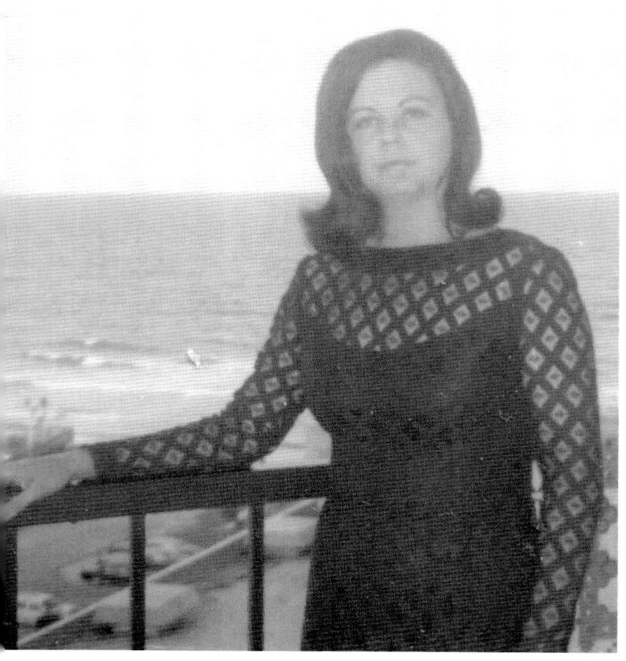

Virginia "Ginny" Carroll

Carroll graduated from Greer High School in 1964 and began her career in journalism with *The State* in Columbia. Her resume included bureau chief for *Newsweek* in Detroit and Houston. She received a Doctor of Journalism in mass communication from the University of North Carolina, Chapel Hill, and had just moved to Chicago to teach at Northwestern University when she died suddenly. (Courtesy of Wayne Farmer.)

Suzanne Greene

Greene was Greer's artist. Born in 1928, she studied art in college and began her career as a technical illustrator in 1952 for Western Electric in North Carolina. She worked for various companies in illustration and design. She was a popular art instructor and watercolorist. Her son Pepper, inspired by his mother, is also an artist. She died in 2004. (Courtesy of Greer Heritage Museum.)

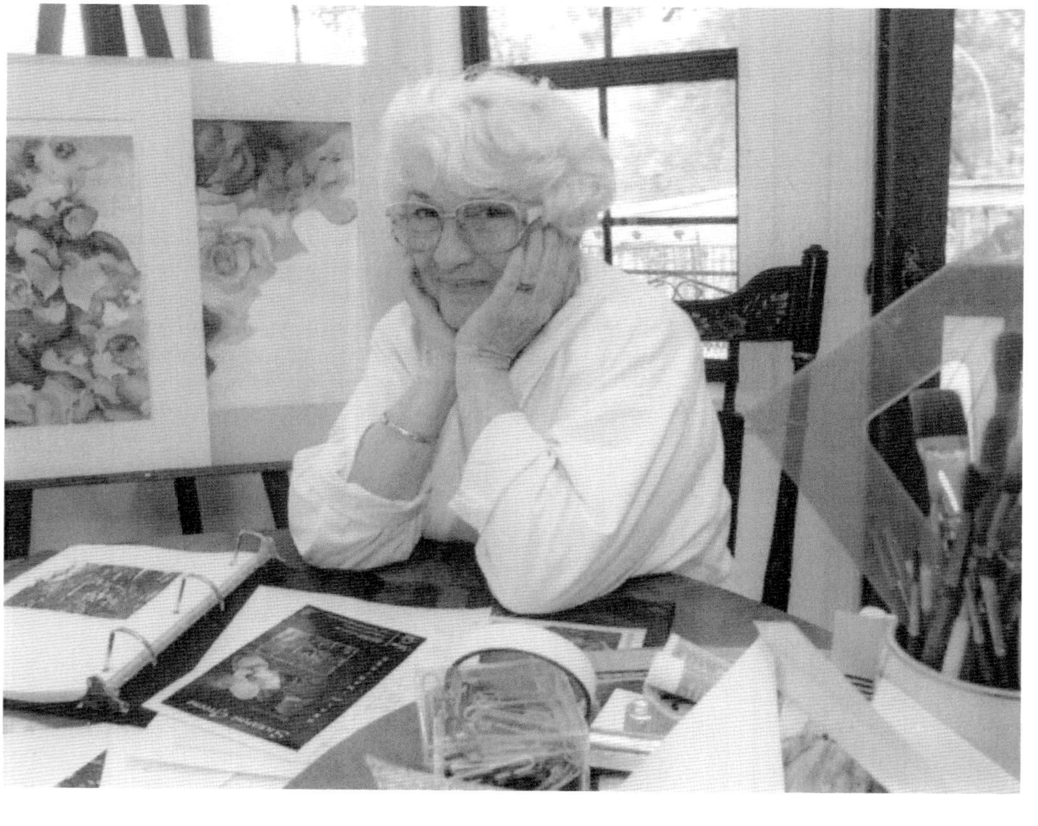

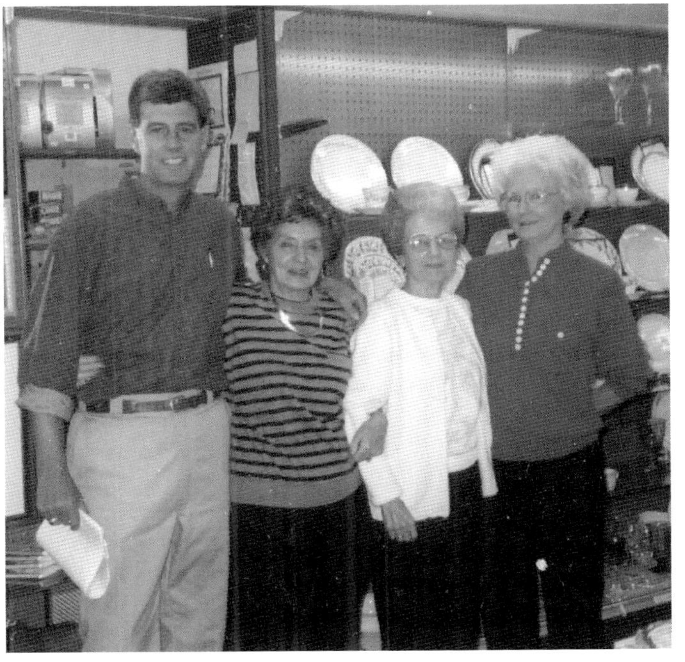

Dobson Hardware

The people of Greer have always enjoyed the friendliness and service of the Dobson Hardware Store. Mrs. Vera Dobson kept the bridal register and helped many young ladies choose china and crystal. Shown here in the store are (left to right) Terry Dobson, his mother Vera Dobson, Mildred Lister, and Geneva Waddell. (Courtesy of Terry Dobson.)

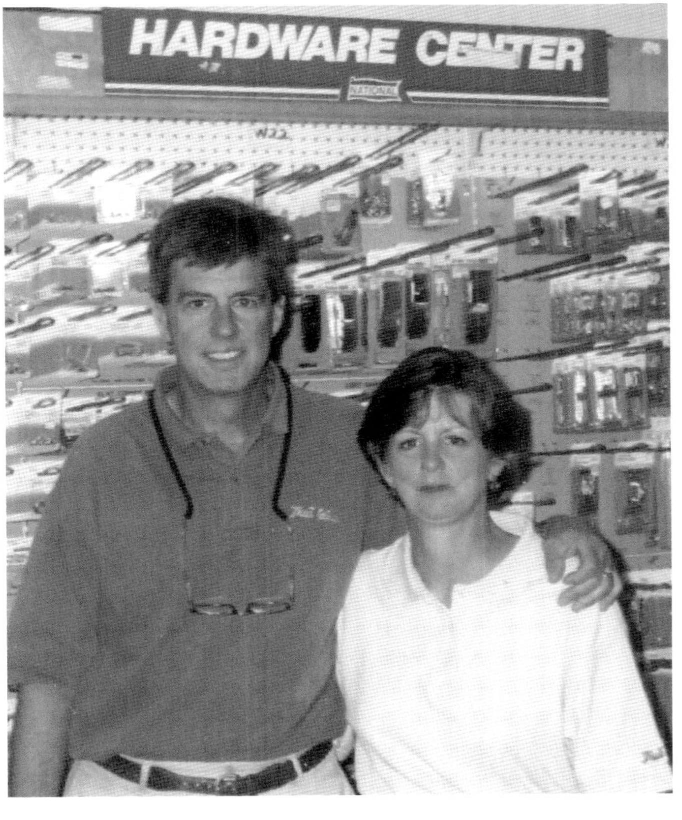

Terry and Debbie Dobson

Terry and Debbie Dobson own Dobson's Gifts and General Hardware on Wade Hampton Boulevard. Terry learned from his father Bill, who started the first store in downtown Greer in 1945. Today, the store offers unique gifts not found in chain stores. The Dobsons epitomize the American dream of the small, successful family-owned business. (Courtesy of Terry Dobson.)

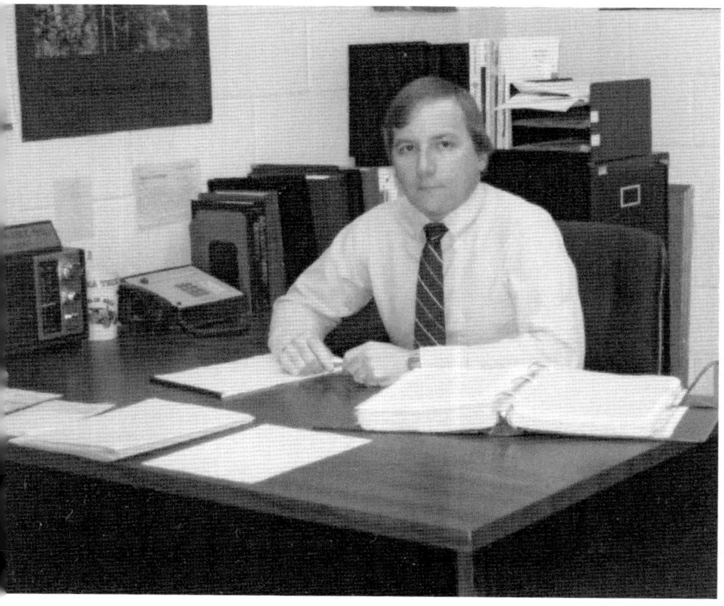

Dr. Thomas McAbee

McAbee represents the vision of individual potential for progress and improvement glimpsed by Greer's early farmers and merchants and later shared by their successors, the cotton mill builders. Greer's founders put their trust in faith, hard work, and a first-rate educational system and built a town that inspired and encouraged the best efforts from succeeding generations. Son of a mill hand, grandson of a farmer, Dr. McAbee, a psychologist, has been active in civic affairs for many years; most recently he served as president of the Victor Mill Community Association in 2009 and 2010. He is currently on the Board of Zoning Appeals for the City of Greer. (Courtesy of Dr. McAbee.)

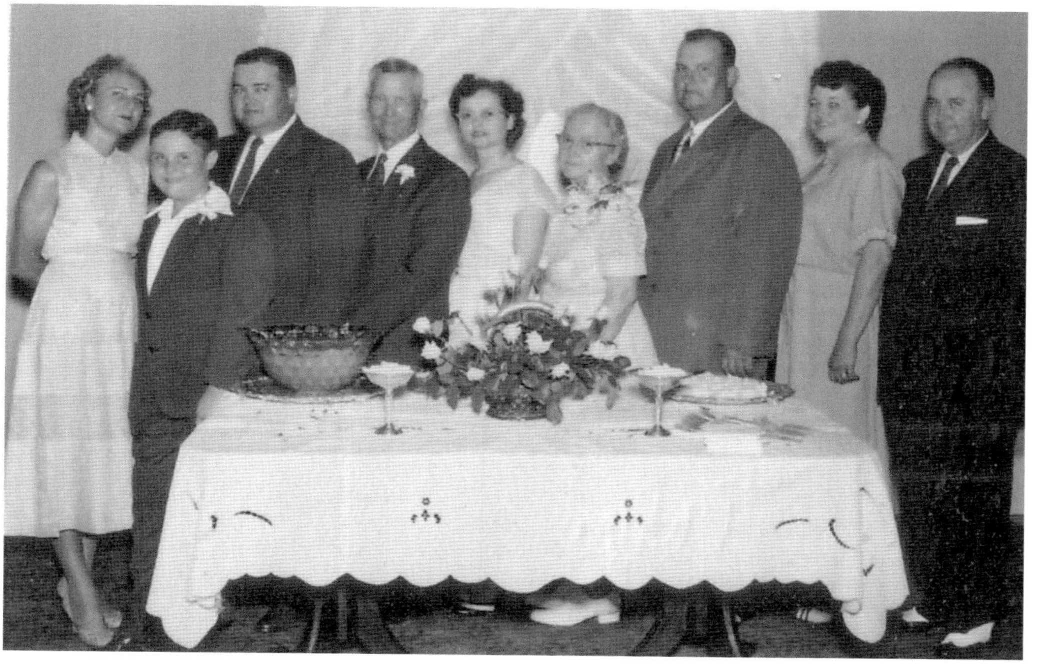

The Henderson Family

The Henderson family had a long history of owning grocery stores, beginning with Mr. Charlie's store on Arlington Road. Most people remember Truman's on North Main Street. The family is celebrating the 50th anniversary of Charles and Rachel in 1953. Shown are (left to right) Laura Henderson, Truman Henderson Jr., Truman Henderson Sr., Charles Henderson, Edna H. Wynn, Rachel Henderson, Troy Henderson, Eva Henderson, and Overton Wynn. (Courtesy of Truman Henderson Jr.)

CHAPTER FIVE

Public Service

In early Greer, through the 1880s, the town's public service was performed collectively by those who lived and operated businesses there, including debris cleanup and street maintenance. Neighbors helped neighbors for the common good.

In modern parlance, when the term "public servant" is used, most people think in terms of elected officials, who preside over the necessary and ceremonial business conducted in a town. The term has a nice ring to it and connotes individuals who work, often unselfishly, and often unremunerated or even at a loss for the time they spend on city business. The towns and cities of the nation could not and would not be the same nor exhibit any unique character and charm were it not for those who serve.

But aside from the business of presiding over or planning for the future of a town, there are the numerous duties and day-to-day tasks performed by the employees of the municipality. City hall clerical personnel, refuse collectors, animal control officers, cemetery maintenance employees, and police and fire departments all come under this category. Greer has been fortunate to have the services of many longtime employees like Joe Johnson, who was street supervisor for many years before retiring and going into business for himself. Claude Cannon served Greer as city clerk and treasurer for many years beginning in 1945, keeping consistently perfect books and offering a ready smile to anyone he met.

Public safety was not a great concern when Greer was young and small. Fire protection was nonexistent, but horse troughs and buckets were always available. Law enforcement fell to the county sheriff. Since the sheriff's office was located a dozen miles away, the closest thing Greer had before it hired a town marshal was the mayor. Mayoral prerogatives extended to the power to make arrests. William A. Hill, one of Greer's first merchants and an early mayor, was the first public servant in Greer known to have used his arrest powers when he and a posse of townsmen captured an escaped horse thief in 1880.

Only after the turn of the century did Greer finally have its departments of the "finest" and the "bravest." And these terms are especially appropriate for the two public servants in Greer's history who lost their lives in the line of duty.

The rapid growth of Greer, especially after the arrival of the cotton mills, required the presence of regular law enforcement. McDuff Littlefield was hired as police chief early in the century with the authority to employ officers as needed. The most common offenses in Greer revolved around bootleg whiskey: drunkenness, fighting, and domestic abuse. To head off these crimes, Littlefield focused on stopping the traffic in illegal whiskey.

William Foster, from the Oneal community, was hired in late spring 1904 as night policeman.

Married, he was the father of two children, Cohen and Lucille, and had earned his living as a farm laborer much of his life. Police duties in Greer of that era primarily involved walking the beat. The presence of an officer served as a deterrent. The vast majority of petty criminals would tend to flee rather than resist unless drunk. In that case, either Chief Littlefield or Officer Foster, both large men, could subdue the miscreant.

On the evening of July 2, the first day he had worn the new uniform that he had paid for out of his own pocket, Foster was instructed to be on the lookout for a whiskey wagon from the mountains rumored to be arriving late in the day on the north end of town near where the Tire Exchange building is located now.

Around 10:00 p.m., customers in the stores along Emma Street heard shots ring out and rushed to the scene of the shooting. Officer Foster had been hit twice by gunfire before he could defend himself. The wounds were fatal; he died in the street. He was buried in his uniform a couple of days later. The town council paid for the monument placed at his grave and provided a sporadic pension for his widow, Martha. Illegal whiskey traffic continued to be a problem in Greer for decades afterward until traffic in more dangerous substances became the norm. One result of Foster's sacrifice was the employment of more officers, both full- and part-time, to combat the problem.

Fire protection in Greer originated with the bucket brigades, which lined up from horse troughs to the blaze. By the 1920s, Greer had an all-volunteer fire department and little in the way of equipment. Building ordinances and safety were insufficient to eliminate the threat of fire. Fire broke out on the second floor of McLellan's Five and Ten in November 1927. Since the store was located mid-block on Trade Street, flames threatened the entire center of town if not contained. The Greenville Fire Department was alerted as Greer firemen rushed to the scene. Carl Miller, who worked at a nearby café, was the first volunteer to respond. Greenville sent a crew that arrived in 17 minutes. By that time, a half-dozen Greer firemen had responded to the fire including Russell DeShields, Chief Leon Flynn, Vernon Flemming, Hollis DeShields, and J.B. Mendenhall Jr. With Miller they had fought their way to the second floor of the building. Greenville firemen entered the building as the two trucks poured streams of water onto the roof from the street. The combined weight of a dozen firemen and the water-saturated merchandise in the storeroom brought down the floor, pinning Miller under "a mountain of wreckage," according to the *Greenville News*. In all, 10 firemen were injured; Miller was trapped and dying. As his fellow volunteers worked to free him, Miller pleaded with rescue workers to "free other firemen." Rescuers had to cut through the side of the first floor to get at the injured fireman; it took half an hour to move enough debris to extract him. By then, Miller had died. His badge number was 13.

William Foster

This photograph of night patrolman William Foster was made the day he was killed in the line of duty, wearing, for the first time, the new uniform he was required to purchase as an officer on Greer's police force. (Courtesy of the Carman family.)

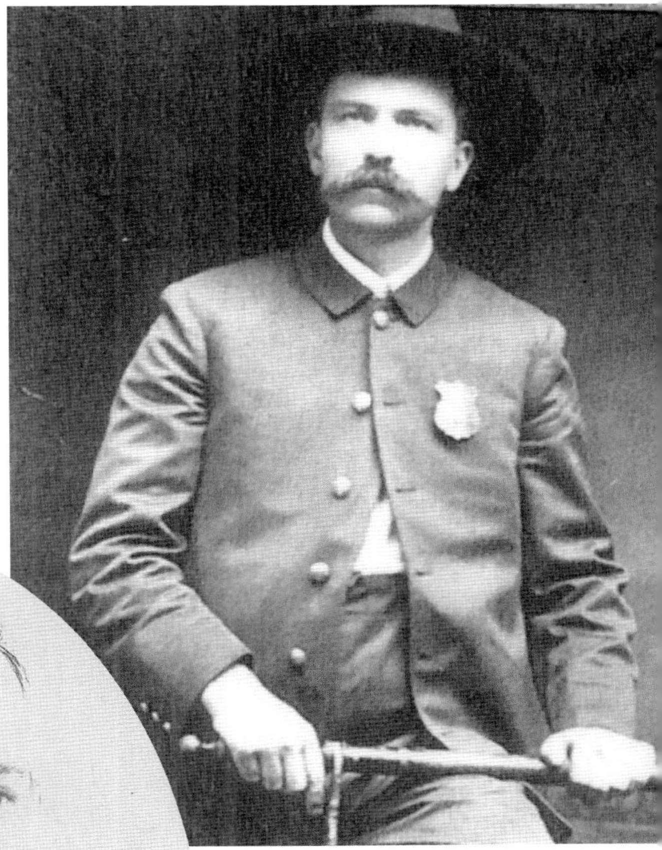

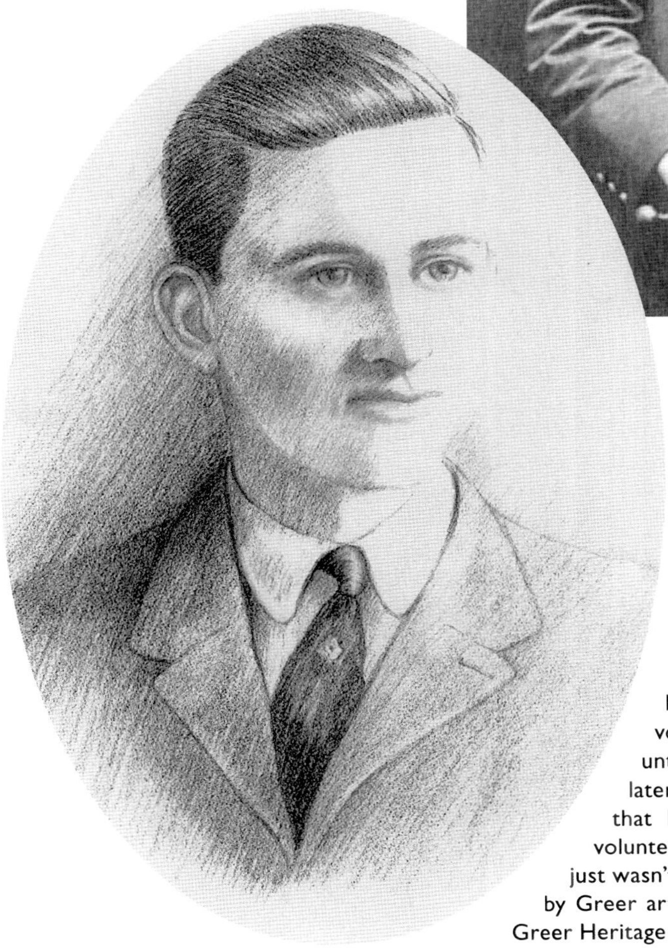

Carl Miller

Miller operated a tiny café, which made him more friends than money. Recently married, Miller continued to serve on the volunteer fire department until his untimely death. A Greenville fireman, later reviewing Miller's last fire, noted that Miller and his fellow firemen, all volunteers, handled it by the book; luck just wasn't with them. This sketch was drawn by Greer artist Rebecca Penland. (Courtesy of Greer Heritage Museum.)

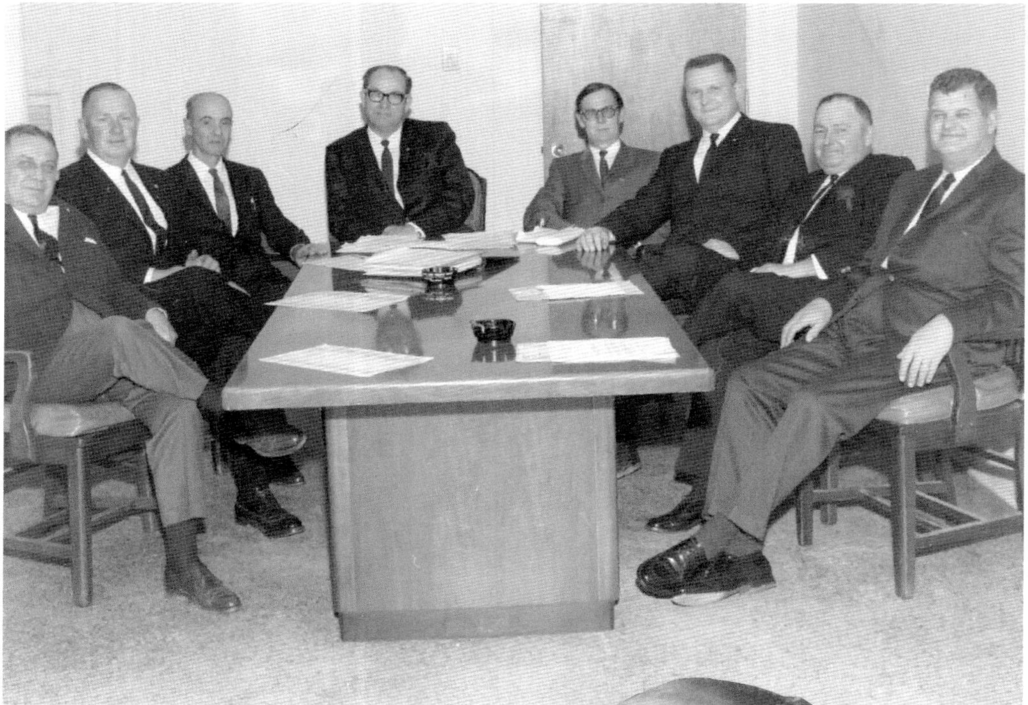

Greer City Council 1965
The 1965 Greer City Council poses with the mayor and city clerk in their offices on Trade Street. Shown here left to right are R.W. "Dub" Johnson, Broadus Dobson, Claude Cannon (city clerk), Everrett Edwards, W.M. "Runt" Mason, Keith Smith, Basco Coggins, and Worth Barnett, mayor. (Courtesy of Katherine Johnson.)

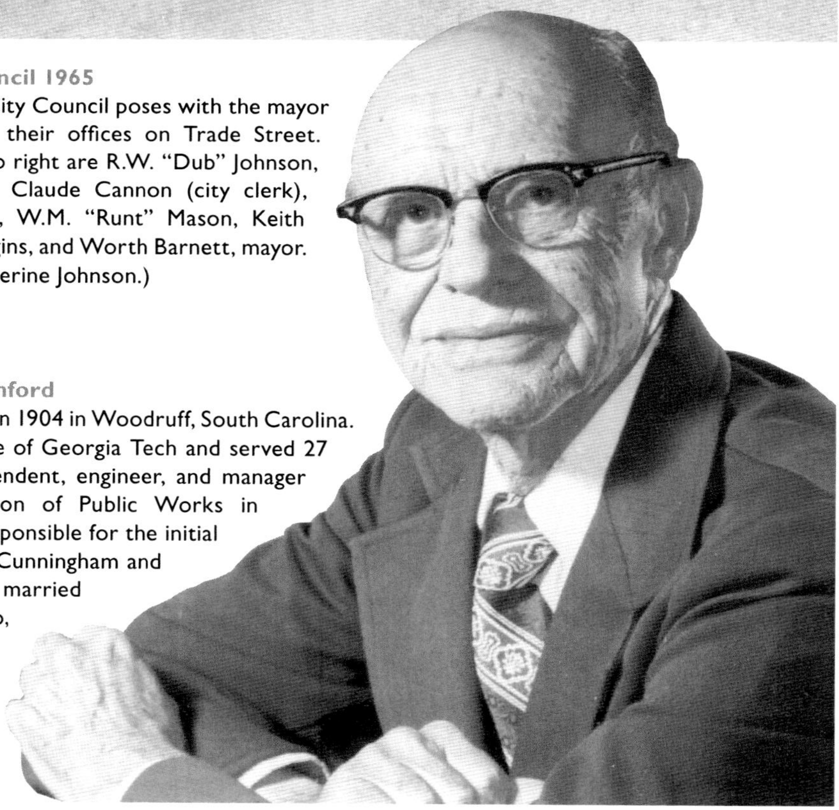

Carl Clinton Lanford
Lanford was born in 1904 in Woodruff, South Carolina. He was a graduate of Georgia Tech and served 27 years as superintendent, engineer, and manager of the Commission of Public Works in Greer. He was responsible for the initial planning for Lake Cunningham and Lake Robinson. He married Mary Sue Bobo, and they had four children. He died in 1982. (Courtesy of Clint "Pepper" Greene Jr.)

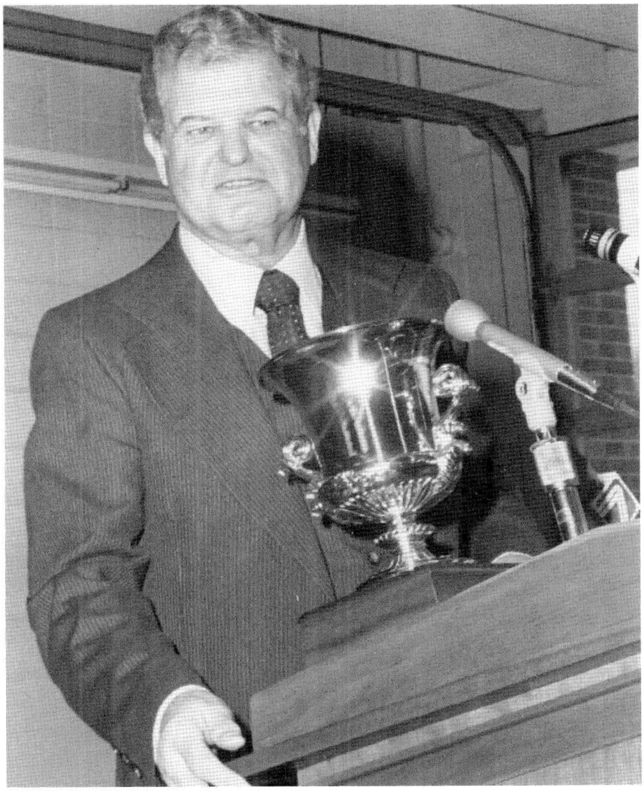

Worth Barnett

Barnett, a native of Chesnee, South Carolina, was mayor of Greer from 1967 to 1979. The owner of Barnett Auto Supply, he first served as councilman for the 1955–1959 term and again from 1961 to 1966. The Worth Barnett Overpass on South Main Street over the Southern Railroad tracks was dedicated in his honor in 1986. He died in 1998. (Courtesy of Greer Heritage Museum.)

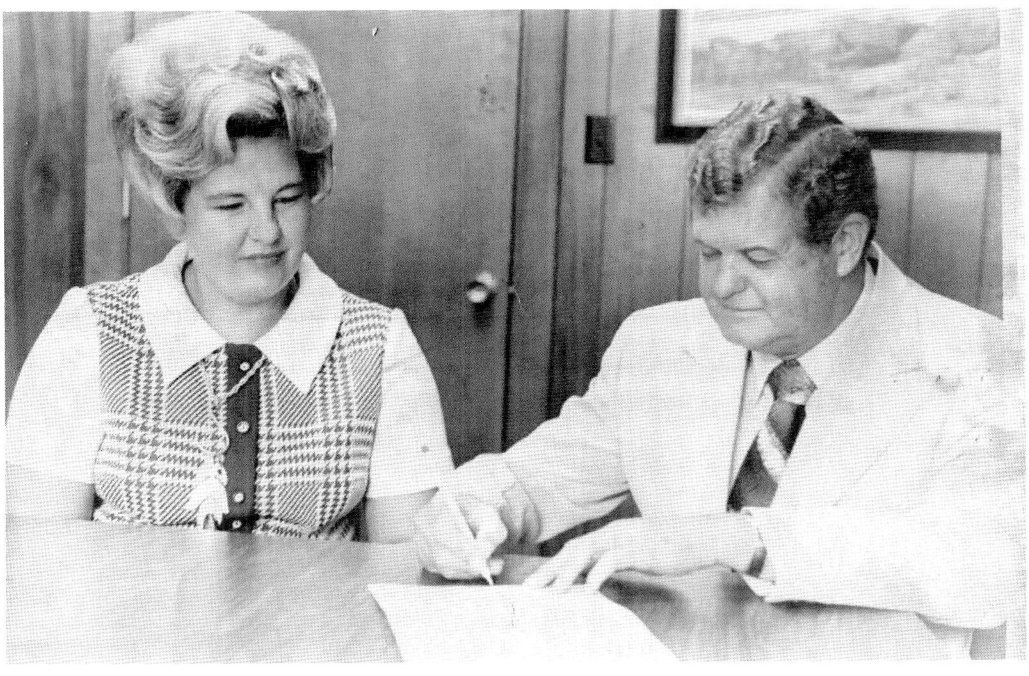

Shirley Rollins

Rollins has the distinction of being the first elected female city council member and the first female mayor in Greer. She was elected mayor of Greer in 1988 and served one term. Here Councilwoman Rollins talks to Mayor Worth Barnett. (Courtesy of John M. Rollins Jr.)

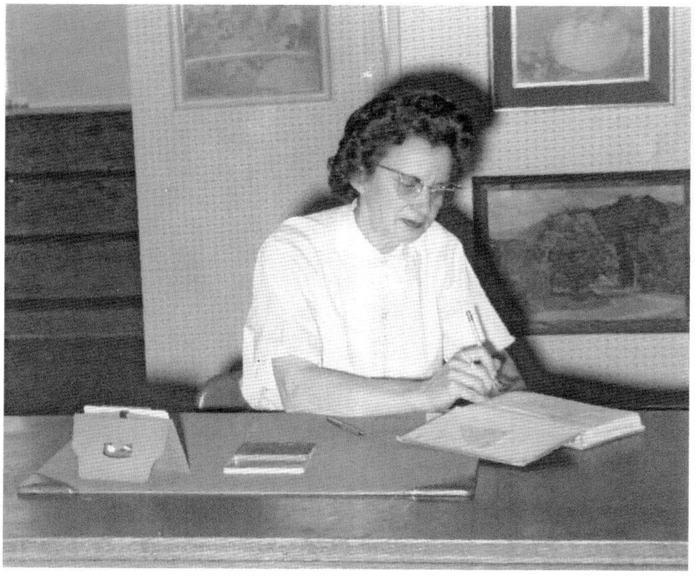

Cartland Berry Hiatt, Librarian

Hiatt served as librarian at the Greer Branch Library on School Street during the 1960s. A graduate of William Penn College in Oskaloosa, Iowa, she came to Greer in the early 1950s with her husband Jack, who opened and managed the Culler-Jackson Furniture Company on Highway 29. She was a member of Memorial Methodist Church where she started the first church library. (Courtesy of Susan Hiatt Maybin.)

Greer Commission of Public Works

In February 1913, Greer City Council authorized $67,000 in bonds to finance the construction of a public works. The first commissioners elected by popular vote were John A. Robinson (chairman), E.C. Bailey, and H.B. Posey. Shown here are (left to right) South Carolina representative Bob Inglis, Commission of Public Works chairman David Duncan, and general manager Jerry Balding as they plan for the arrival of BMW. (Courtesy of David Duncan.)

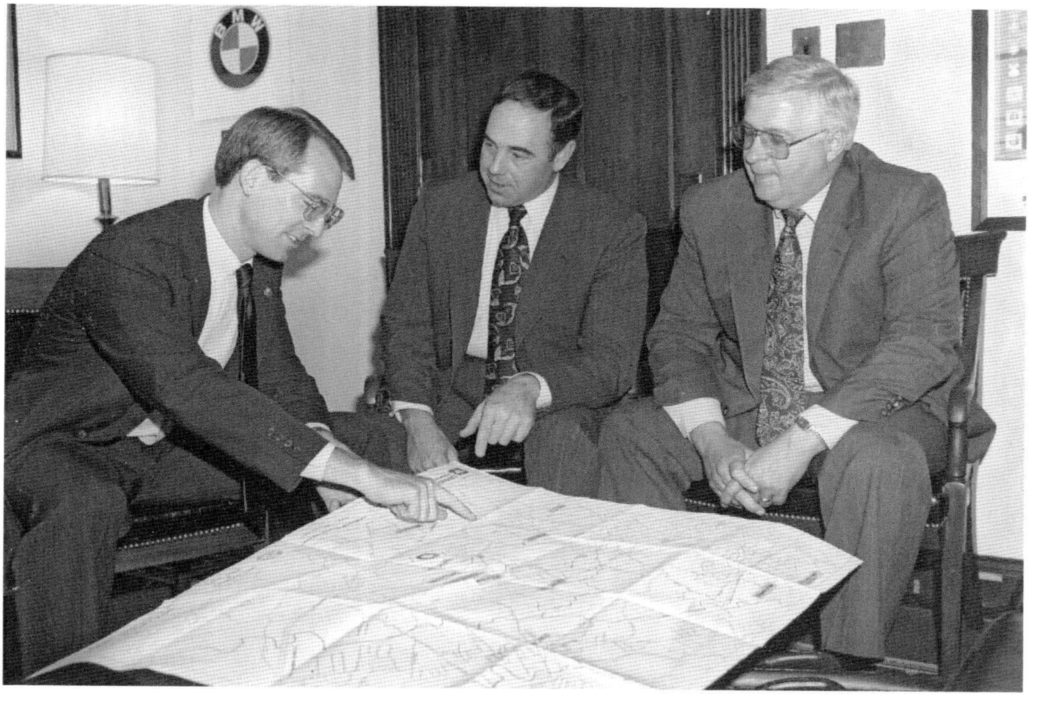

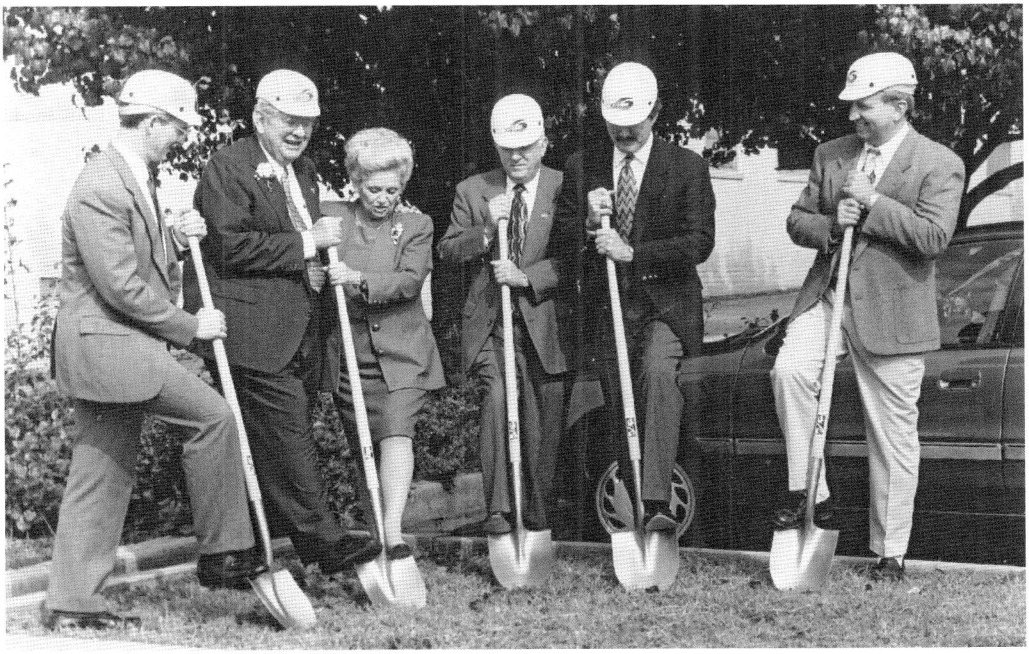

Square One 1981
In an effort to revitalize downtown, Square One was built as a farmers' market. At the ground breaking are (left to right) unidentified, State Senator Verne Smith, State Representative Rita Allison, State Representative Lewis Vaughn, Bob Peeler (later lieutenant governor), and businessman Don Wall, who would later become mayor. The short-lived market opened in September 1981 on Depot Street. (Courtesy of Greer Heritage Museum.)

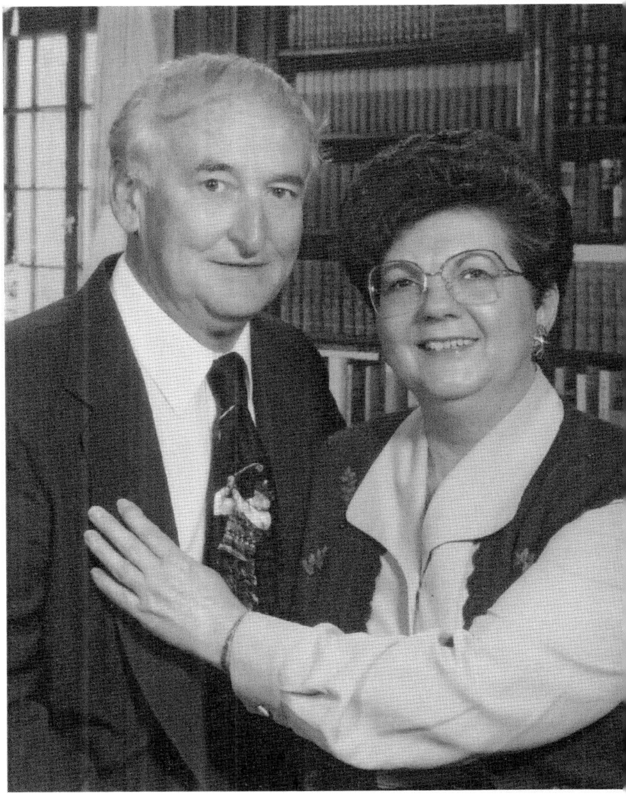

Martha and Verner King
When Martha King was 17, she skipped classes from Greer High School and stopped by Verner King's store. That chance meeting led to a long family and business partnership when they married in 1958. Martha served her district well on the Greer City Council from 1987 to 1999 and continues to serve the community as the kitchen manager at Greer Community Ministries. (Courtesy of the King family.)

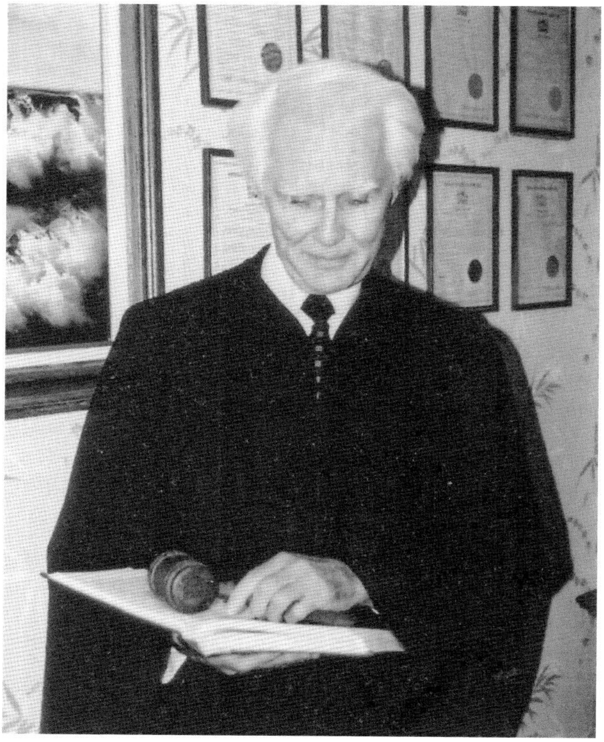

Judge R. Carey Werner

Judge Werner graduated from Draughon's Business School and began a career in the textile machinery industry. In 1967, he was appointed judge of the Magisterial Court by Gov. Robert McNair. A popular local judge, he was reelected for three consecutive terms. After judges were no longer elected, he was reappointed by each succeeding governor until his retirement in 2006. He and wife Sue continue to live in Greer. (Courtesy of Carey Werner.)

Mayors of Greer

Since its incorporation in 1876, the City of Greer has had 29 mayors. Shown here (left to right) are the last three mayors: Richard W. Danner (2000–present), Shirley Rollins (1988–1991), and C. Don Wall (1992–1999). (Courtesy of the City of Greer.)

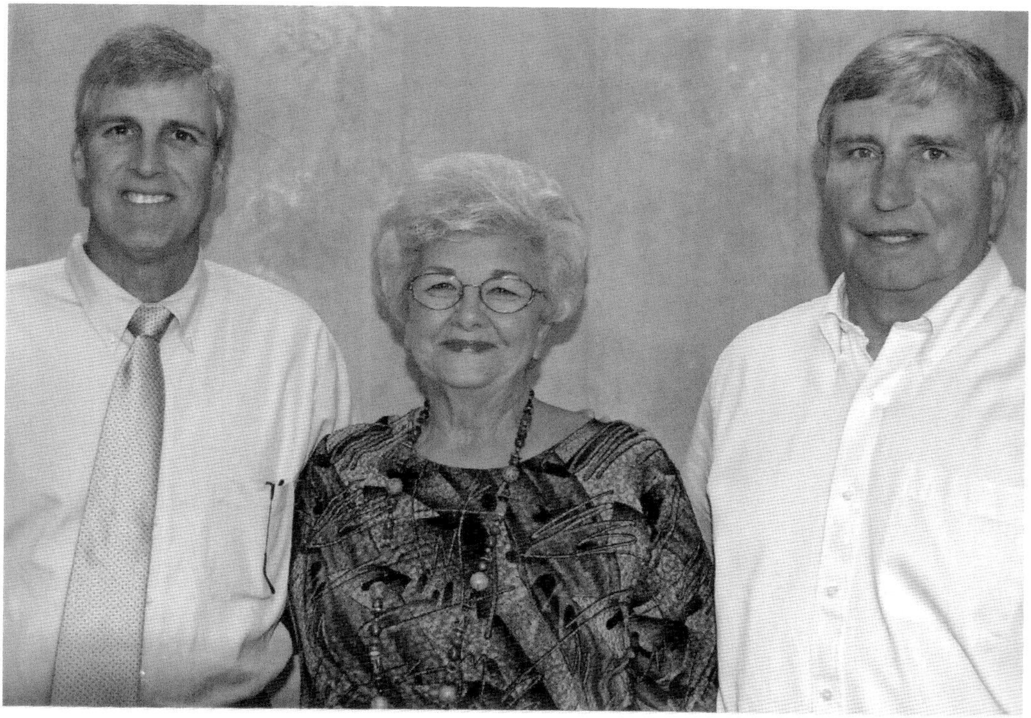

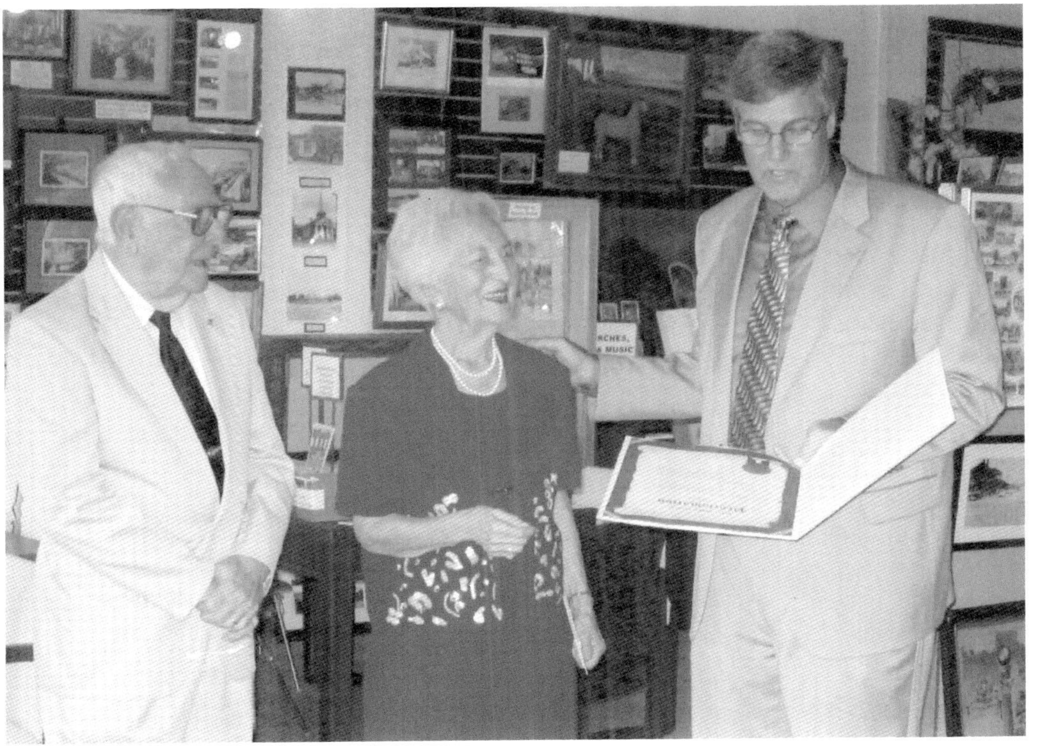

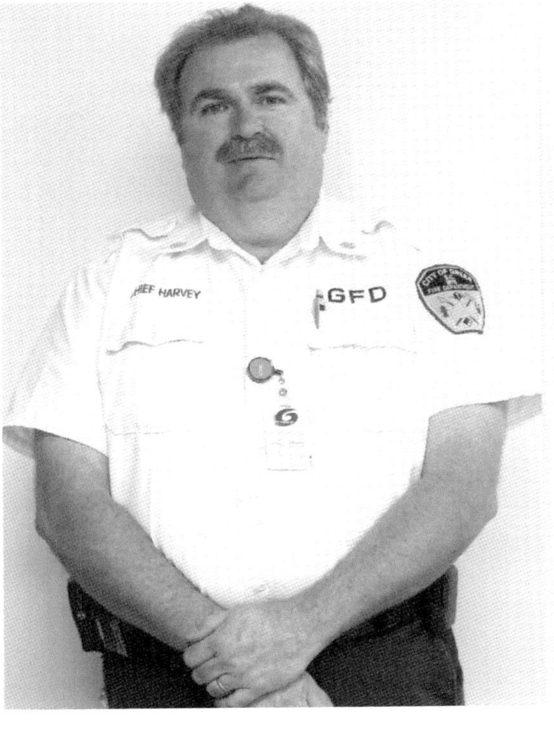

Carm and Earl Hudson
In 1993, the Hudsons organized the Greer Heritage Museum. It opened three years later in the old Bailes Collins Store on Trade Street. A retired schoolteacher and librarian, Mrs. Hudson's dream was to preserve local history for the next generation. On their retirement as directors in August 2006, Mayor Richard Danner presented them a City Proclamation, honoring their community work. (Courtesy of Greer Heritage Museum.)

Chief Chris Harvey
Harvey joined the Greer Fire Department in 1977. In 1986, he became assistant chief and was appointed chief in 1996. He is the past president of the South Carolina State Fire Chief's Association. He oversees two stations, 30 personnel, and 18 volunteers. His son is also a firefighter. (Courtesy of the City of Greer.)

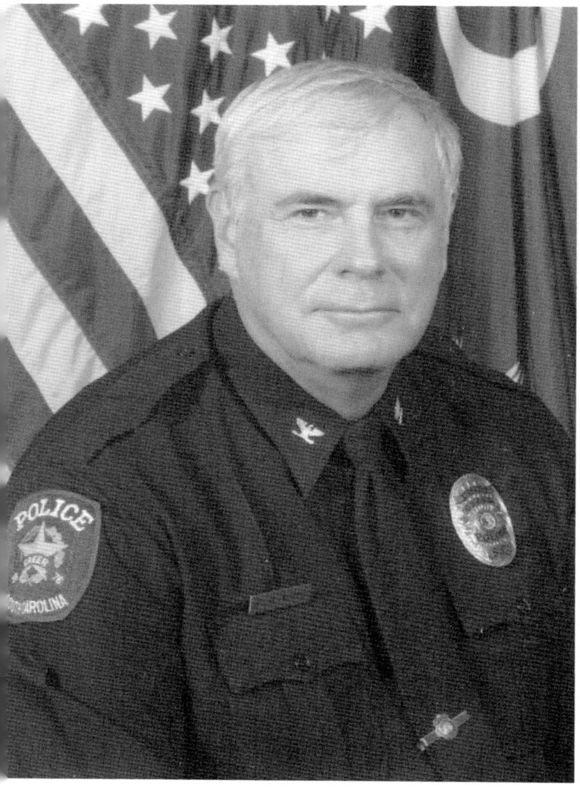

Chief Dan Reynolds
Reynolds assumed the leadership of the Greer Police Department in 2005. Before coming to Greer, he served more than 30 years with the police department in Savannah, Georgia. He holds bachelor of science and master of science degrees in criminal justice from Armstrong Atlantic State University. He received his master's degree in public administration from Columbus State College. (Courtesy of City of Greer.)

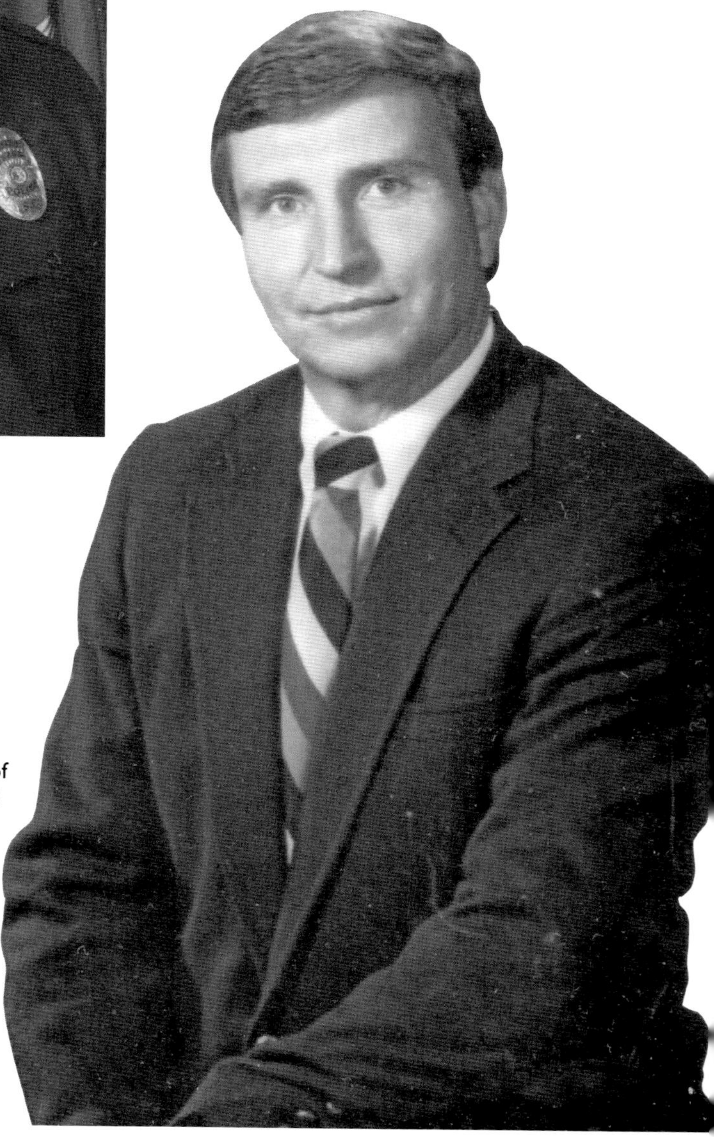

C. Don Wall
Wall graduated from University of South Carolina in 1967 and returned to Greer as a pharmacist. After purchasing Professional Pharmacy, he added more locations. Starting in 1992, he served two terms as mayor. His wife Ellen, also civic-minded, helped start the Greer Art Reach Program and has been active in downtown revitalization. They have two sons, one of whom is a pharmacist with the family business. (Courtesy of Don Wall.)

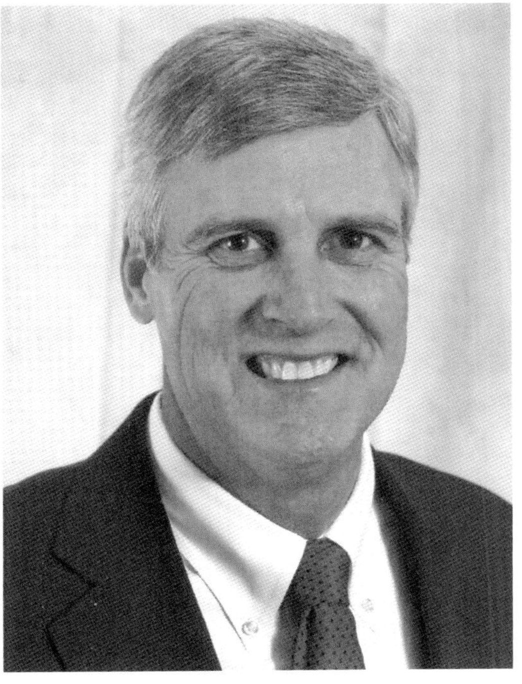

Richard Danner
A native of Knoxville, Tennessee, Danner began his service as mayor of Greer in 2000 and continues to serve. He received his BS from Clemson University and was the owner of Danner Landscape Management for 20 years. In 2002, he joined Greer State Bank as vice president of human resources and security. He and wife Rita Howell have two sons. (Courtesy of City of Greer.)

Mary Clark-Greer
A Blacksburg native, Greer attended Durham Business College. In 1977, Mary broke racial barriers when she was hired as the City of Greer's first minority office employee. When city administrator Ken Westmoreland resigned, she was appointed as interim city administrator. Upon the hiring of an administrator, she was appointed assistant administrator/municipal clerk, the position she held until retirement in 2003. She is shown with one of many awards. (Courtesy of Mary Greer.)

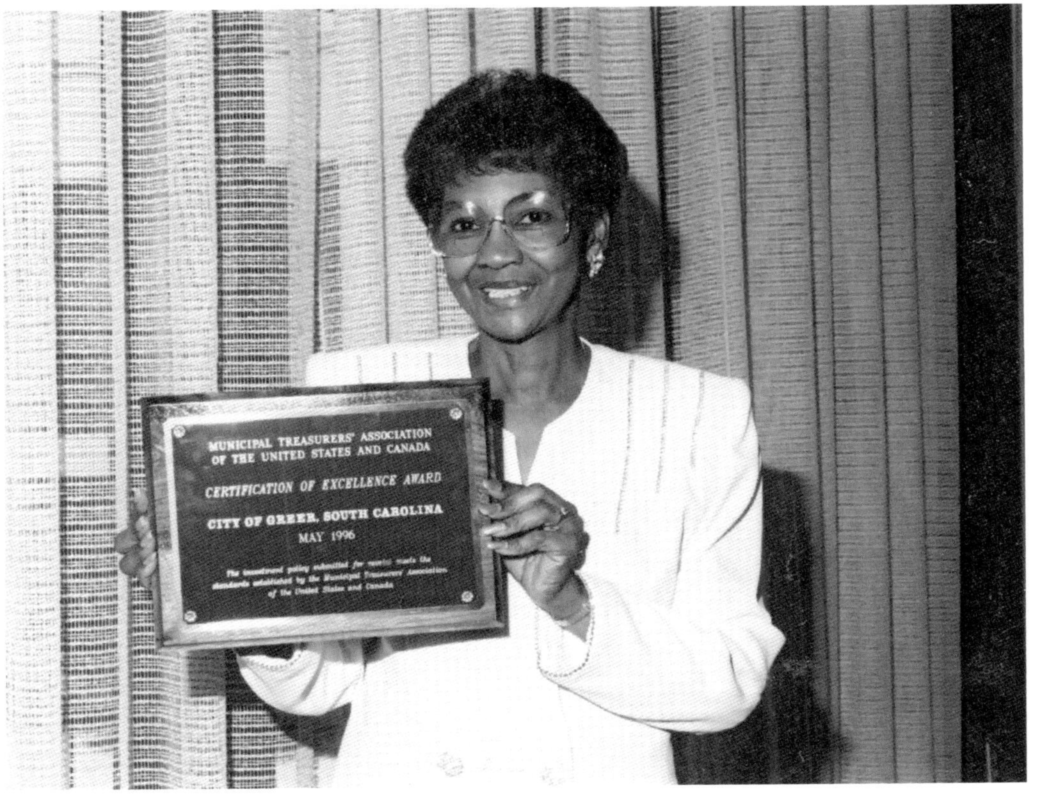

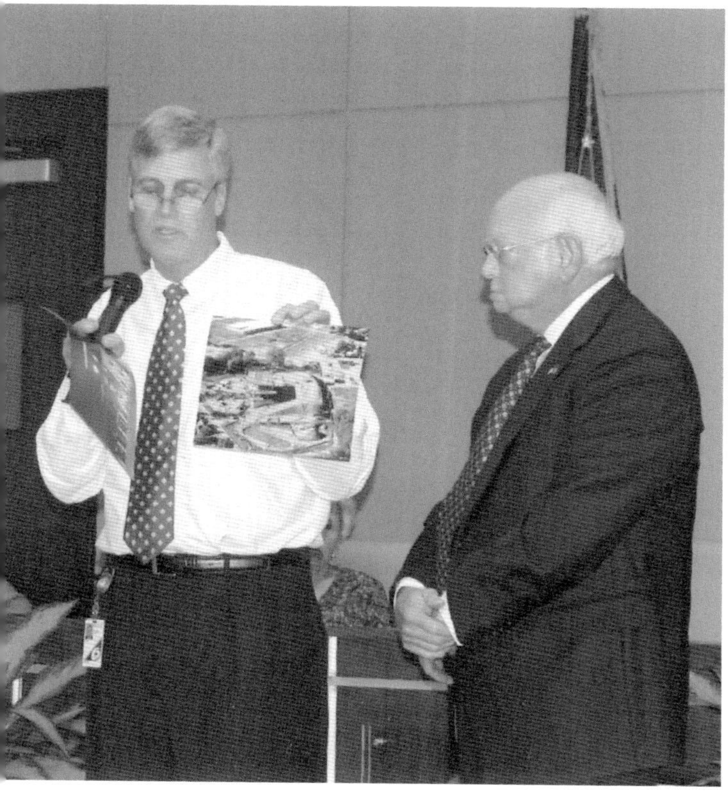

Gerald M. Davis

Mayor Rick Danner (left) presents a Key to the City to Gerald Davis. Davis began his career with J.P. Stevens Company, but after the textile mills closed, he found another career at Wood Mortuary. In retirement, he has voluntarily photographed much of Greer, recording the rapid changes in the community as it has moved from a small town to thriving city. (Courtesy of City of Greer.)

J. Verne Smith Jr.

Smith was elected to the South Carolina State Senate in 1972 and served until 2006. He was so popular that he often ran unopposed. He was the champion of the disadvantaged and helped shape the state's Medicare system. This proud moment at the State House with his wife Jean was the dedication ceremony for the hanging of his portrait. (Courtesy of Carole Smith Olmert.)

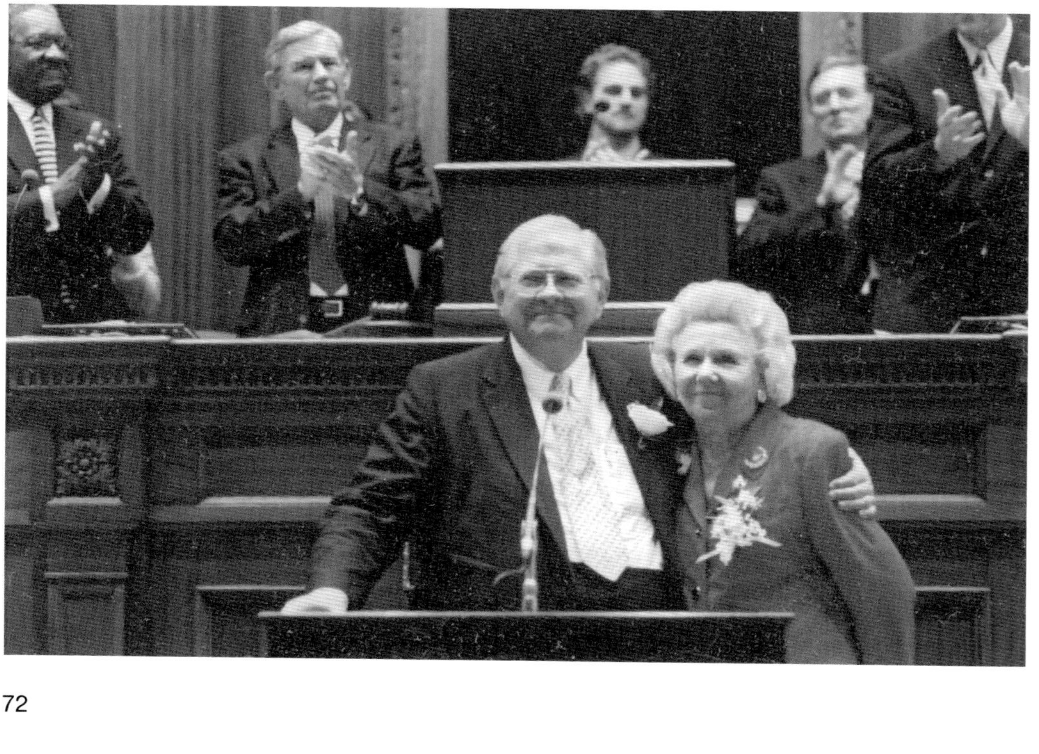

CHAPTER SIX

School and Church

Churches are one of the important indices of human progress and civilization; to that end, Greer's founder W.T. Shumate offered free building lots to congregations of Methodists, Baptists, and Presbyterians who would build their churches in Greer. The Baptists were the first to take Shumate up on his offer, putting up their meeting house by mid-1880. In November of the same year, the Presbyterian congregation at Bailey's Crossroads secured title to their lot and hauled their one-room meeting house on log rollers pulled by mule teams the two miles to Greer. Organized September 5, 1841, at Bailey Crossroads, the church retained that name until the 1920s when it officially became First Presbyterian Church of Greer. Methodists of Greer worshipped in the storeroom of H.P. Moore, general merchant, until their church was constructed in 1887.

Greer residents have always valued education. In the town's early days, children attended school in a cabin. In 1880, citizens formed a joint stock company, the Greer Educational Association, to raise construction money to build a proper school for the growing population of school-age children. A board of trustees was created consisting of six men, two of whom were Baptists, two Methodists, and two Presbyterian. The first board consisted of W.E. Carver, John Landrum Carman, A.A. Dempsey, Cunningham Pennington, J.H. Boyd, and John M. Dickson. The first public school building was completed by March 1881. Education had been optional for the farmers of 50 years earlier, but in the New South, it was viewed as critical for economic recovery. Greer had provided haphazard schooling supervised under minimal state laws and county supervision since 1876. The job of the new board was to create a school district that would function independently. To get the task underway, the Greer Board of Education hired Murray Manley as the first principal of the Greer schools. He left the next year and was succeeded by Joseph W. Kennedy, whose vision for public education had a lasting impact on the Greer School District. Kennedy was only 27 when he came to Greer, but by the end of his tenure he had become known statewide as a voice for reform of the state's educational policies. Kennedy promoted the hiring of well-qualified teachers and encouraged greater local funding for which Greer was known as a pioneering district. Kennedy was elected as county school commissioner in 1883, a position he held the remainder of his tenure at Greer.

After the Kennedy years, the Greer School District was unable to attract another long-term superintendent for many years. State funding was weak and the national economy suffered a recession in 1893 and again in 1907. Despite national economic issues, Greer continued to expand, because of the cotton mills.

Student population outgrew the facility built in 1881, requiring another major construction in 1904. Greer Graded School, later known as Central Elementary, boasted four teachers, Maggie Garlington,

Leila Cunningham, Bess Owings, and Lura Langston, all unmarried as required by the district on the theory that married women had family duties in the home and should not be engaged in public work.

Again, the number of school-age children in Greer outpaced the ability of the district to build. By the World War I era, the district had to rent floor space for classes from merchants who had unused areas in their buildings. At last, a new high school was completed during the early 1920s and named for its principal benefactor, D.D. Davenport.

The period from 1920 to the end of World War II saw more changes and more substantial changes than any other time before the end of the dual school system. During that time, Greer Schools had four superintendents, W.H. Ward, Edmund Wroe, S.W. Rabb, and William Albergotti. As the school population continued to increase, philosophical differences arose between superintendents and the local board. Amid the controversy, Greer schools were falling behind where they should have been. There had been some criticism of the quality of education in the past, most notably near the turn of the century when local mill schools were, for a time, able to offer more consistent education than the Greer School District, but the board of education had always managed to meet most of the district's needs. The pace of growth continued to be strong throughout the 1920s, but the Depression era of the next decade slowed things down. During the late 1930s, there were some questions about priorities that were put on hold during the war years.

Issues came to a head in 1946 when Greer High School lost its longtime superintendent, William Albergotti, who elected to complete a career in the military. The same year, Greer High lost its national accreditation. Thereafter strong arguments built for the consolidation of Greenville County's many small school districts in a quest for uniform quality throughout the county. Accreditation was regained the next year and the board approved plans for two new high schools, one for white students and one for black students.

In 1949, the County Legislative Delegation, which served in the capacity of a county council, appointed a 15-person committee to study the administration of schools within the county. At the time, there were 86 districts. The committee drafted a statement in June 1950 endorsing the consolidation but called for a gradual approach to something less than total consolidation. The first action on consolidation of schools took place in Greer area districts. Youthful administrators Charles Chewning and B.L. Frick oversaw the first consolidation in the country, which became official July 1, 1950, as six rural districts joined with Greer. Victor, Apalache, Zoar, Pelham, Ansel, and Pleasant Grove added over a thousand children and a hundred teachers to the Greer district. Chewning, of Bishopville, was a former principal at Fountain Inn; Frick, former superintendent-principal of Ninety-Six Schools, came to Greer initially as principal of Davenport High School.

The majority of the county's citizens opposed consolidation; a vote held on July 11, 1950, demonstrated the will of the people. Despite the public's voice, the General Assembly passed a General School Law, Act 379 in early 1951, which gave the county board of education the authority to consolidate the small districts, which they did on August 23, 1951. After a new high school was constructed in 1953, the district relied again on the leadership of B.L. Frick as principal to make the transition into a new era as smooth as possible.

As a part of the Greenville County School District, Greer Schools did not lose their identity. Greer area superintendent L.L. Holladay and school board member J. Harley Bonds insisted on a degree of independence from the county board. When Bonds left the board in the 1980s after decades of service, he was succeeded by Margaret Burch, who, as a former educator, continued the tradition, giving the students, teachers, and parents of the Greer area a voice in district decisions.

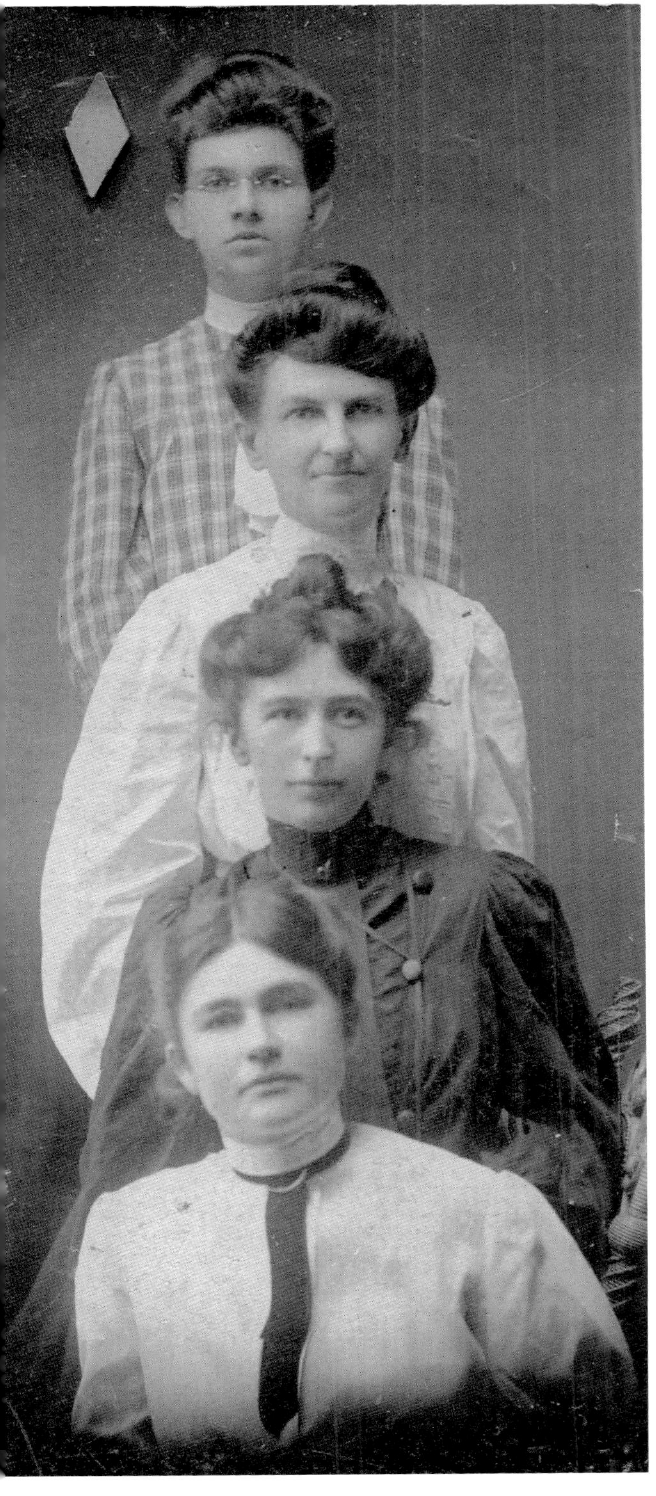

Greer Graded School Teachers
When the Greer Graded School opened the new brick building on School Street, the 1905 teachers were (top to bottom) Maggie Garlington, Leila Cunningham, Bess Owings, and Lura Langston. There were eight grades and the term "graded" indicated a modern school system with teachers assigned by grades. (Courtesy of Greer Heritage Museum.)

Reverend Clinton Lafayette Cox
Cox was born in 1868 and died in 1945. He married Stella Austin and they had 12 children. He was a Baptist minister who served the Flint Hill Church and also traveled the South as an itinerant preacher. He lived variously in Duncan, Reidville, Woodruff, and the Apalache area of Greer where he was a sharecropper. His special talent was caning chair seats. (Courtesy of Nellie Williams.)

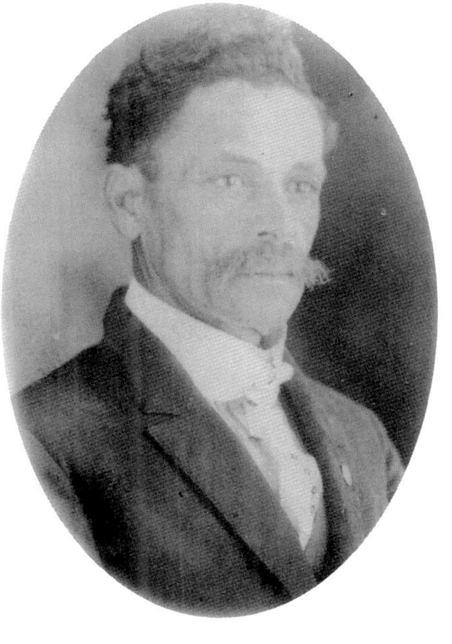

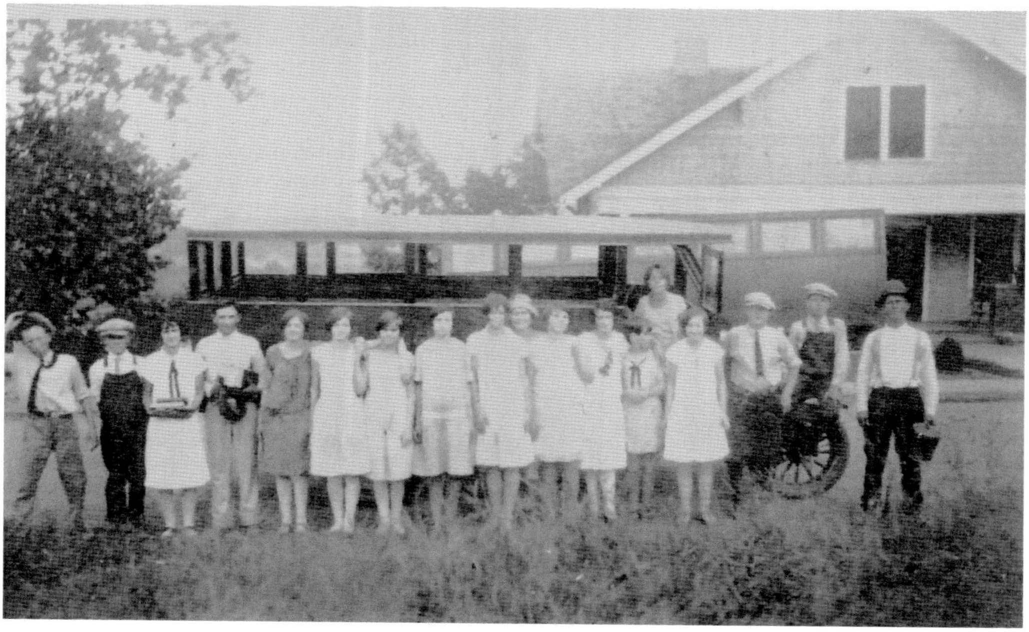

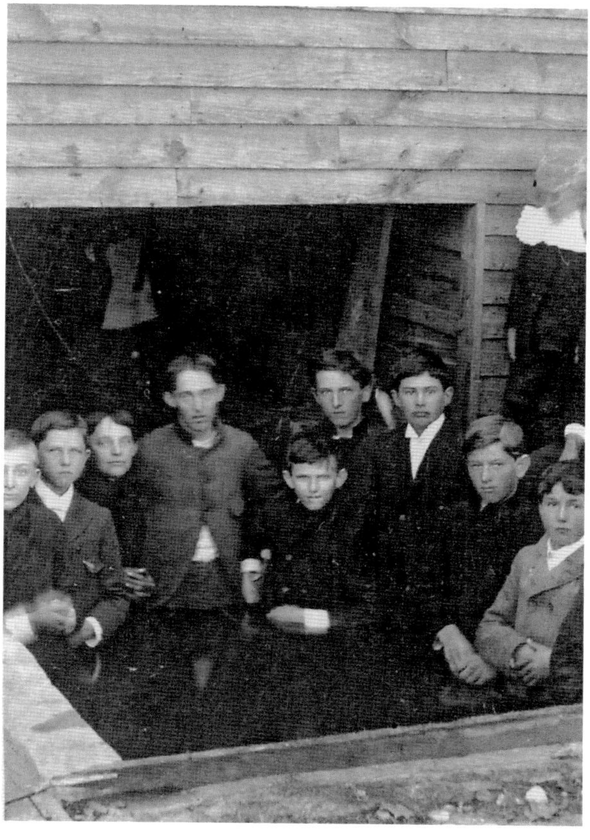

Duncan High School 1926
The students of the Woods Chapel and Abner Creek communities were bused to Duncan High School. The bus driver, seen right with bucket, was John Oliver Edge. Before antifreeze was discovered, drivers kept a bucket to drain the radiator each night. Tipping his hat on the left is Don Smith, who became the mayor of Greer. (Courtesy of F.E. Hendrix.)

Abner Creek Baptist Church Baptism
These young men were baptized on October 26, 1901. Pictured (left to right) are Earle McHugh, Homer S. Brockman, Ernest Coggins, Dexter Coggins, Furman McHugh, Dennie Hendrix, Leroy Brockman, J. Olice Hendrix, Earle Brockman, and Beattie Burnett. Pastor E.C. Ezell (not pictured) also baptized 12 female converts. (Courtesy of F.E. Hendrix.)

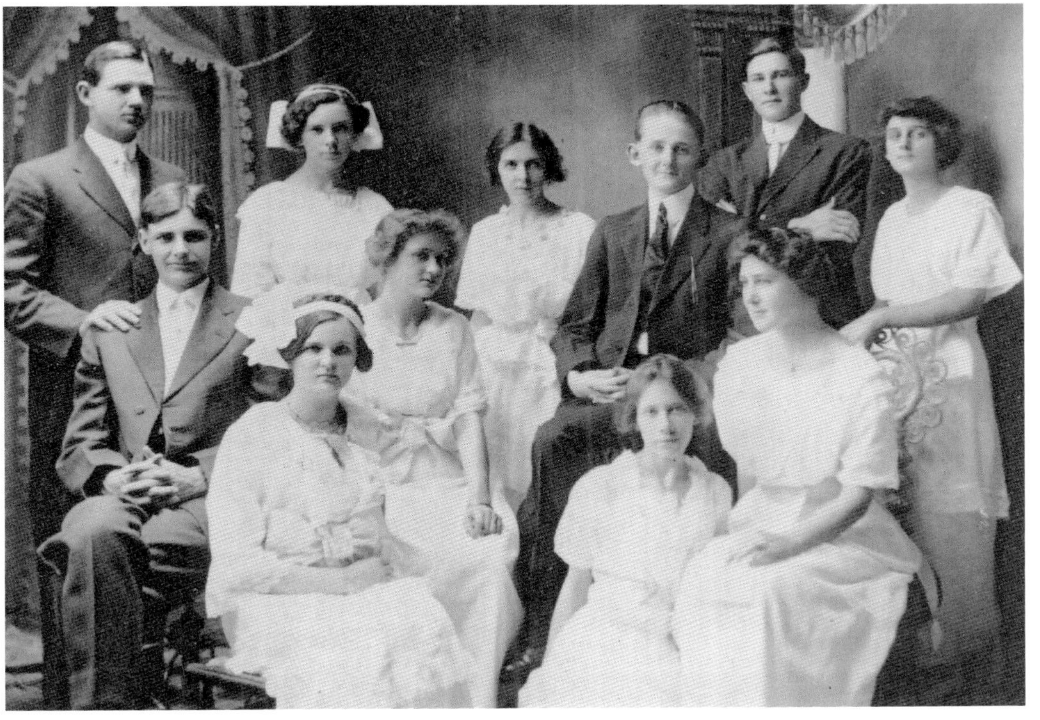

Greer High School Graduation 1913

The class of 1913 represents the early families of Greer. Shown here are (seated first row) unknown; (second row left to right) Robert Alton Few, unidentified, Fitzhugh Marchant, and Louise Cunningham Few; (third row left to right) Paul Brockman, unidentified, Edith Walker, Harry Lee Cunningham, and Eva Green. (Courtesy of Greer Heritage Museum.)

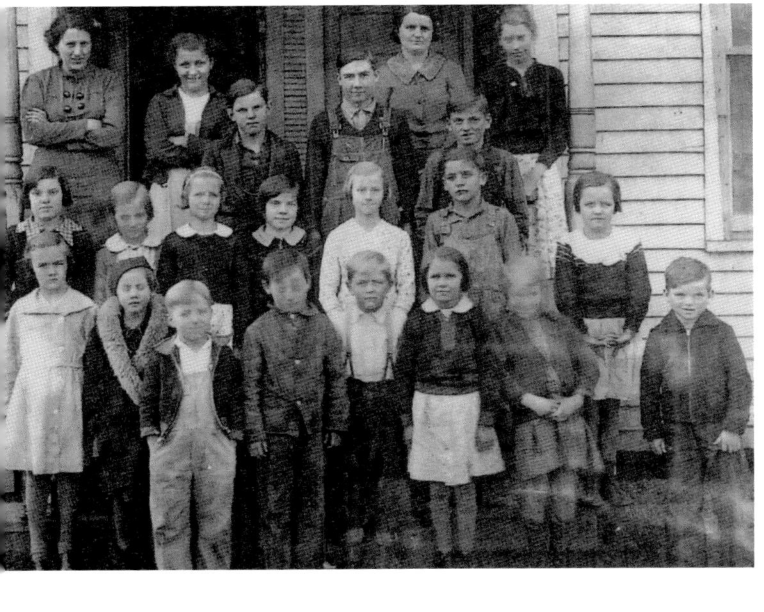

Abner Creek Grammar School 1937

Students are left to right (first row) Obelia Foster, Mary Burch, Milton Waddell, Marchant Greer, Billy Compton, Mildred Nodine, Marvolene Pearson, and unidentified; (second row) Margaret Bentley, Juanita Waddell, Mildred Green, Sarah Bentley, Blanche Waddell, Miles Compton, and Stella Compton; (third row) John Bentley, Judson Burch, Marvin Bentley, Evelyn Brown; (fourth row) teacher Grace Wilson, Vernelle Miller, and teacher Agnes Lister. (Courtesy of F.E. Hendrix.)

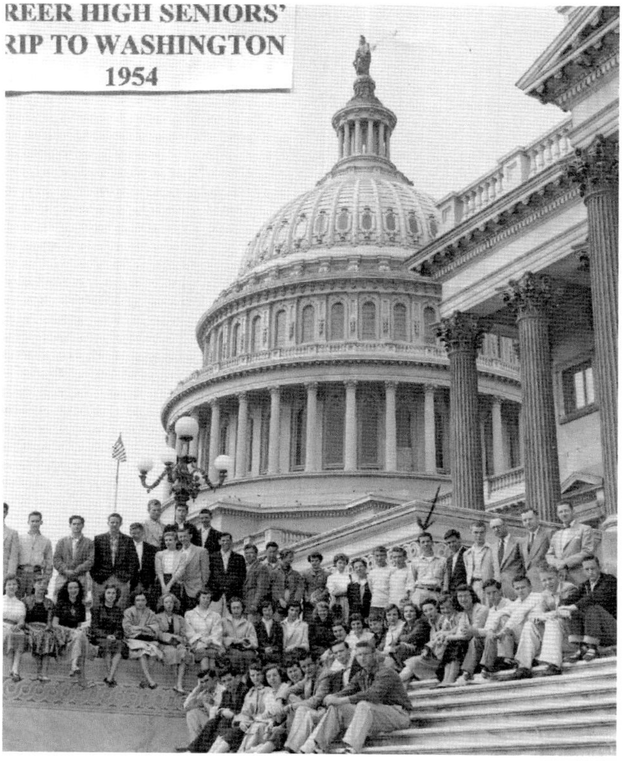

Senior Trip to Washington, DC

The highlight of senior year at Greer High School was the senior trip to Washington, DC. The 1954 class poses on the steps of the US Capitol. Seniors boarded the Southern Railroad in Greer for the trip. As the graduating classes grew, the trips had to be discontinued. (Courtesy of Greer Heritage Museum.)

Dan Davenport

Davenport provided the driver's education car for the classes at Greer High School. Davenport, who bought Thompson Motors in 1937 with Earl Duncan, renamed it D&D Ford. He is shown here at left with Charles Cherning, superintendent of Greer Schools (in the car) and Boyce Lynn, manager of D&D, on the right. His son George and grandson George Jr. (known as "Skip") continue in the business today. (Courtesy of Greer Heritage Museum.)

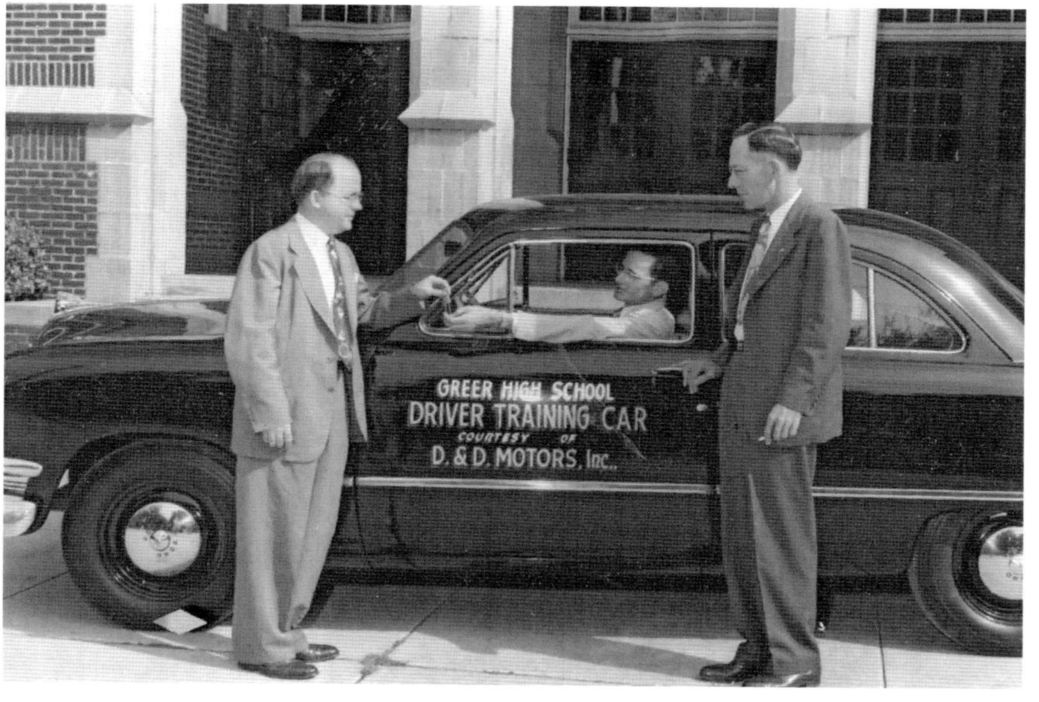

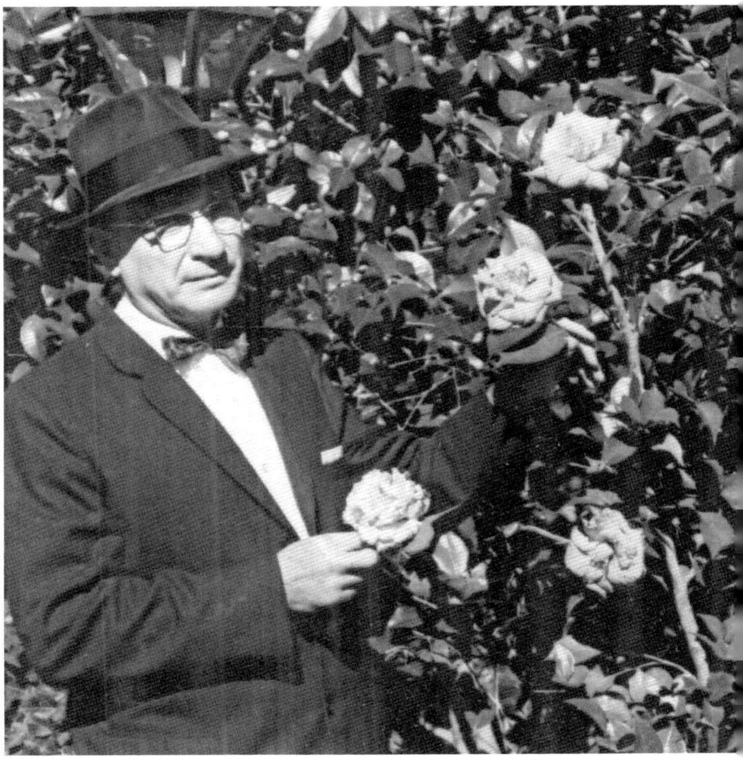

B.L. Frick, Principal
Frick came to Greer as principal of Davenport High School and oversaw the building of the new high school on North Main Street. He also implemented the consolidation of six rural districts with the Greer school district in 1950. An avid rose gardener, the popular principal is shown here in 1959 with his fine roses. (Courtesy of Greer Heritage Museum.)

Home Economics Class 1952
The new Greer High School on North Main Street opened in 1952, a much larger and more modern facility than its predecessor. Shown in the new home economics class (left to right) are Caroline Harrison, Margery Mayfield, and Pattie Lovell. Pattie Lovell Gaddy later became a popular teacher at Tryon Street Elementary School. (Courtesy of Greer Heritage Museum.)

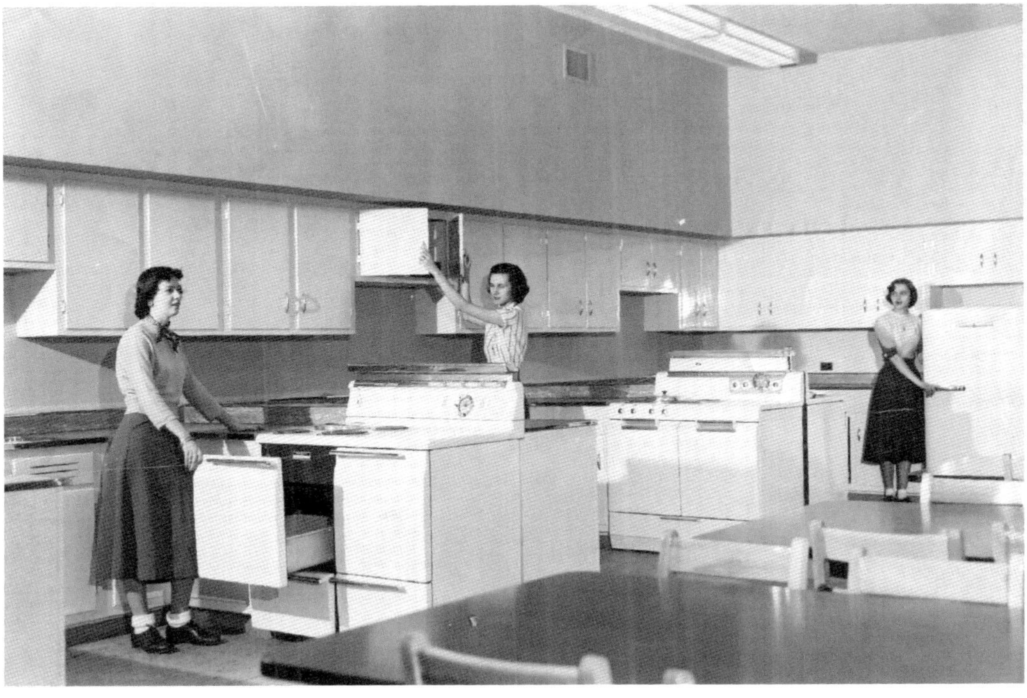

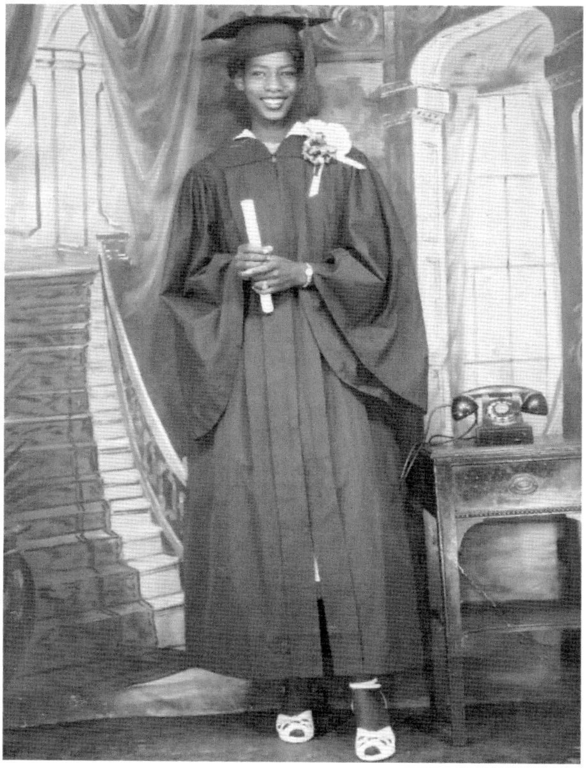

Margaret Durham

Durham poses proudly for her 1953 graduation picture from Dunbar High School. She attended Benedict College and graduated with a degree in education. She had a successful career as a public school teacher. Today, she and her husband James Hill live on the original Durham farm. (Courtesy of Margaret and James Hill.)

Lincoln High School Typing Class

Located in Taylors, Lincoln High School was the facility for black students. This is a 1959 typing class. Pictured left to right are (first row) Jo Ann Gray, Martha Ferguson, and Annie Goodwin; (second row) Donald Cox, Carolyn Mack, and Annette Thomas; (third row) Patricia Hoke, Freddie Bennett, and Hazel Gray; (fourth row) John Carson, Vermal Wood, and Cewell Wood; (fifth row) Joe McJunkin, unidentified; (standing) teacher Thomas Sherman. (Courtesy of Martha Gregory.)

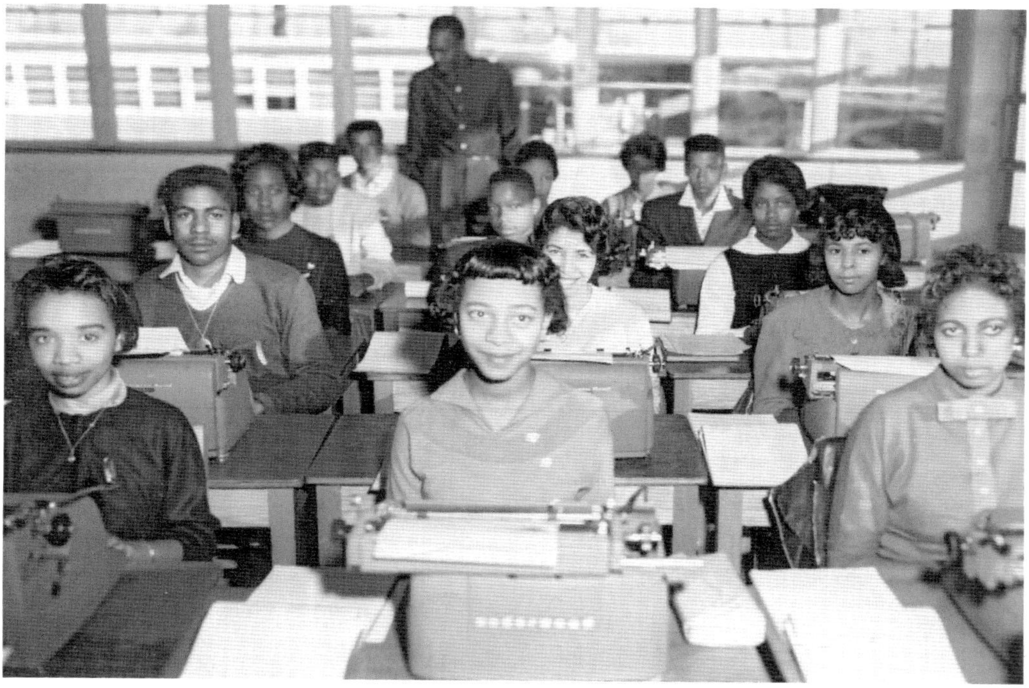

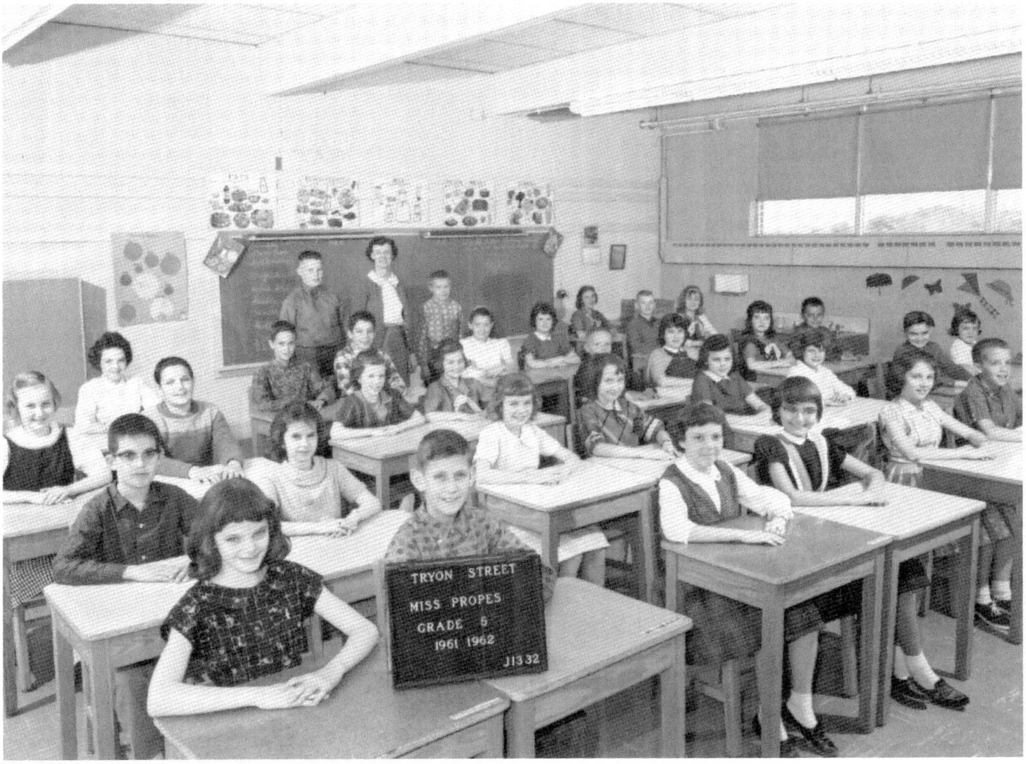

Tryon Street School 1961
For many years, the children in Greer attended Central School. The new Tryon Street Elementary School opened in 1960. Pictured is the 1961–1962 fifth grade class taught by Miss Lib Propes. Miss Propes had been a teacher at Central before moving to Tryon Street. The school closed in 1999 and the children of that area now attend the Chandler Creek Elementary School. (Courtesy of Greer Heritage Museum.)

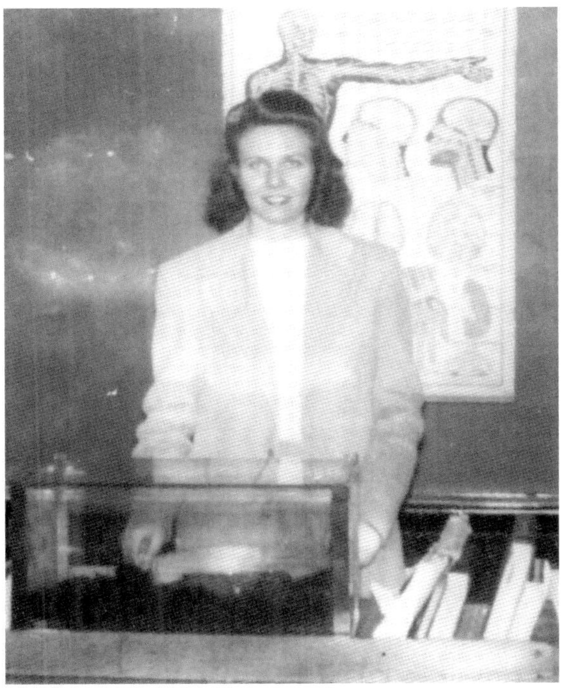

Jean Smith
Smith finished Furman University and accepted a position to teach biology and chemistry at Greer's Davenport High School. She is shown here in her classroom. One snowy day at the Greer Post Office, she met Verne Smith, who was more than helpful to the attractive new teacher. They married and became lifelong partners who loved and served their community and state. (Courtesy of Carole Smith Olmert.)

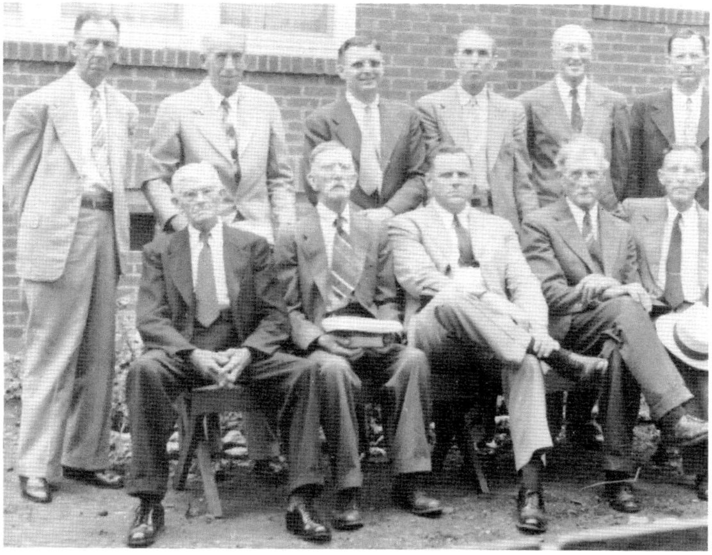

Washington Baptist Church 1946

The deacons at Washington Baptist Church in 1946 celebrate the building of the parsonage. Shown (seated left to right) are Jake Gibson, Jack Ballenger, O.B. Lancaster (Pastor), Bubb Ponder, and Richard Walls; (standing left to right) Herman Ponder, B.C. Berry, Thurman Sudduth, Bommer Wood, Fate Moon, and Harold Hill. (Courtesy of Mary Ponder Vickery.)

Margaret Burch

When Burch ran for her third term in 1990 for Greenville County School Board, she was anxious to receive the results of the election. Husband Leland and friend Debbie Davis (center) tally the votes as Margaret mans the phone. She had good news that evening with a win. She was the first female chair of the school board for the year 1988–1989. (Courtesy of Leland and Margaret Burch.)

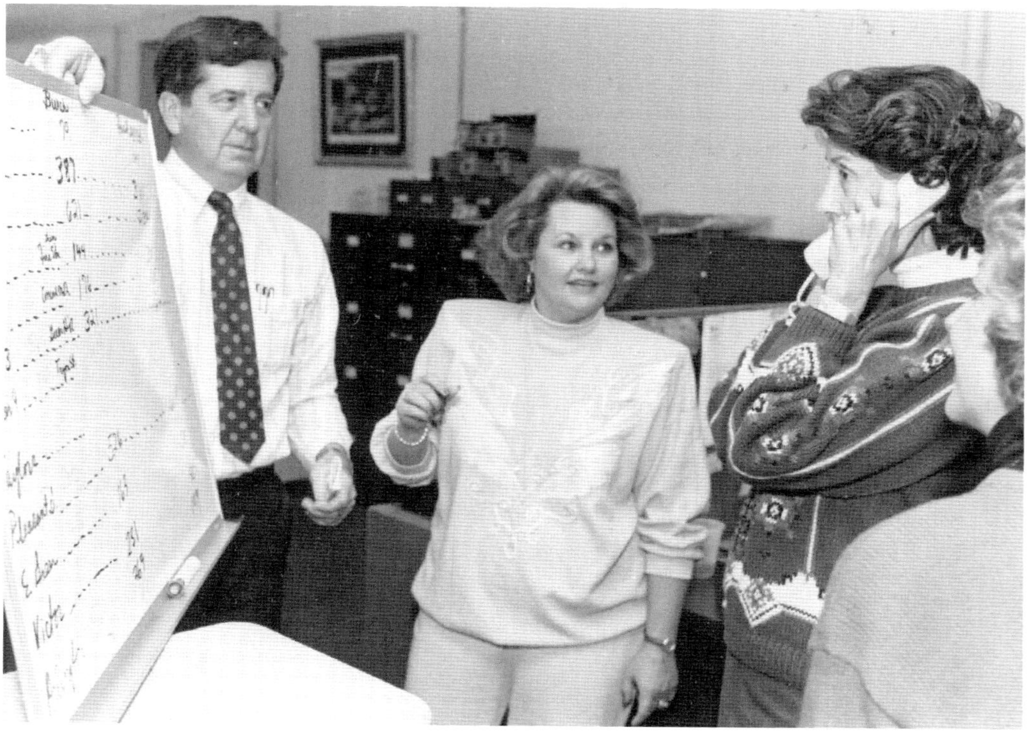

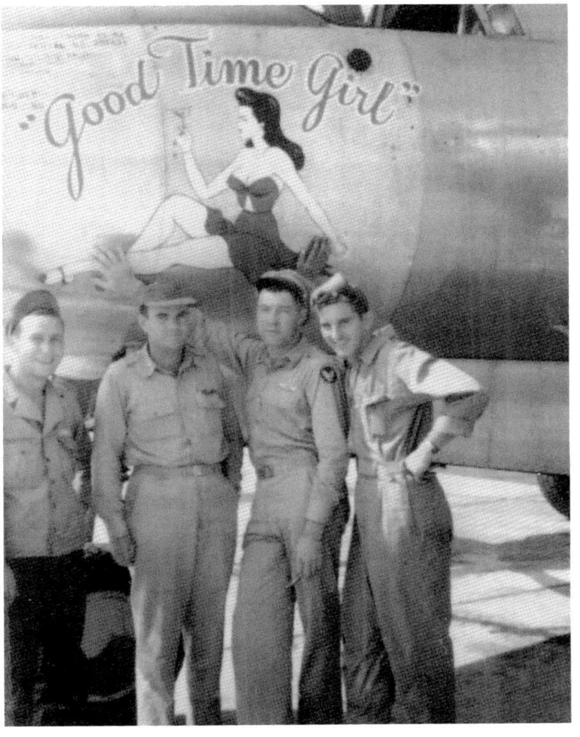

David Sheppard

In October 1939, David Sheppard held the first organization meeting for a Greer High School band. Confident of his musicians, Sheppard took the band to Columbia to enter a state contest. Despite the fact they had no uniforms, they won. Sheppard was drafted in late 1941. He is shown here (second from left) with the plane he used to train pilots in the Army Air Force. (Courtesy of David Sheppard Jr.)

Tommy Hughes

After a long career with Greenville County Schools, Hughes became the popular principal of Mountain View Elementary School. Worried about family literacy, he initiated a visitation program to the homes of all kindergarten students. Students chose books for the principal to read from the book bag, and they would also get to keep their books. Here he reads to Rebecca Yates. (Courtesy of Tommy Hughes.)

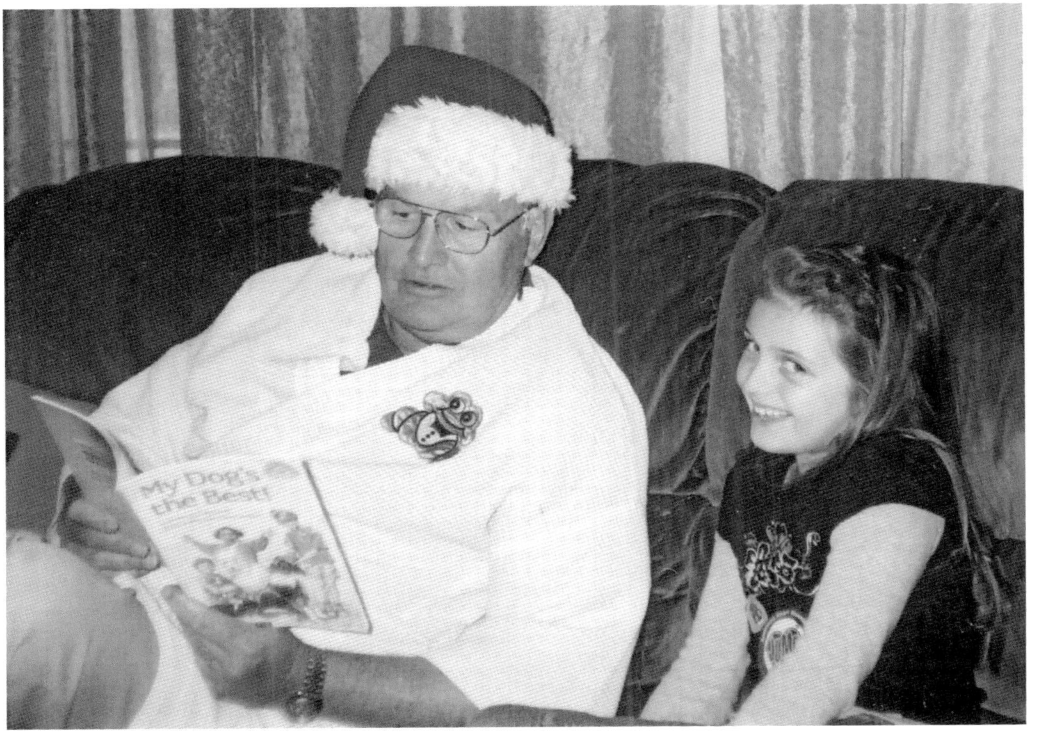

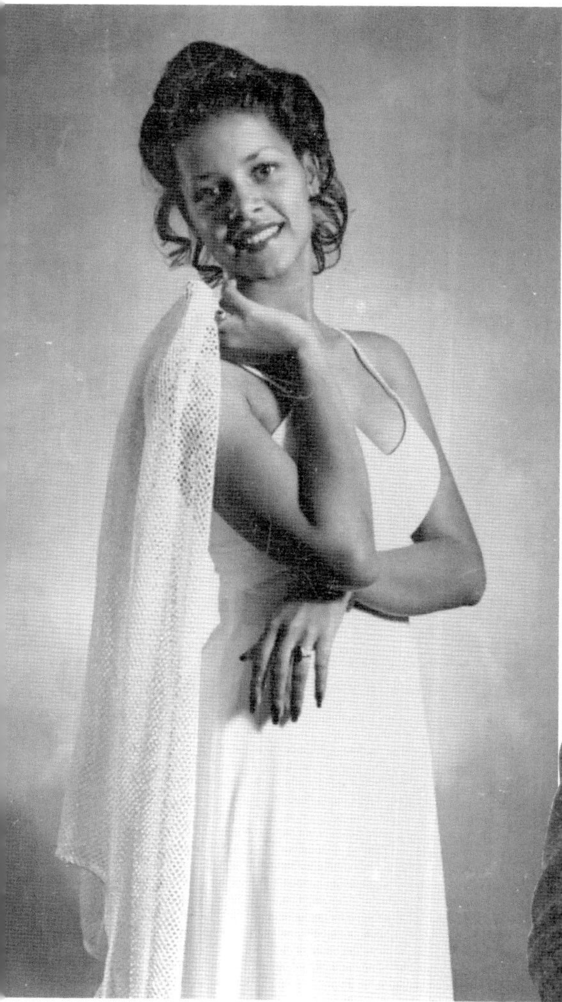

Demetra Elizabeth Gregory

Gregory, daughter of Martha and J.W. Gregory, was chosen Miss LeFlambeau of 1980. *The LeFlambeau* is the Greer High School yearbook and honors one young lady every year for outstanding beauty, intelligence, and school spirit. Demetra, who was an outstanding choice, had the distinction of being the first black young woman to hold the title. (Courtesy of J.W. and Martha Gregory.)

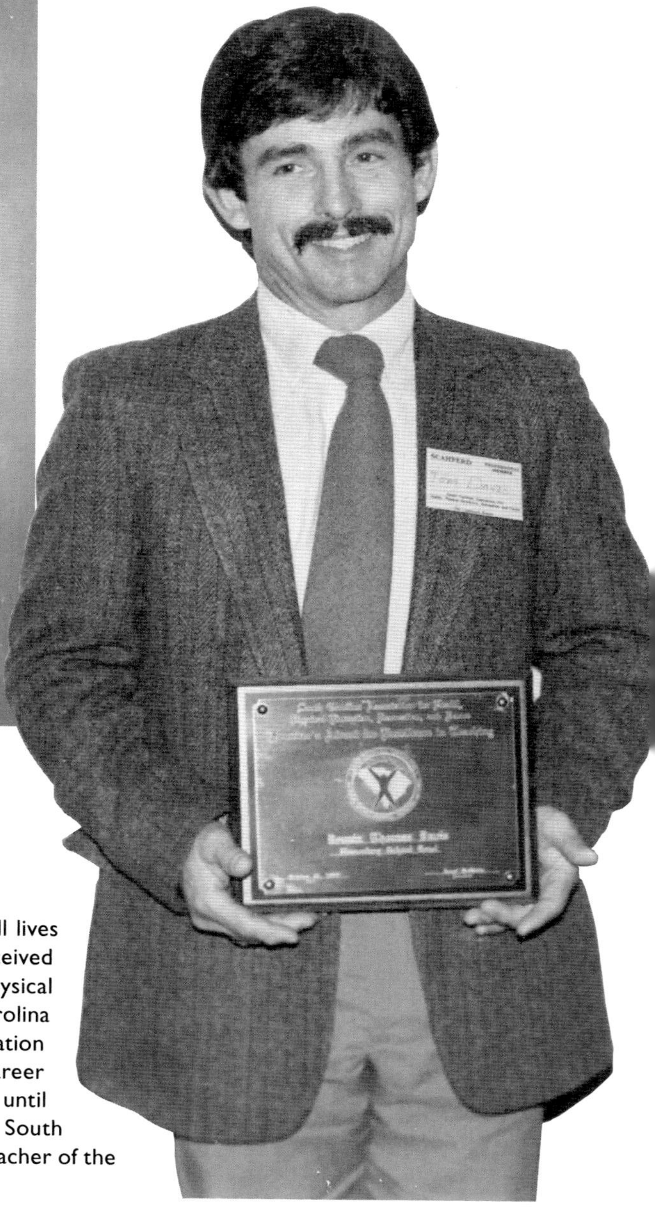

Tom Davis

Dennis Thomas Davis, known as Tom, still lives on River Road where he grew up. He received a bachelor of science in health and physical education from the University of South Carolina and a master of arts in health and education from Furman University. His teaching career was spent in elementary schools from 1974 until he retired in 2004. Among his awards was South Carolina Elementary Physical Education Teacher of the Year in 1987. (Courtesy of Tom Davis.)

CHAPTER SEVEN

Sports

Listen closely, and you can hear the sounds of the past. Do you not hear the call "Play Ball!", the crack of the bat, the roar of the crowd, the slap of skin against pigskin, the squeak of the rubber soles on the hardwood floor? Greer has always been serious about its sports. There are pictures almost as old as the town itself of men outfitted to play baseball, girls in basketball dresses, and boys in old woolen football pants and leather helmets.

The local textile mills organized many of the earliest sports teams to provide relaxation for workers who put in long, hard hours. Quite early, textile owners recognized the value of recreation and built YMCAs, ball fields, and swimming pools in the villages. Public recreation today owes much of its origins to textile programs for children and adults. Baseball and basketball teams were organized for adult workers; junior league teams provided the children with healthy activities after school and on weekends. Greer Mill even had a golf course, although it also served as a grazing pasture for the villagers' cows.

After Victor Mill built a baseball field for its textile league team, it allowed the community at large to use it. Greer High School played football there until a stadium was built in the 1930s. During World War I, teams from Camp Sevier in Greenville and Camp Wadsworth in Spartanburg met halfway on Victor Field for a baseball tournament on April 5, 1918. Since most of the Greer men were stationed at Sevier, the citizens cheered for Sevier, who defeated Wadsworth 7 to 1.

As textile league baseball grew in popularity, there was active recruitment of good players for the mill teams. In 1908, Shoeless Joe Jackson played for the Victor Pirates. In turn, major leagues looked at the textile teams for some of their players. It was not unusual for young men to turn down the major leagues, because the textile mills paid much better. Dennis Smith, known as the "Greer Peach," played for the 1937 New York Yankees but returned home to play for Greer Mill for more money.

Flint Rhem was one of the greatest pitchers in the majors to come out of South Carolina. One of nine children, he was born in 1901 in Rhems, a town named for his grandfather. He had begun playing baseball when he was nine even though his father considered baseball the sport of roughnecks. Expected to enter the family wholesale business, he entered the engineering program at Clemson University with no plans to play ball. Once the coach became aware of his talent, he recruited Rhem to play for Clemson his last two years. At the time, he was considered the leading South Carolina college pitcher, averaging 15 strikeouts a game.

Before he went to the majors, he played some textile league ball for Belton in the Saluda Textile League. Even at the end of his first professional season with the St. Louis Cardinals in 1924, he made an appearance with the Brandon Mills team against Judson. It was not uncommon for the mill teams to bring in a heavy hitter for the fiercely competitive textile league.

Rhem is credited with helping his team win the 1926, 1931, and 1934 World Series. His best season was 1926; his salary was $5,000. He always said that his biggest thrill was playing against the Babe in that 1926 series.

The Phillies purchased him in 1932. He returned to St. Louis only to be sold to the Boston Braves. In 1935, he spent a season with the Cincinnati Reds before returning to the Cardinals and retirement. During his career he acquired the nickname "Shad." Players gave it to him because he always had a "fish story."

In 1930, Rhem married Lula Dillard, a Greer schoolteacher, and Greer became his home. He died in 1969. His only child, Charles "Sonny" Flint Rhem Jr., born in 1936, still lives in Greer today.

As the textile leagues began to wane, high school football took its place as a popular pastime in Greer. Friday nights in Greer found cars lining the narrow streets around the stadium. Residents in the surrounding neighborhood followed the band as it marched from Davenport High School to the stadium just a few blocks away. Greer High School won State Football Championships in 1956, 1989, 1994, and 2003 and State Basketball Championships in 1931, 1955, 1959, and 2005, according to available records.

The winning 1956 team was coached by Phil Clark, head coach; Eddis Freeman, line coach; and Lewis Phillips, B team coach. Staff writer John Wilson of the *Spartanburg Herald* interviewed a local service station operator in Greer. "Y'know," he said, "Before Greer High went on that long winning streak Phil Clark was a real regular guy. Now they've won 17 straight games, Phil Clark is still a regular guy." Perhaps he summed up the community's feeling about Coach Clark, who came to Greer High in 1951 as assistant coach and served from 1952 until 1970 as head coach.

Several Greer high school players have gone on to bigger and better things. Nelson Welch was an outstanding kicker for Clemson University. Today Kris "Hi-Lite" Bruton plays for the world-renowned Harlem Globetrotters.

The mills and their teams are gone. The Victor YMCA closed in the early 1980s, but the Friday night lights still burn for the local high schools. Fishermen can be found on Lake Cunningham and Lake Robinson; golfers tee off at Greer Country Club. For both spectators and participants, sports are alive and well in Greer.

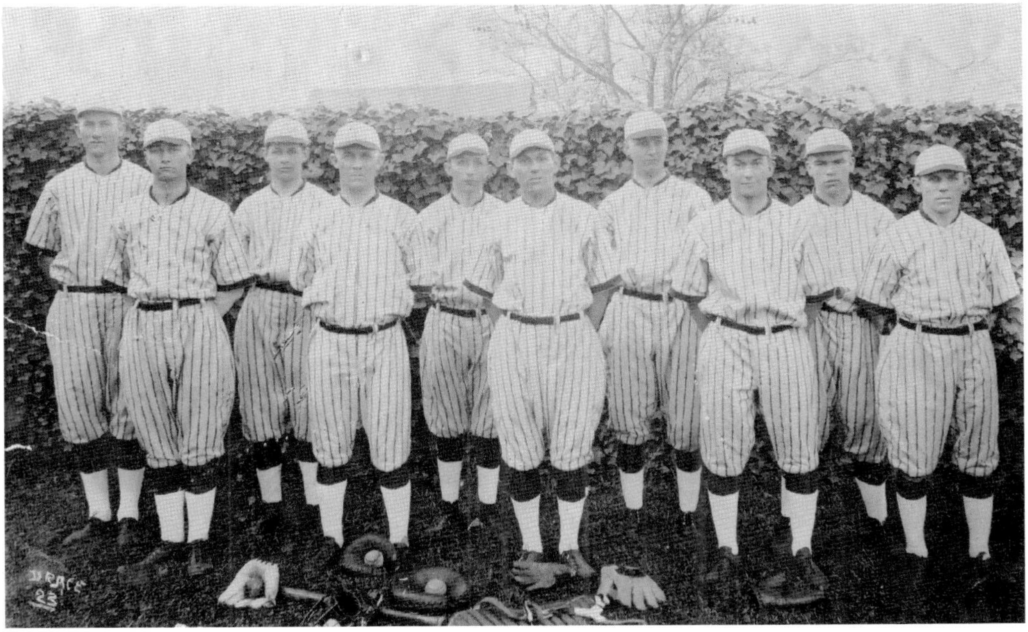

Greer High School Baseball 1923

This 1923 Drace photograph of the Greer High School baseball team shows (left to right) Jones Clement, Paul Bonham, J.W. Gibson, Roy Campbell, Fred Shore, ? Smith, Lewis Cunningham, Ray Norman, Sewell Hawkins, and Elford Campbell. It is believed that this was the first high school baseball team at the new Davenport High School. (Courtesy of Greer Heritage Museum.)

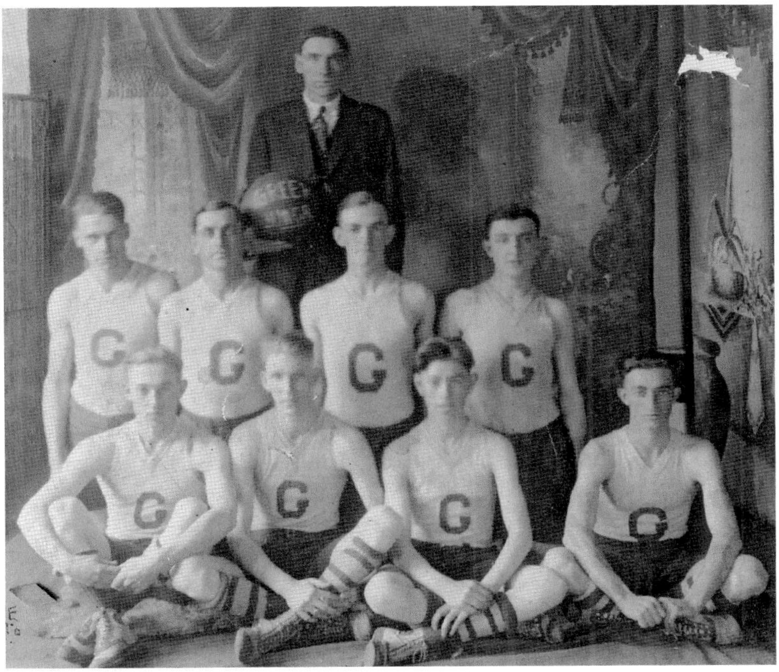

Greer Mill YMCA Team 1922

The Greer Mill YMCA team of 1922 is unnamed except for Coach Wilton Pruitt. Local textile mills had YMCA programs with active sports teams for the residents of their villages. There were youth teams as well as teams for workers. Before the advent of public recreation, the mill owners realized the value of recreation in people's lives. (Courtesy of Greer Heritage Museum.)

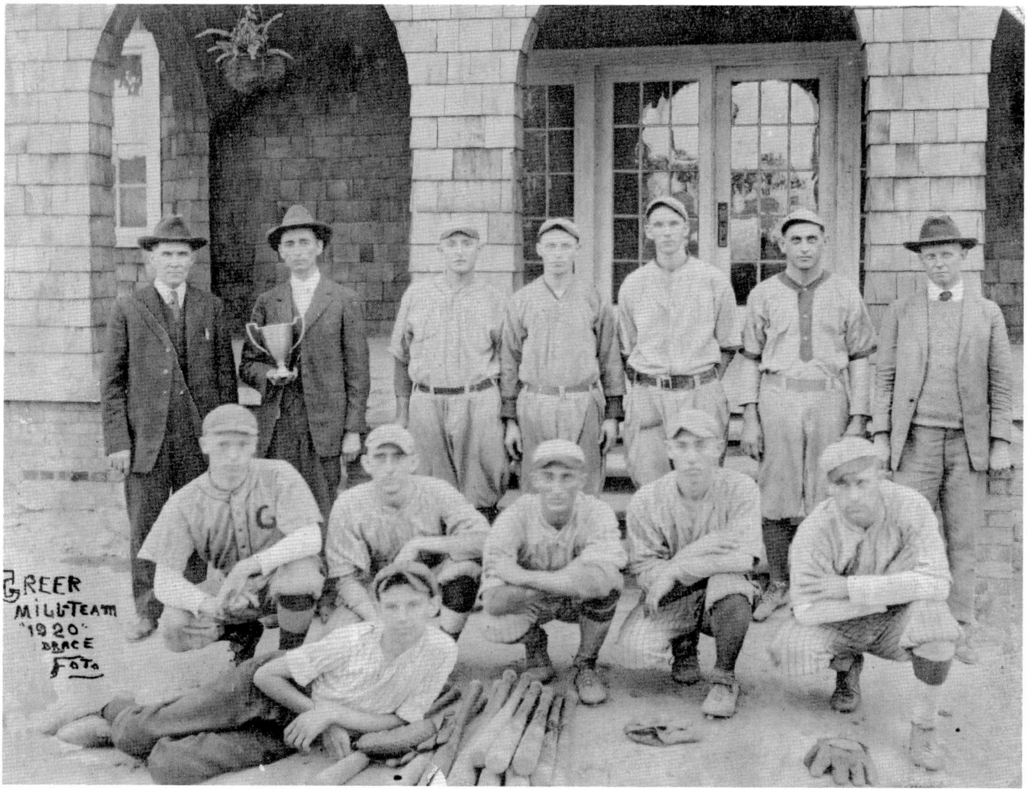

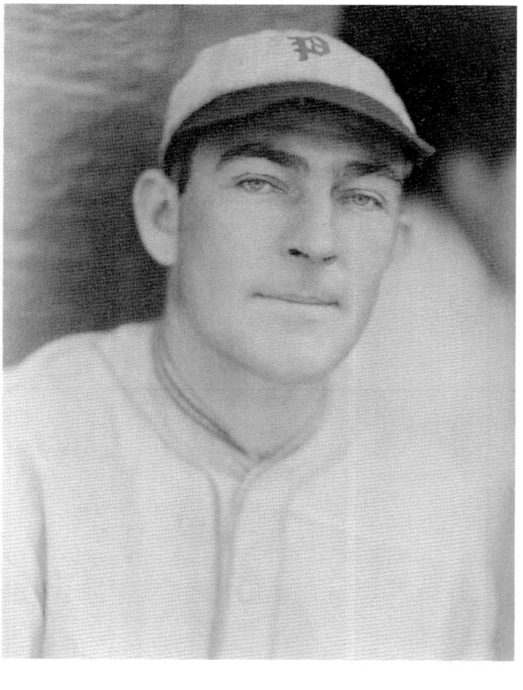

Greer Mill Baseball 1920

The textile league baseball teams were as popular as major league baseball. Mill owners recruited heavily to employ the best players. This unidentified 1920 Greer Mill team posed with their trophy for the locally famous photographer Charles Drace. Teams from all the area mills played each other. Shoeless Joe Jackson played one season with the Victor Mill team. (Courtesy of Greer Heritage Museum.)

Flint Rhem

Rhem was an outstanding Clemson baseball player who joined the St. Louis Cardinals in 1924 as a pitcher. In 1926, he won 20 games to help the Cardinals win their first National League pennant. He is shown here in 1933 in his Philadelphia Phillies uniform after being traded. After 10 seasons of baseball, he settled in Greer. (Courtesy of Sonny Rhem.)

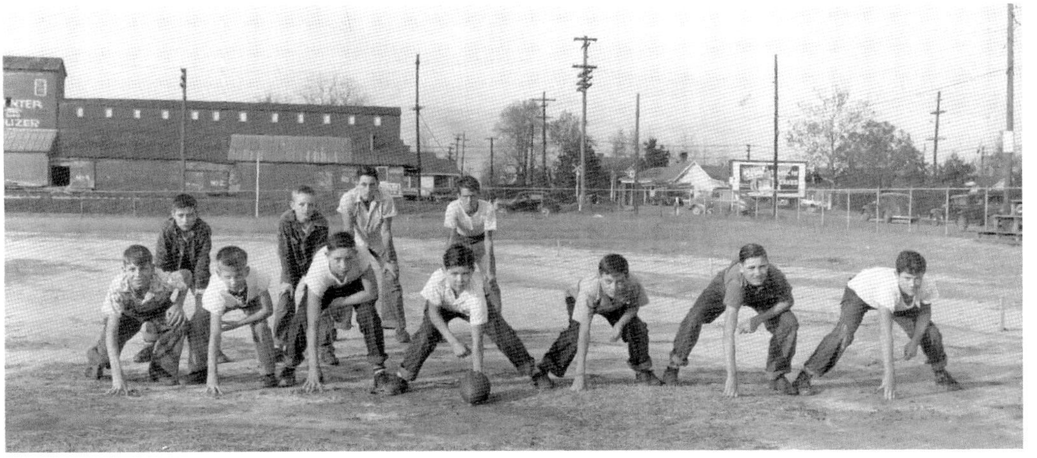

The Victor Wildcats 1948

In 1948, the Victor Wildcats were the two-hand touch football champions. Shown here on the Victor Field are (left to right) Bobby Lemmons, Butch Miller, Bobby Spearman, Don Godfrey, Jimmy Jackson, Jack Gorman, and Millard Leonhardt; (back field) Gary Hollaway, Don Elder, Billy Joe Sanders, and Kenneth Moss. (Courtesy of Butch Miller.)

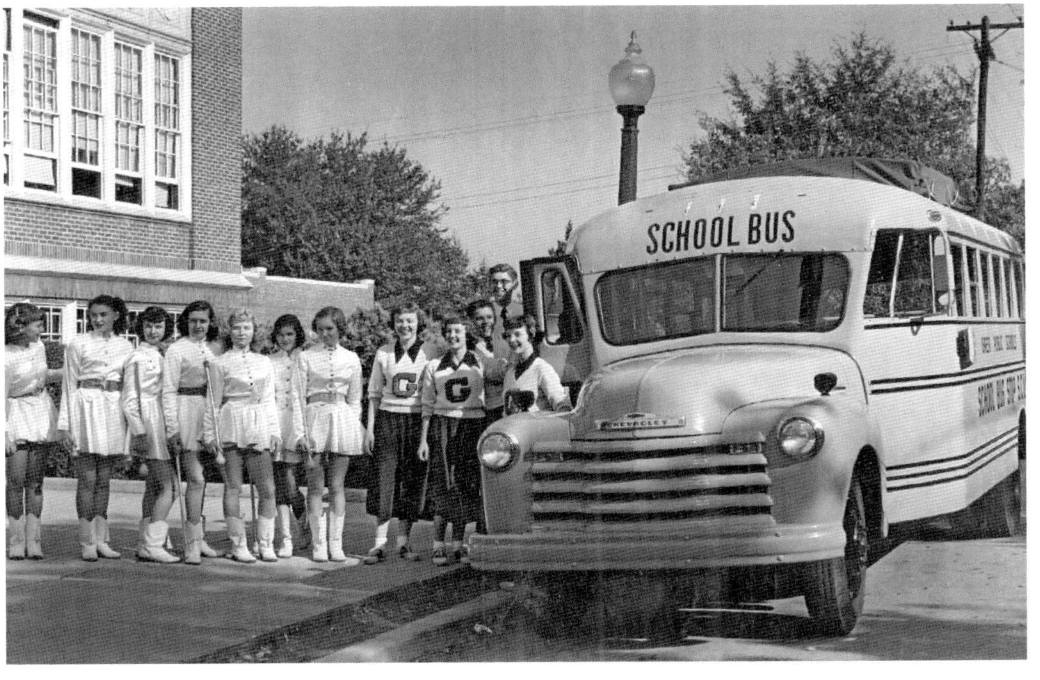

Greer High Majorettes and Cheerleaders

In this 1951 picture, the Greer High School majorettes and cheerleaders board the bus for a game. The picture was taken in front of the old Davenport High School. The majorettes are not identified, but the cheerleaders are (left to right) Patsy Terrell, Patsy Cole, Jonnie Sue Jones, Walter Peterson, and Billy Black. (Courtesy of Greer Heritage Museum.)

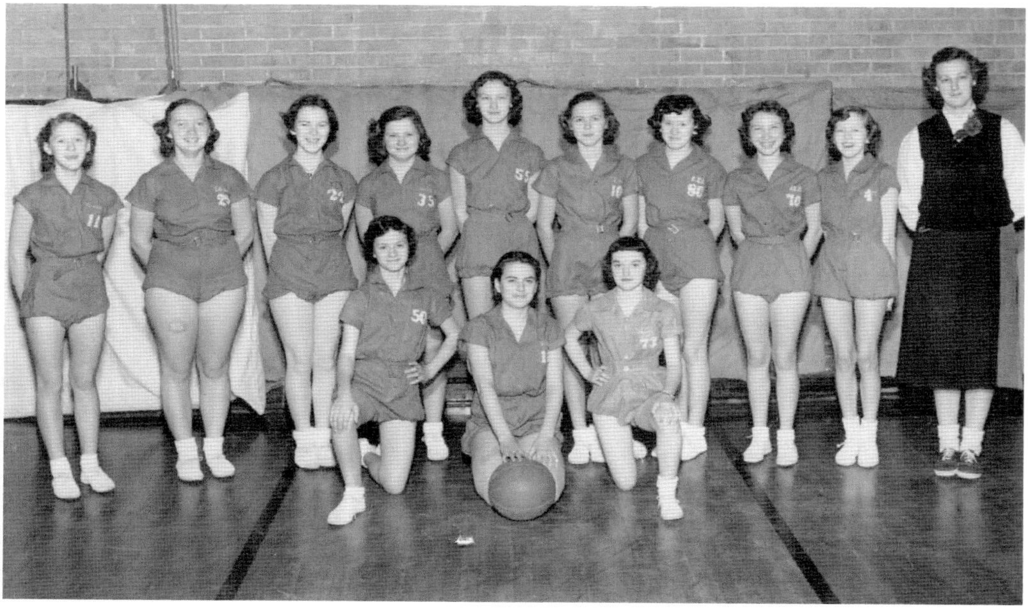

Davenport Junior High Girls' Basketball
After a new high school was built on North Main Street, Davenport became the junior high school. Shown here is the 1954 girls' basketball team: (back row left to right) Jo Ann Stoddard, Elinor Copland, Judy Cox, Jerry Sue Wood, Sarah Smith, Eleanor Hannah, Eurcel Laws, Ann Dillard, and Sharon West; (front row left to right) Ruby Loftis, Sarah Sanders (Captain), Deloris Owens, and Coach Ellen Meadow. (Courtesy of Ann Dillard Withrow.)

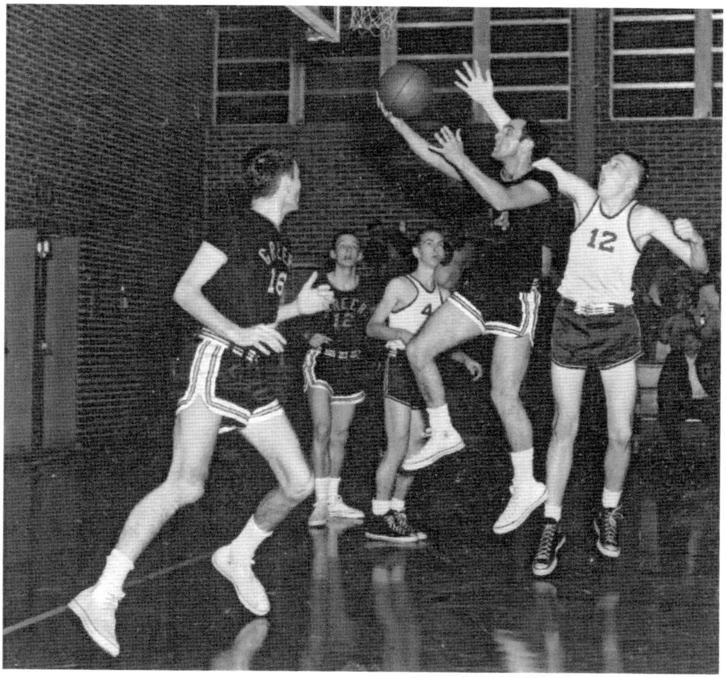

Greer High School Basketball 1956
The 1956 Greer High basketball team is shown in a game against Taylors High School. In this photo are Micky Flynn #16, Chick Smith #12, and Don Jones #14 jumping. (Courtesy of Butch Miller.)

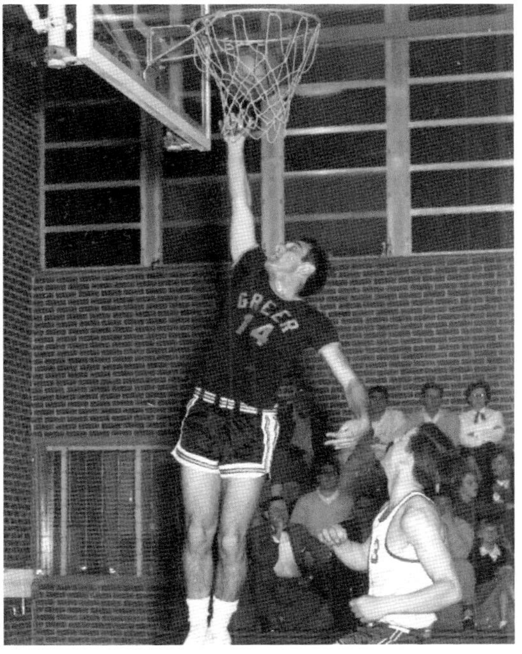

Don Jones
In another shot of the same game, Jones, #14, lays up a shot against Taylors High School. (Courtesy of Butch Miller.)

State Basketball Champions 1955
Greer High School's championship team in 1955 were left to right (first row) Butch Miller, Buck Black, Leon McElmore, Don Jones, and Harold Durham; (second row) ? McGowan, Steve Satterfield, Mike McCallister, Mickey Flynn, and Chick Smith; (rear) Eddis Freeman, coach. (Courtesy of Butch Miller.)

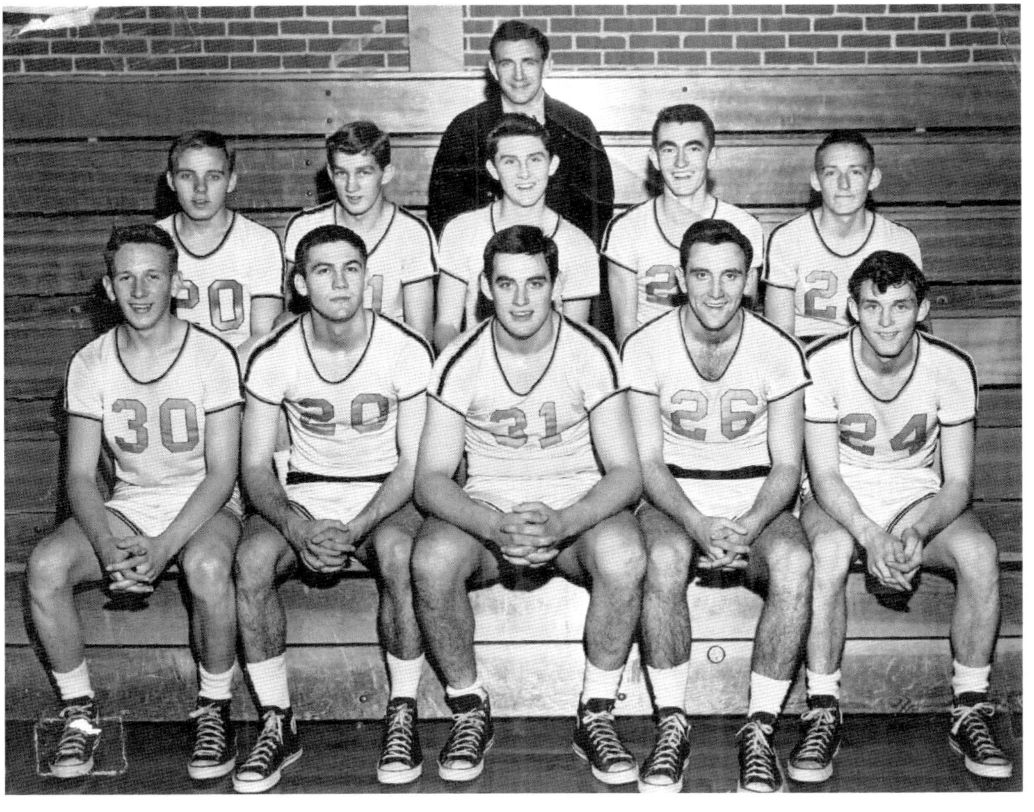

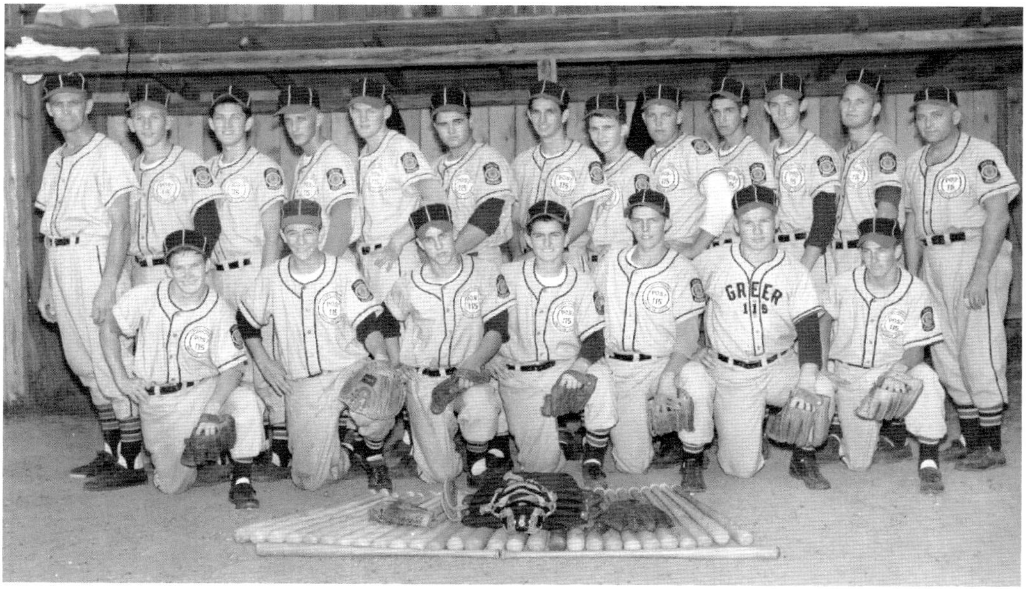

American Legion Baseball 1956

This American Legion Baseball team was runner-up to North Charleston in the 1956 tournament. Shown here left to right are (front row) Dickie Gravley, Larry Johnson, Mickey Stickland, Donnie Carruth, Larry Stokes, Clyde Weaver, and Bobby Gravley; (back row) Paul Edwards, Butch Miller, Murray Hall, Ken Waddell, Wayne Blackmon, Billy Cooper, Toby Foster, Benny Atkins, Sonny Lanford, Donnie Dill, Barry Bolding, Richard Robinson, and Dudley Tollison. (Courtesy of Butch Miller.)

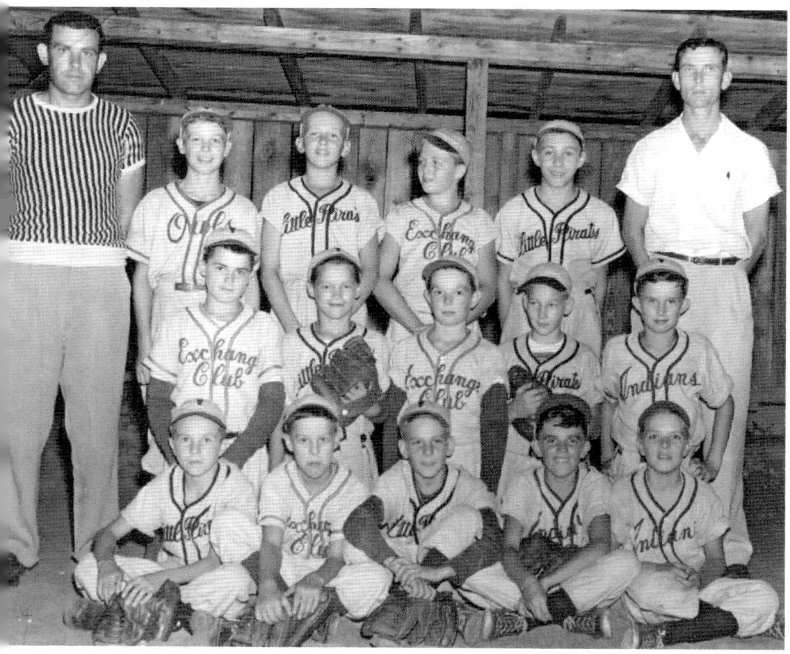

Little League All-Stars 1950

The first Greer Little League franchise in 1950 consisted of four teams: the city's Exchange Club, the Owls of Greer Mill, the Indians of Apalache Mill, and the Little Pirates of Victor Mill. The season all-stars are shown here left to right (first row) Dan Harvey, Mickey Strickland, Jimmy Taleff, Riley Beeks, and James Garrett; (second row) Billy Cooper, Jack McKinney, Jerry Jones, Earl Southerland, and Benny Atkins; (third row) Coach Ralph Bogan, Fred Ellenburg, Butch Miller, Mike Sudduth, George Jones, and Coach Fred Snoddy. (Courtesy of Butch Miller.)

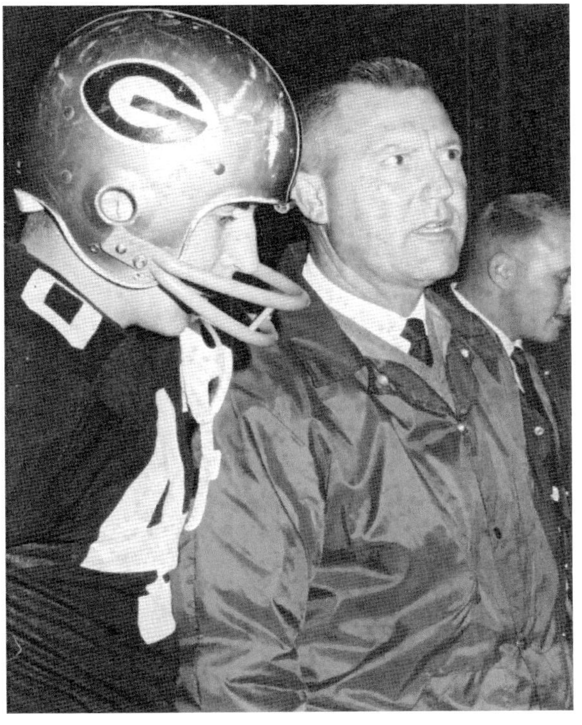

Phil Clark

Legendary coach Phil Clark began as assistant football coach at Greer High School in 1951. The next year he became head coach and served in that capacity until 1970. In 1956, his team won the State AA Football Championship. He was well respected by the community. After his coaching and teaching days were over, he was active in church and community activities. (Courtesy of Lynn D. Clark.)

Greer High School Football 1955

It was Friday night in the old Greer High School stadium in 1955 when Dicky Gravley ran a 23-yard kick return after a Spartanburg High School touchdown. Spartanburg won, beating Greer 20 to 12. Visible players are Gravely #22, Jack Allen #36, and Butch Miller #31. (Courtesy of Butch Miller.)

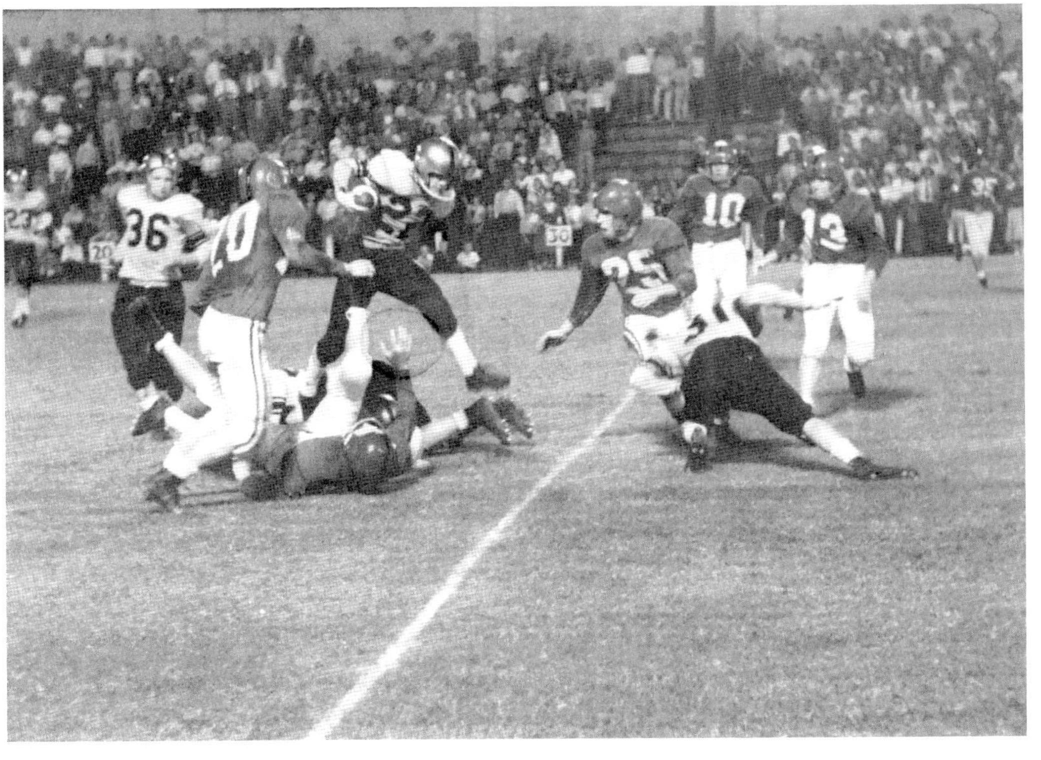

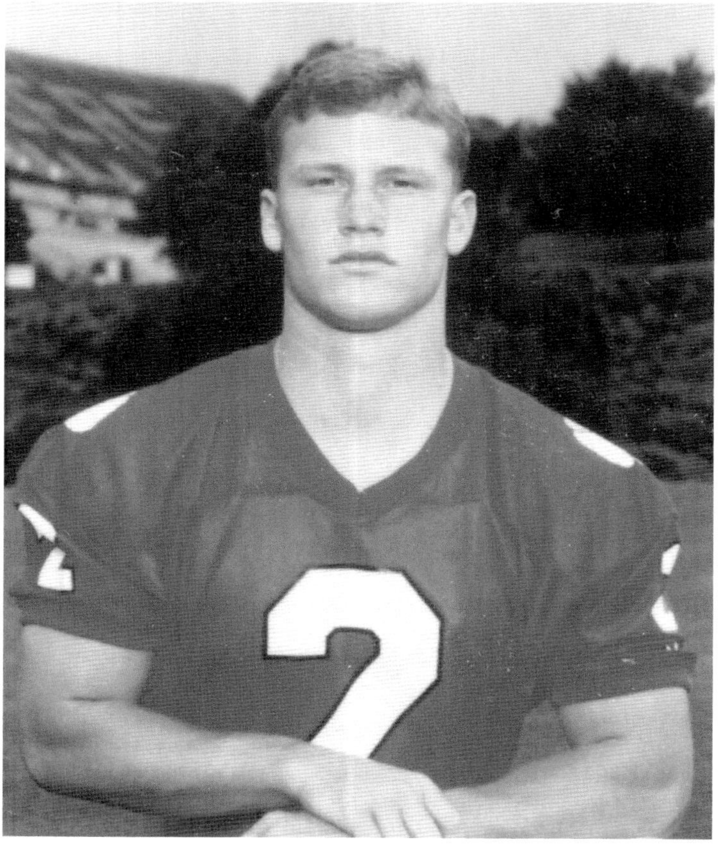

Nelson Welch
Welch was a winning kicker for both the Greer High School and Clemson University football teams. He was a member of the 1989 Greer State Championship team. (Courtesy of Butch Miller.)

State AAA Football Champions 1989
The 1989 State AAA Championship football team stand on the steps of the State Capitol in Columbia. Coach Stuart Holcombe and his team were welcomed by State Senator Verne Smith and State Representative Lewis Vaughn. (Courtesy of Greer Heritage Museum.)

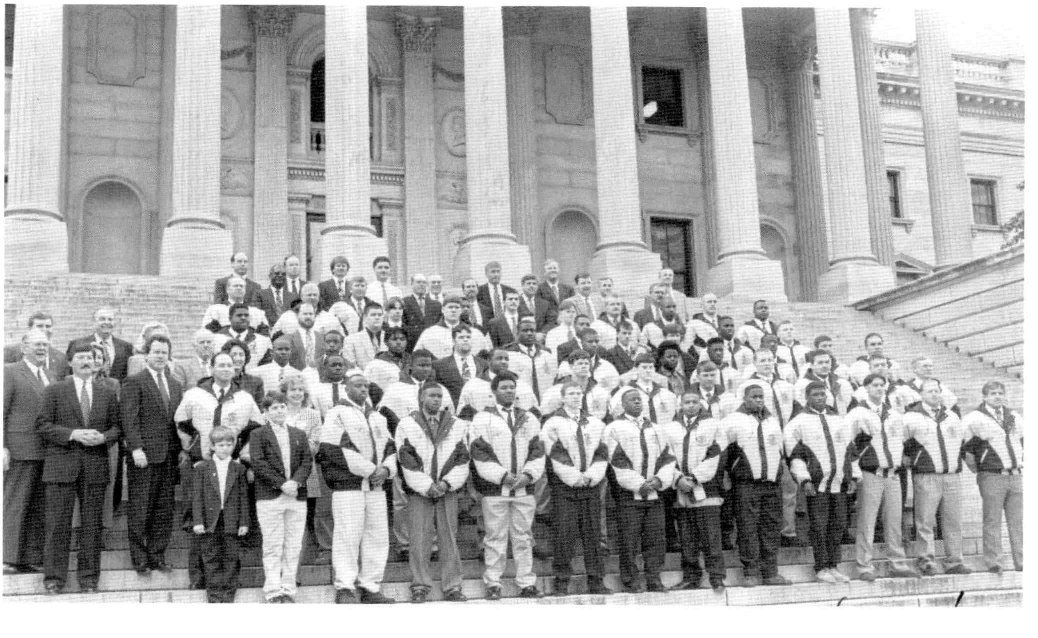

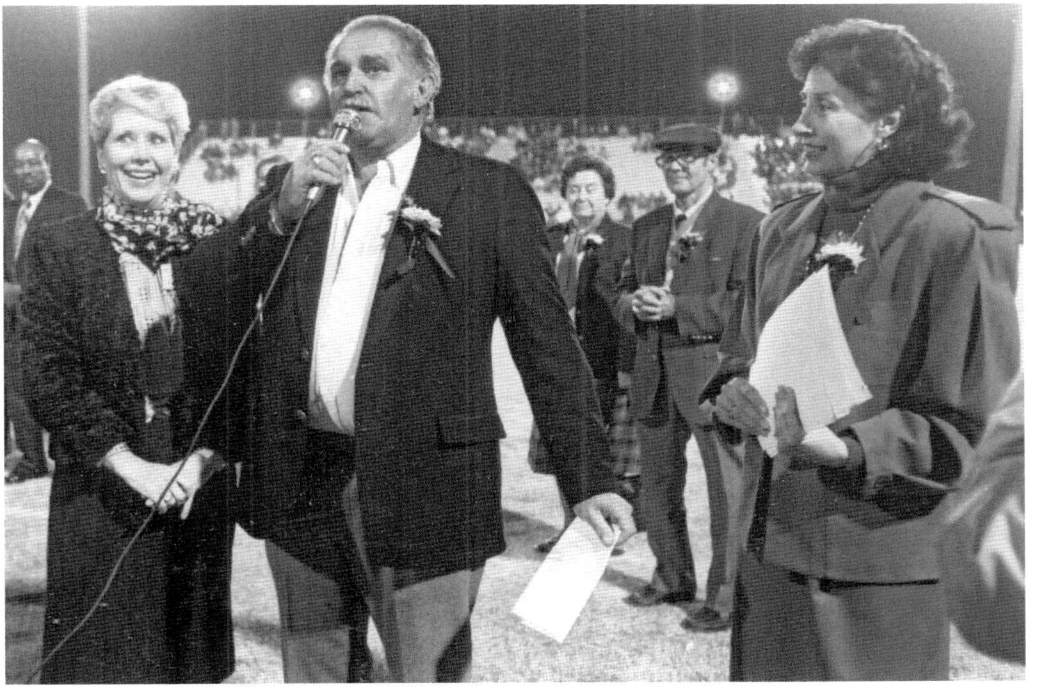

Roy Dooley
When Greer High School needed a new football stadium, many local citizens raised money, but none was a bigger booster than Dooley. The field was named in his honor, and Nancy Welch (left) and Margaret Burch, Greenville County School Trustee, listen as he speaks to the crowd at the dedication in 1987. (Courtesy of Leland and Margaret Burch.)

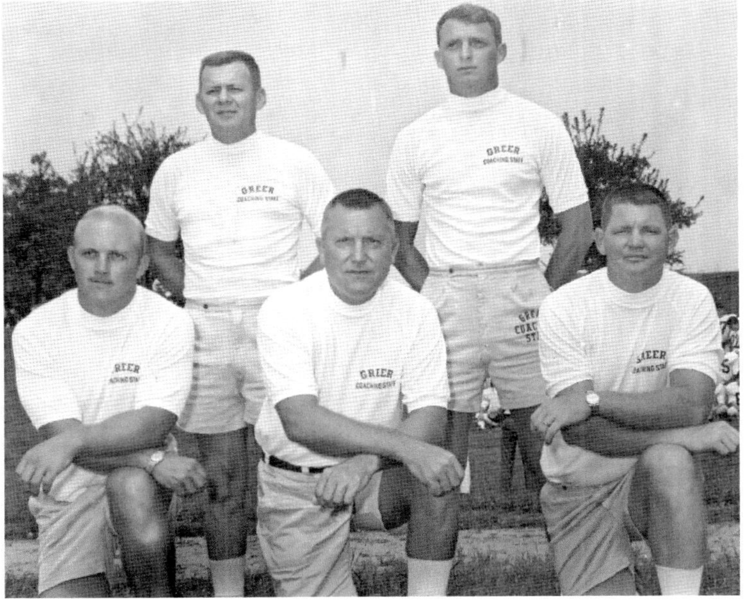

Greer High School Coaches
Greer High School coaches in 1969 are left to right (front) Pat Sudduth, Phil Clark (head coach), and Jim Few; (back) Lewis Phillips and Stanley Godfrey. Few succeeded Clark as head coach. Phillips, a longtime coach and educator, became a South Carolina state representative. Sudduth, a retired principal, now serves on the Greenville County School Board representing the Greer area. (Courtesy of Lynn D. Clark.)

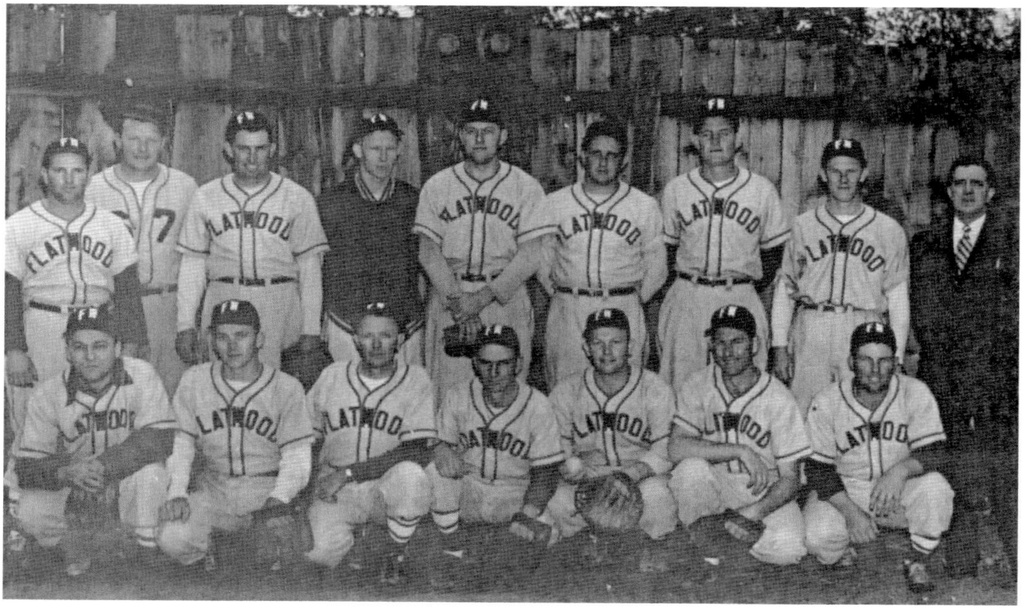

Flatwood Baseball Team 1952

This team played in the Twilight League, which was active from 1946 to 1955. Pictured here left to right are (front row) J. Wohonick, Dude Waddell, P. Wood, Poss Dillar, H. Davis, R. Duncan, and J. Davis; (second row) W. Davis, B.C. Hawkins, G. Carlton, R. Cox, F.E. Hendrix, C. Davis, Hoss Owens, Bob Cox, and Les Tillotson. (Courtesy of F.E. Hendrix.)

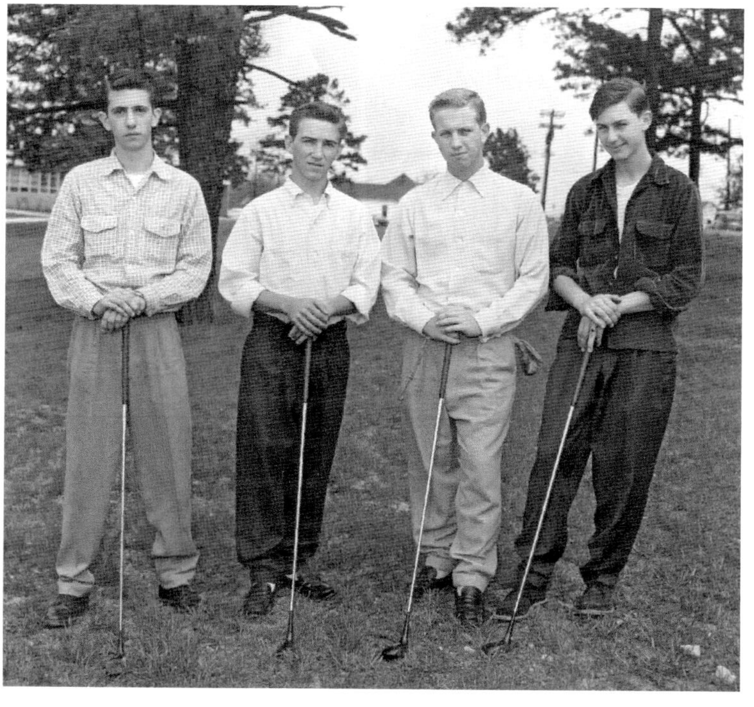

Greer High School Golf Team

The 1954 Greer High School golf team played at the Greer Country Club. Pictured here from left to right are Ben Padgett, Jerry Hemphill, Norman Davis, and Bill Van Arsdale. (Courtesy of Greer Heritage Museum.)

CHAPTER EIGHT

Cultural and Social Life

In the early years of Greer's history, the founders spent their time developing the community. Homes, churches, and schools were built; shops opened along Trade Street; textile mills began operating to provide employment. The last stage of development of any community is its cultural and social life. Greer was no different. Citizens began to form clubs and organizations, both social and civic. They built a library and encouraged the arts with a Music Club. The Greer Garden Club built a city park. Parades and festivals provided needed breaks from work and social occasions for the whole community to enjoy.

The oldest organization in Greer is Bailey Lodge #146, a Masonic lodge that was founded in 1868 in the Bailey's Crossroads area of Pleasant Grove. William Clark Bailey, the first railroad station agent and mayor of Greer, sought a charter in 1868 even before Greer was imagined. The lodge began meeting in 1869, but when the Greer's Depot was built in 1873, the group moved their meetings to the depot. Needing more space, they built a small building near the new depot. Today, they continue as an active organization.

With an established community, the people began to seek social life through clubs in the 1920s. Among the early organizations was the Greer Garden Club, organized October 15, 1928. During the height of the Great Depression, this club built City Park on Cannon Street. It wasn't until after World War II that additional clubs were organized. In 1947, the Camellia Garden Club formed, followed by the Azalea Garden Club in 1948, the Primrose Garden Club in 1952, and the Briarcliff Garden Club in 1959. Finally, the White Pines Garden Club organized in 1960. Today only three clubs remain: Camellia, Azalea, and Primrose. The citizens of Greer have been the benefactors of their projects to plant trees and flower beds in public areas, to encourage laws to protect birds, to develop parks, and promote public interest in beautification and conservation.

While the women were gardening, the men organized civic clubs. In January 1929, the Greer Lions Club was organized. The Greer Kiwanis International Club chartered in 1933. Rotary and Jaycees have also had chapters in Greer. These various civic clubs have worked to make Greer a better place.

In 1957, the merchants approached the Greer Chamber of Commerce about a festival to highlight Greer and create commerce downtown. Chamber of commerce president Paul Smith appointed Laurens James as chairman. The first Peach Festival was held on May 16 and 17, 1957. It made sense to celebrate peaches with the many orchards dotting the hillsides around Greer and the upstate area. The first festival had a pageant to pick a Peach Queen, a parade, a golf tournament, and a community barbecue. After that first year it grew in popularity, adding other events such as street dances, drag races at the Greer Dragway, coin shows, and bowling tournaments. In 1968, the festival ended for lack of volunteers.

In 1985, businesswoman Martha King became concerned that Greer no longer had a festival to compete with the many popular ones in neighboring communities. She convinced the city and merchants to plan a new festival for families, aptly named the Greer Family Festival. Today, it continues under the name Greer Family Fest. During its first couple years, it was held on the old Wesleyan Campground in August. Location and date changed when it moved to the downtown on Mother's Day weekend. The streets of Greer teem with visitors for the Fest on the first weekend of May every year.

Both the Peach Festival and the Family Festival owe a lot to artist Suzanne Greene. Loving her community, she was always more than anxious to promote it. Over the years, the community organizations called upon her to create posters, logos, and other visuals to promote festivals and the arts in Greer. She illustrated the Community Ministries cookbook. Seeing a need for an arts program for young people, she was one of the founders of the Greer Art Reach Program. Her community volunteer work and her awards are too numerous to list.

Suzanne, the daughter of Carl Lanford and Mary Sue Bobo Lanford, was born in Atlanta, Georgia, November 11, 1928. After graduating from Georgia Technical College, Carl Lanford became the superintendent and engineer for the Greer Commission of Public Works. After Suzanne graduated from Greer High School, she attended Mars Hill College and Wake Forest College. In 1952, she took her first job as technical illustrator for Western Electric in Winston Salem, North Carolina. When she returned to South Carolina and home in Greer, she worked for Henderson Advertising, Ivey's Department Store, and Piedmont Engineering as an illustrator. Over the years, she taught arts and crafts and even had her own shop for a while. Although she had used different media, she was best known for her watercolors, which are seen in many local homes and businesses. She spent her last years in a studio near Travelers Rest and died in 2004.

Another legend in the community is Nancy Welch, who like Suzanne Greene, has always shared her talents for the betterment of Greer. Nancy was born in Nashville, Tennessee, but home was wherever her Presbyterian minister father had a church. From the third grade until high school graduation, the family called Ocala, Florida, home. After graduating from Florida State University with a degree in interior design, she was hired as decorator for Zeta Tau Alpha houses in colleges along the East Coast.

In 1966, she moved to Greer with her husband, and the next year she went on the air March 20, 1967, with the live and in color *Nancy Welch Show* on WSPA Channel 7 television. A month contract became 23 years of weekday shows, popular with women in the Greenville/Spartanburg television viewing area. Over the years she interviewed many celebrities. One of her favorite memories, according to her website, was mending Phil Donahue's pants with him still in them just before airtime.

Dr. Tom Barton hired Nancy in 1991 to help develop a Greer satellite campus for Greenville Technical College. She returned to school to prepare and earned a doctorate in education in technical and career technology from Clemson University. After 18 years with the school, she resigned in 2008 as vice president of student services.

Welch is the Renaissance woman. She is an author, educator, television personality, quilter, crafter, chef, speaker extraordinaire, wife, mother, one-time innkeeper, and committed church and community volunteer. She approaches everything with optimism and good humor and has been a friend to all.

Greer is a better place because of the many social, charitable, civic, and religious organizations and the people who belong to them. They believe that their lives are better when they volunteer to help someone else.

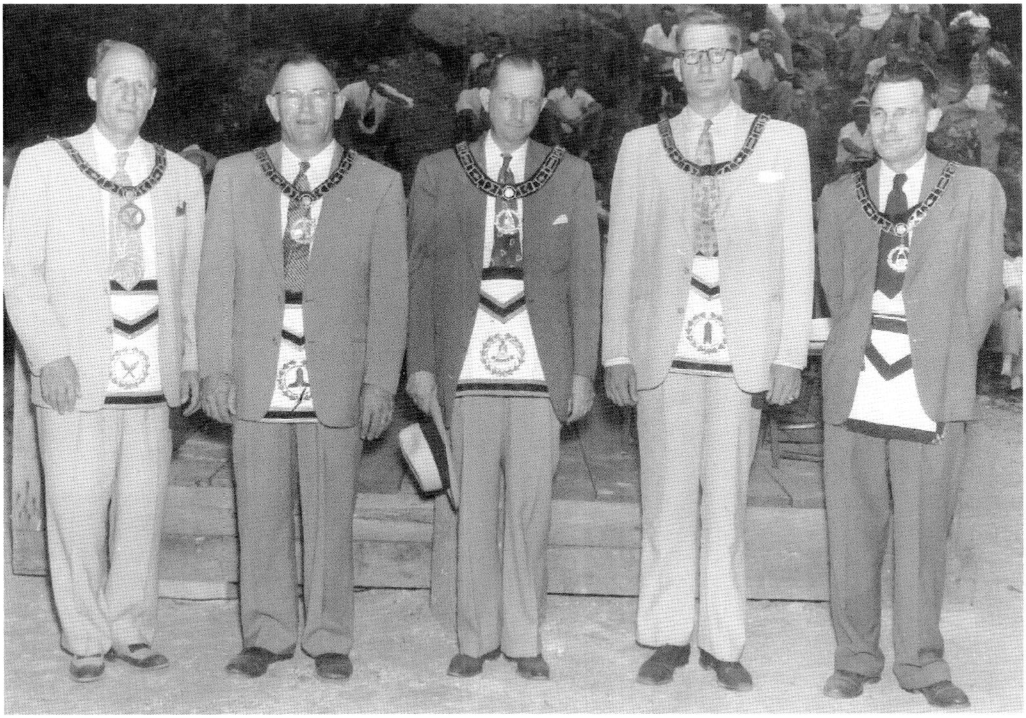

Bailey Lodge No. 146

Bailey Lodge #146, the oldest fraternal organization in Greer, was organized in 1868 at Bailey's Crossroads. In 1873, t moved its meetings to Greer's Depot, and by 1876 had a building beside the depot. This 1951 Rock Quarry Meeting, held in Travelers Rest, shows (far right) Roy C. Hefner, grand master of the 14th District and past master of Bailey Lodge. Others are unidentified. (Courtesy of the Greer Heritage Museum.)

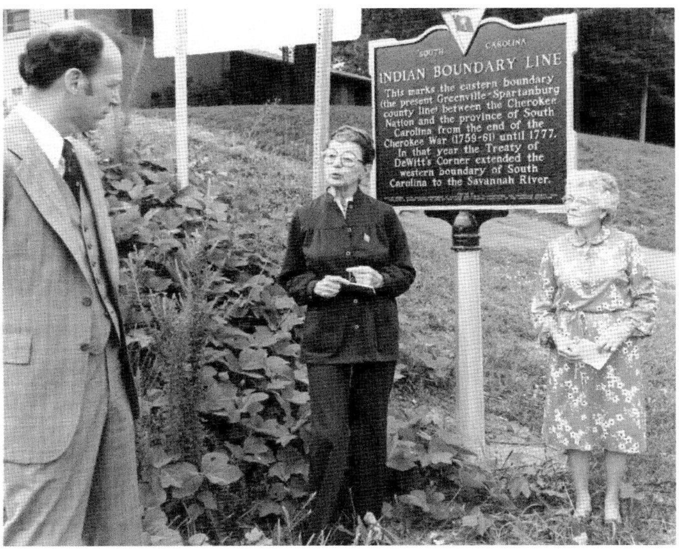

Joyce Scott Chapter, Daughters of the American Revolution (DAR)

On May 9, 1952, the DAR dedicated this historical marker on Wade Hampton Boulevard to remember the Indian Boundary Line, a significant part of Greer's history. Today it is the county line. After restoring the old marker, the members rededicated it. Shown here are (left to right) Reverend Ray White of the First Presbyterian Church, Eulalia Walker, and Mrs. Ansel Hawkins. (Courtesy of the Joyce Scott Chapter DAR.)

Greer Lions Club 1947

Since its beginnings in January 1929, the Greer Lions Club has had a long history of service in Greer. The officers for 1947–1948 were (left to right) Charles Smith, Edgar Bruce, Harley Bonds, Harold Davis, and Miller West. Bonds represented Greer on the Greenville County School Board for many years. (Courtesy of Greer Heritage Museum.

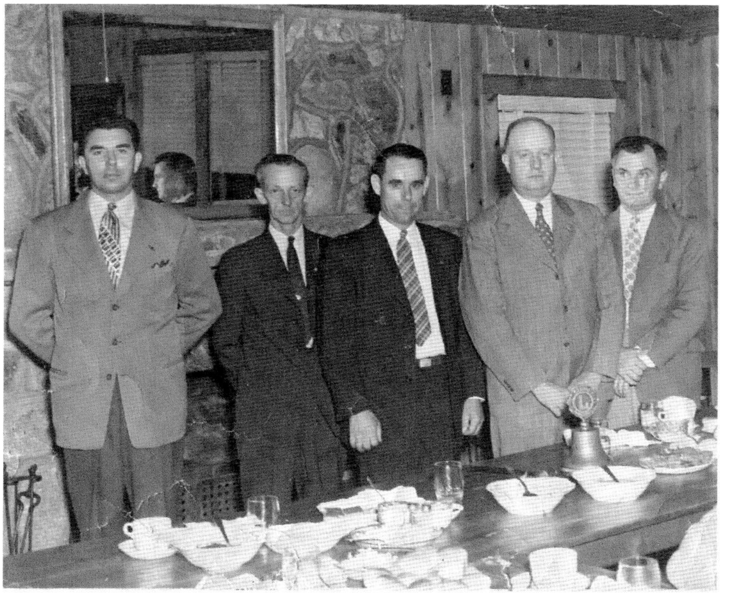

Greer Lions Club 1960

In 1960, the officers were left to right (seated) Dub Bruce, Dub Johnson, Tom Stroud, and Carl Stack; (standing) Steve Abraham, Will Free, Dan Leach, Bill Richardson, Morris McElrath, Tom Duncan, Kent Bridges, Ken Stigberg, and W.J. Gibson. (Courtesy of Greer Heritage Museum.)

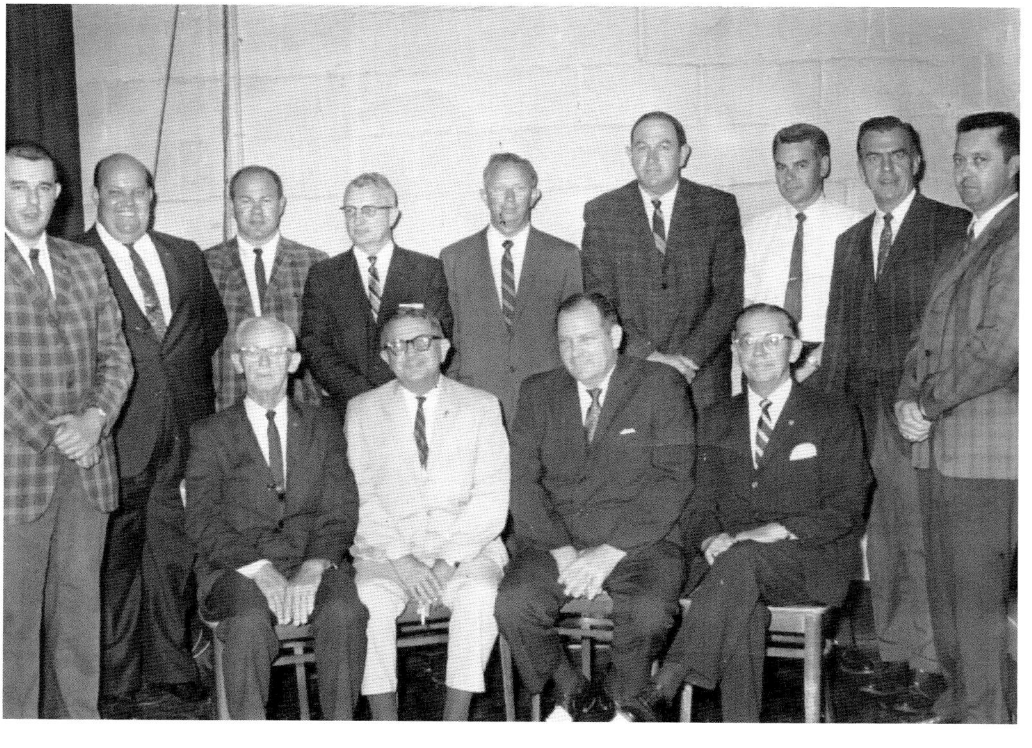

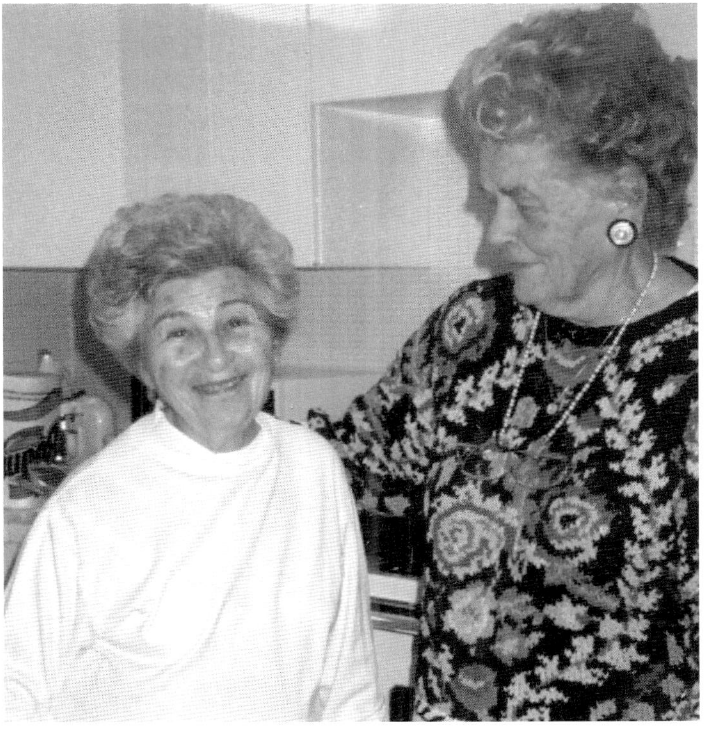

Azalea Garden Club
On April 15, 1948, the Azalea Garden Club organized, choosing their name because the azaleas were blooming profusely in Greer. The only charter member living is Sara Crain (shown at right) with other longtime member Leah Lurey. An award-winning club, it was responsible for Greer Ordinance No. 633, making the city a bird sanctuary. (Courtesy of Azalea Garden Club.)

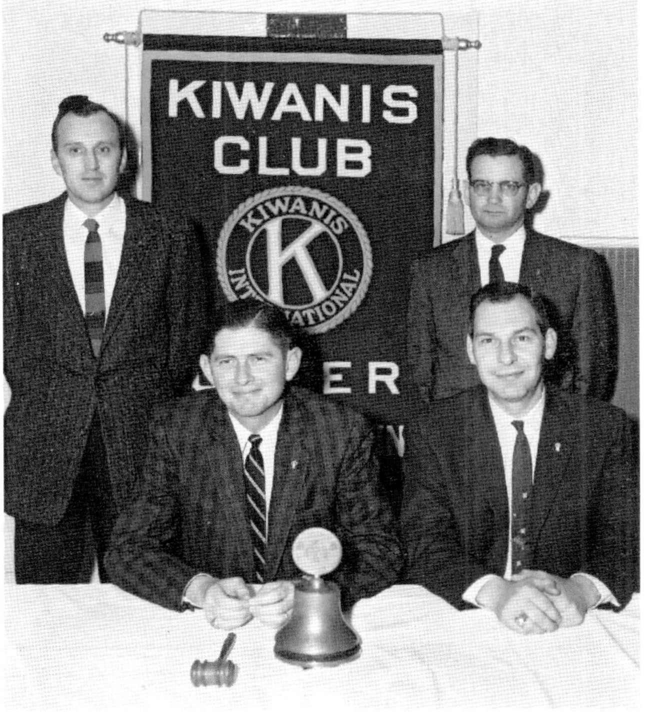

Kiwanis Club of Greer
The Greer Kiwanis Club was chartered October 11, 1933. This 1957 picture shows the officers left to right (seated) Verne Smith, president and Dennis Dobson, vice president; (standing) Woody Morrow, secretary and Jake Morgan, treasurer. (Courtesy of Carole Smith Olmert.)

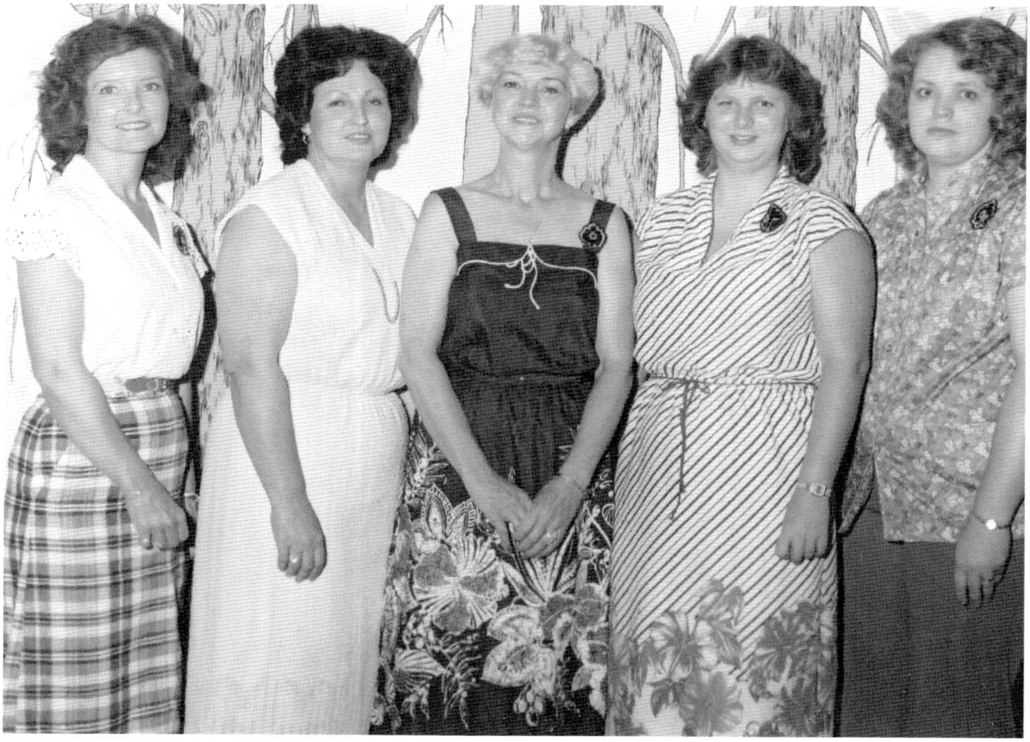

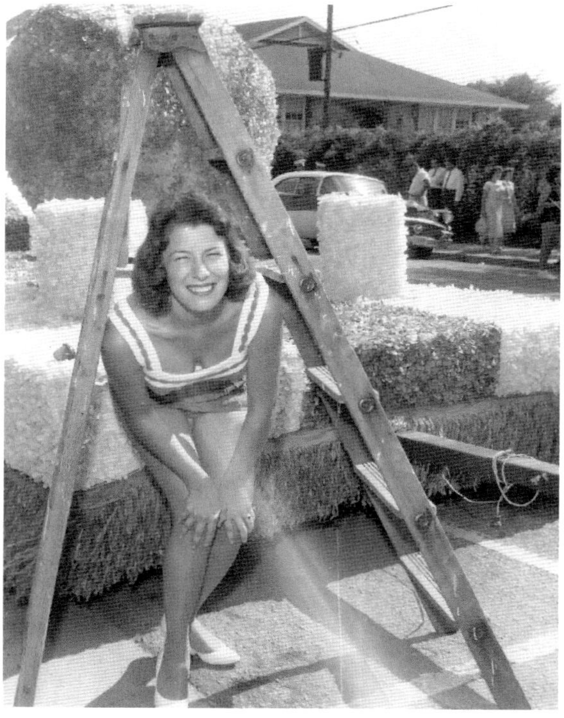

American Business Women's Association

The 1981 officers of the Greer Chapter of the American Business Women's Association (left to right) are Janice Sudduth, vice president, Iris Bateman, Pat Duncan, president, Melinda Roberts, and Kandy Powell. (Courtesy of Greer Heritage Museum.)

Phyllis Parker, Peach Queen

Phyllis Parker, daughter of Mr. and Mrs. Henry Parker, was the only Greer girl to serve as Peach Queen for the Peach Festival. She attended Limestone College and won her title in 1961. This photograph by Joe Jordan captures Phyllis having fun before the festival parade began. (Courtesy of Greer Heritage Museum.)

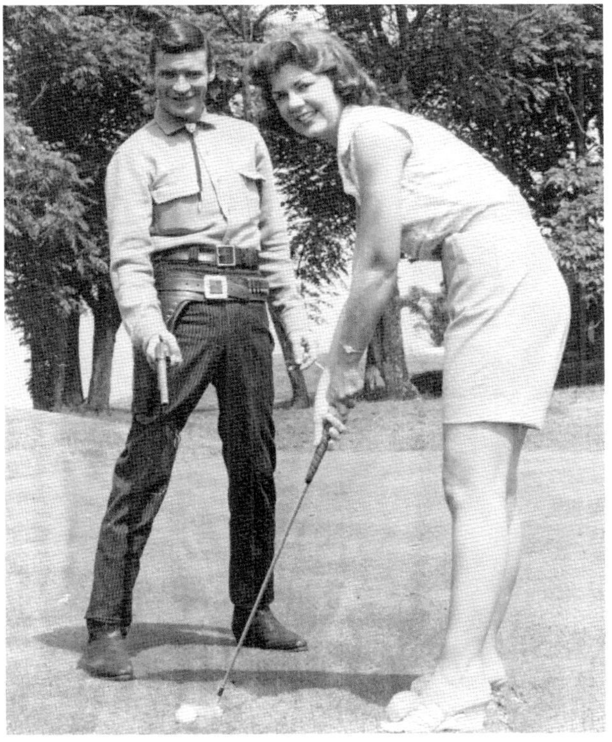

Frances Hambright, Peach Queen
Western star Peter Breck was the nationally known celebrity for the 1958 Peach Festival. Here he appears with Peach Queen Frances Hambright in this photograph by Joe Jordan. Peter Breck was the star of *Black Saddle*, a popular television show. (Courtesy of Greer Heritage Museum.)

Easter Parade
Easter Parades in Greer were rare, but this 1950s parade featured a Kiwanis Club float with children promoting "Fix up, Clean up" in Greer. The only one identified is Susan Clark (Moon), the blonde girl in the middle. (Courtesy of Greer Heritage Museum.)

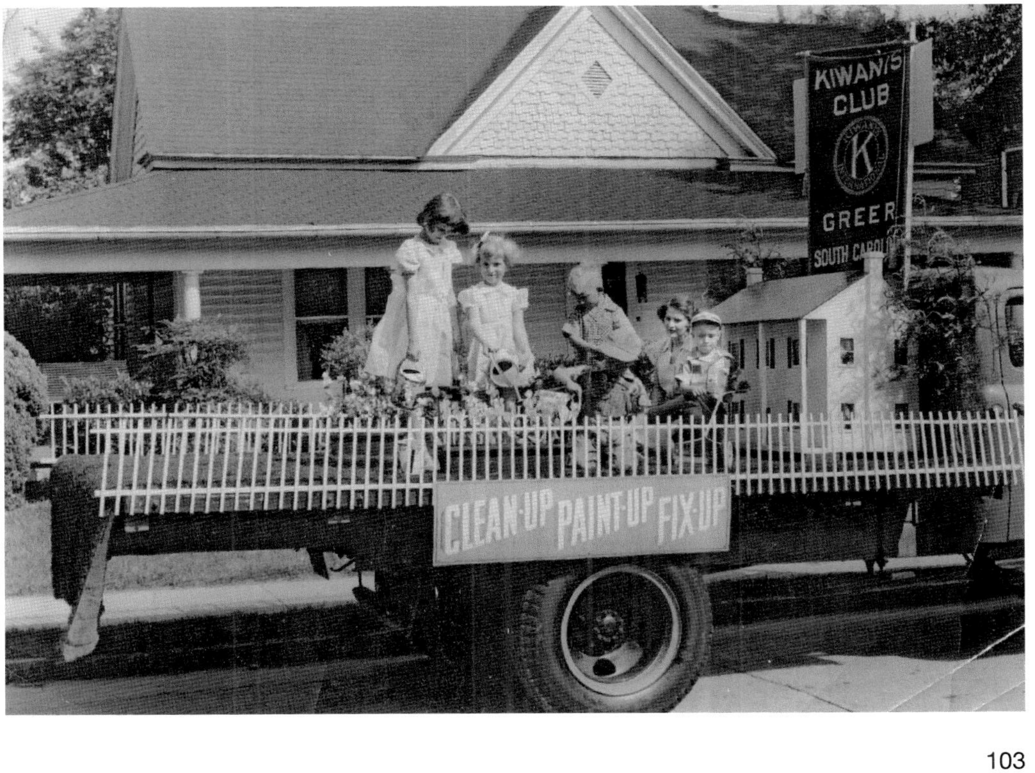

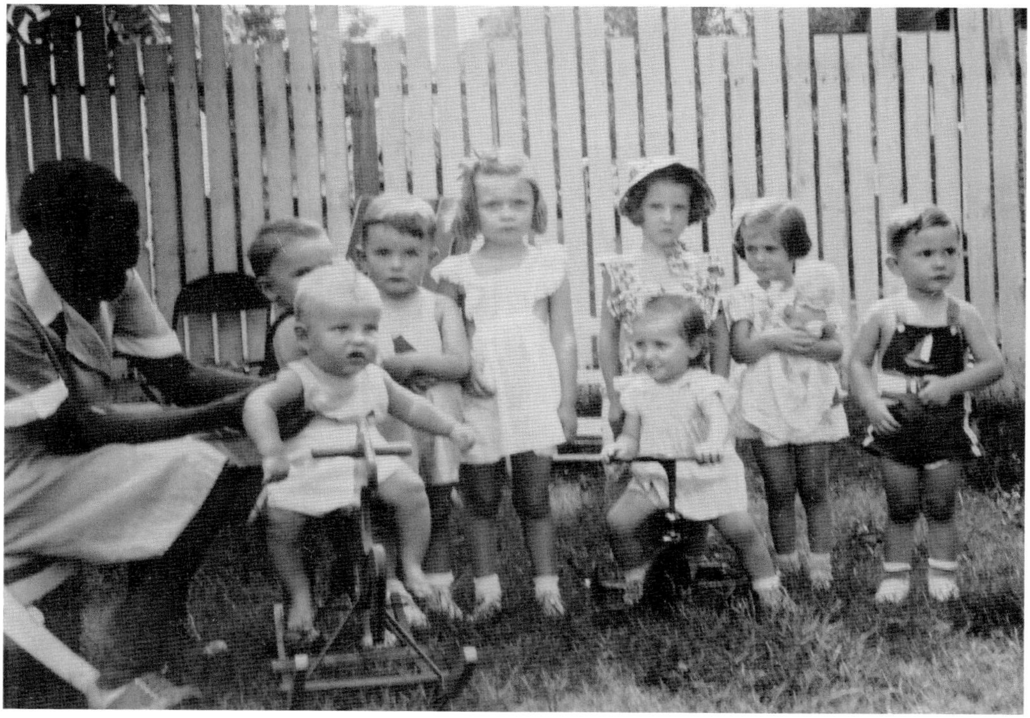

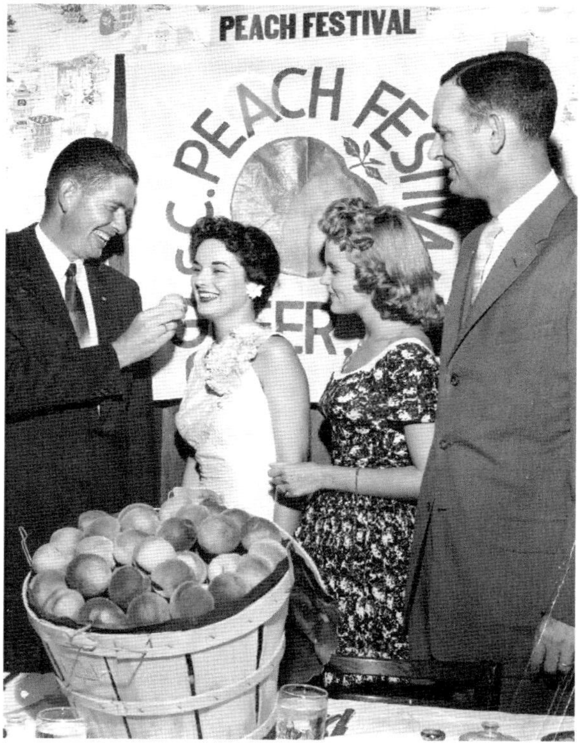

Bill Moore's Birthday Party

Birthday parties in Greer were occasions for fun. At this birthday party for Bill Moore, the participants line up for a photo op. "Are we having fun?" asked the unknown photographer. Shown left to right are unidentified adult, unknown child on rocking horse, Dick Wood, Jimmy Hughes, Miriam Hughes, Jean Olive Lane, Karolyn Kendrick, Bill Moore, and Betty Gail Brunson on the tricycle. (Courtesy of Karolyn and Richard Taylor.)

Peach Festival 1957

The first Peach Festival was held in Greer on May 16–17, 1957. Local merchants approached the chamber of commerce president Paul Smith, who appointed Laurens James as chairman. Shown here are (left to right) businessman J. Verne Smith, whose family had early peach orchards in Greer, the first Peach Queen Martha Brannon of Bishopville, and the chamber of commerce director James "Dutch" Boling. (Courtesy of Frankie Boling.)

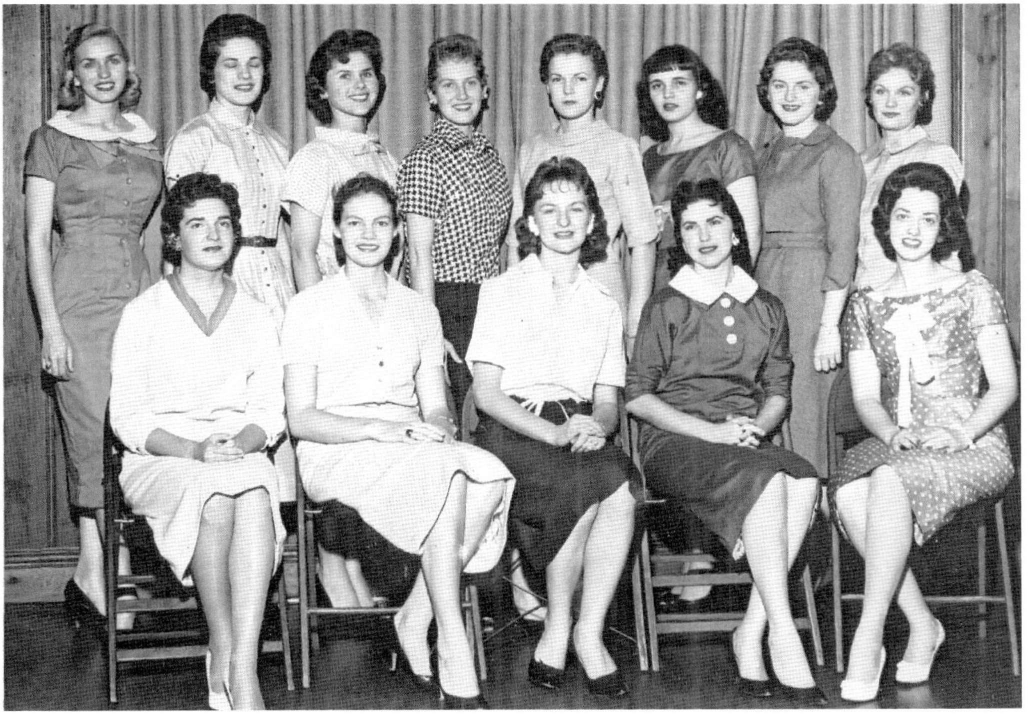

Miss Greater Greer 1958

Mayor Lloyd Hunt proclaimed May 2, 1958, as Miss Greater Greer Day. The first contestants from left to right are (seated) Ruth Boling, Gail Brookshire, Sylvia Bishop (elected queen), Pat Culbreth, and Martha Jordan; (back row) Lorita Miller, Janice Collins, Wilda Corley, Martha Corne, Norma Jean Stokes, Carole Stewart, Jane Wade, and Rita Nichols. (Courtesy of Greer Heritage Museum.)

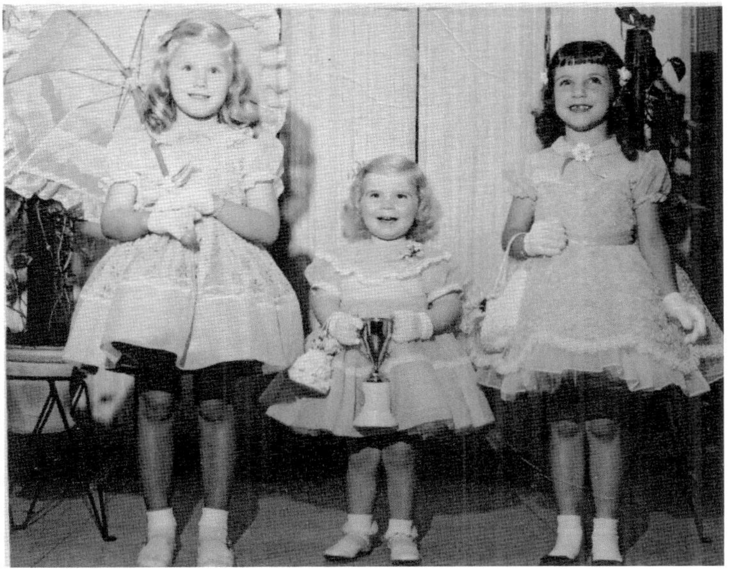

Little Miss Greer 1958

The first Little Miss Greer contest was part of the 1958 pageant. These cuties from left to right are Paula Tate, Cheryl Stokes, and Jeannie Lister. (Courtesy of Greer Heritage Museum.)

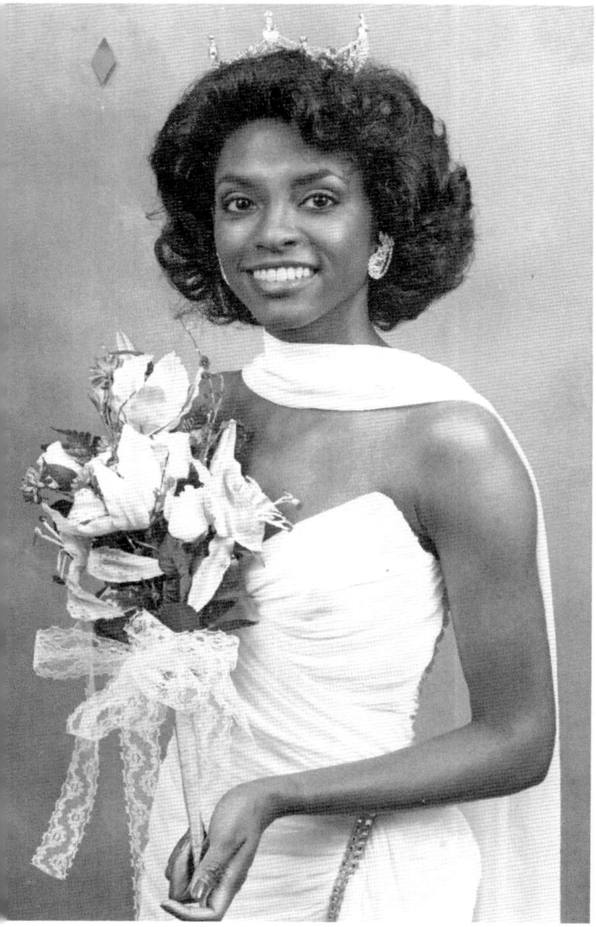

Stephanie Taylor, Miss Greer 1989

In 1989, Miss Stephanie Taylor became the first black Miss Greater Greer in the Miss America sanctioned pageant, representing Greer in the Miss South Carolina pageant. She has had a successful banking career in North Carolina as a vice president with Bank of America. In 2007, she was elected Miss Queen of Queens. (Courtesy of Greer Heritage Museum.)

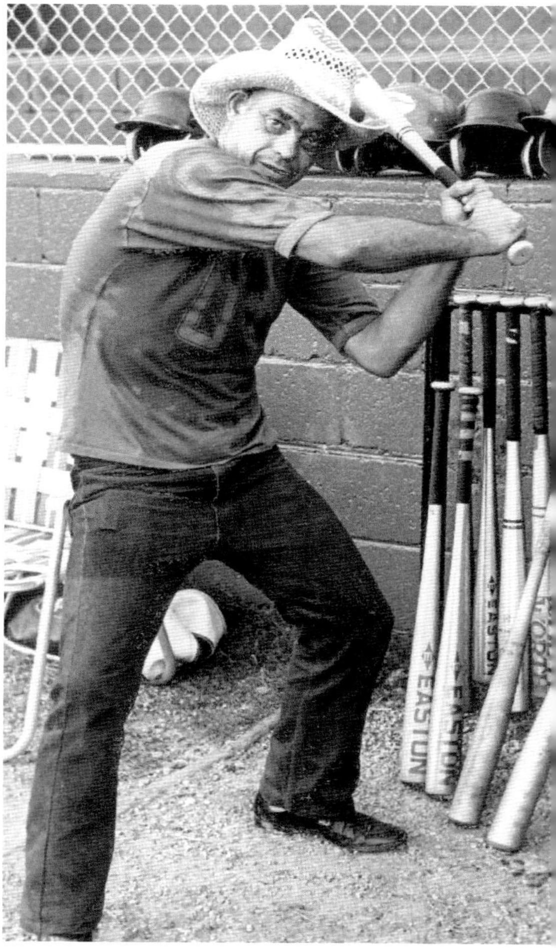

"Housecat" Hawkins

An enthusiastic supporter of all Greer sports, Hawkins was known for his signature cheer, not unlike the sound of a bellowing bull. *Greer Citizen* photographer Eddie Burch captured Housecat at one of the American Legion games where he had designated himself as the bat boy. (Courtesy of Greer Heritage Museum.)

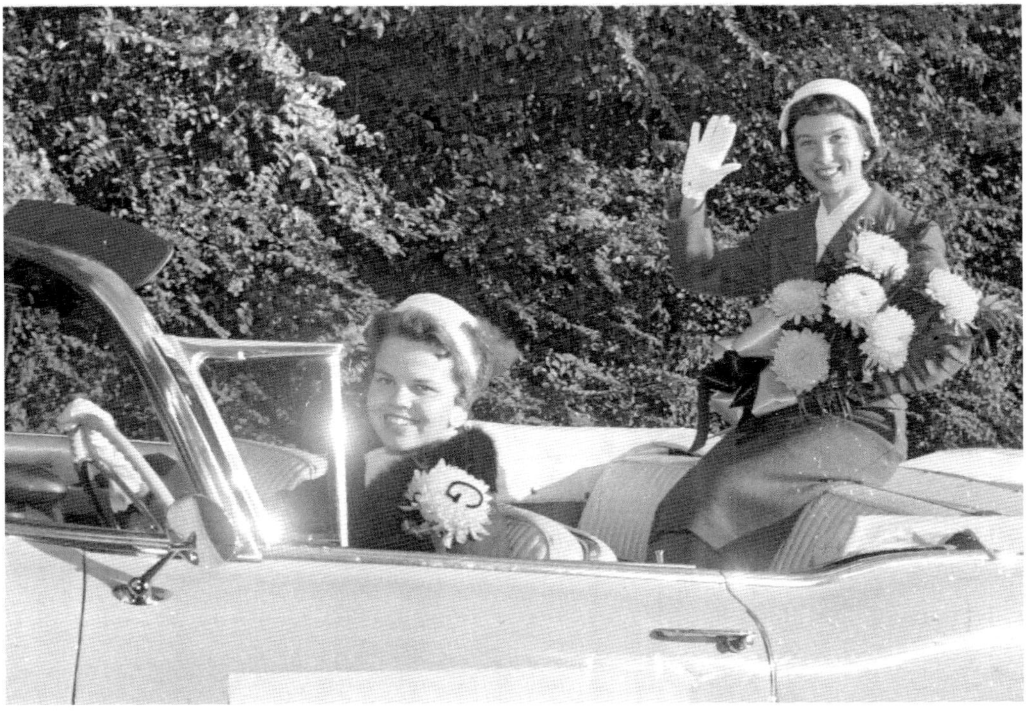

Ann Dillard
Dillard, daughter of peach grower Palmer Dillard, is shown riding in the Peach Festival Parade. The parades were a highlight of the festival with ornate floats, beauty queens, peach trucks, and tractors. Her driver is Brenda Jones. (Courtesy of Ann Dillard Withrow.)

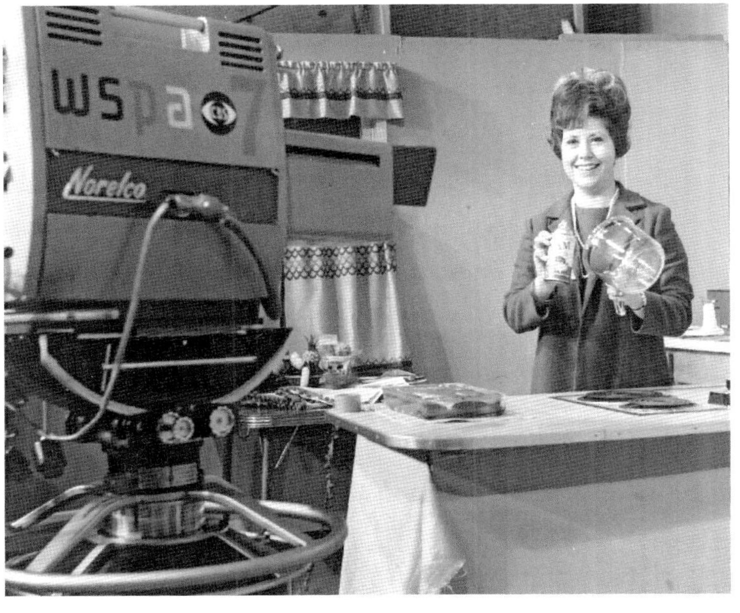

Nancy Welch
Welch appeared on WSPA TV 7 from 1967 to 1988. Her popular weekday morning show offered more than recipes. Nancy, the daughter of a Presbyterian minister, was born in Nashville, Tennessee, but has called Greer home since 1966. After television, she earned an EdD from Clemson University and led the Greer Greenville Technical College branch through its developing years. (Courtesy of Nancy Welch.)

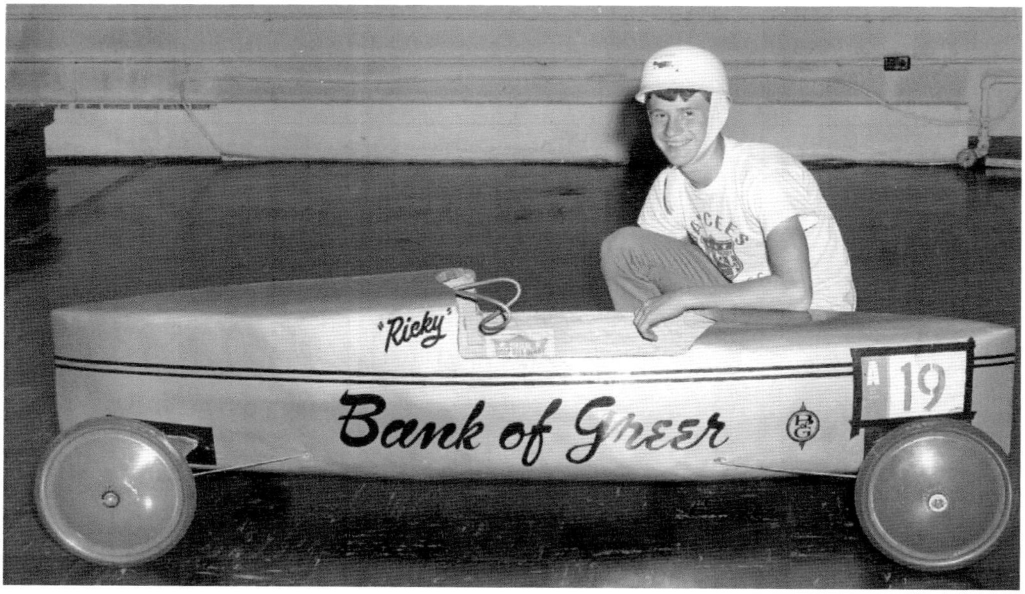

Ricky Boozer
Ricky Boozer proudly shows off his official Soap Box Derby entry sometime in the 1950s. His sponsor was the Bank of Greer on Trade Street. (Courtesy of Greer Heritage Museum.)

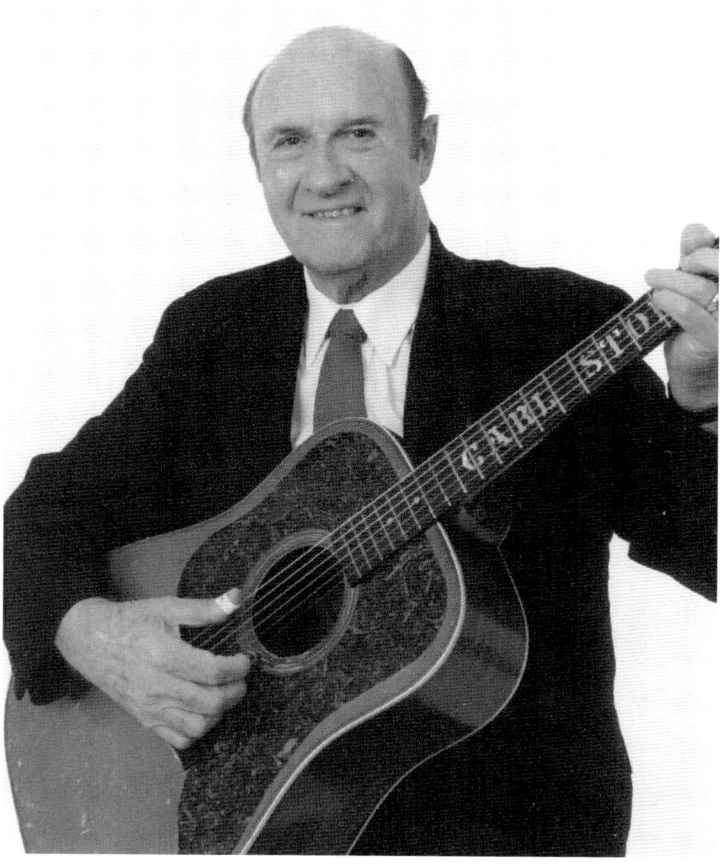

Musician Carl Story
Story was born and reared in Lenoir, South Carolina, and came to Greer's WCKI Radio in May 1964. In 1934, he formed his own band the Rambling Mountaineers and had a 60-year career with 66 albums. Called the Father of Bluegrass Gospel Music, he performed on the Grand Ole Opry, Tennessee Barn Dance, and at Greer's own Greer Opry House. (Courtesy of Greer Heritage Museum.)

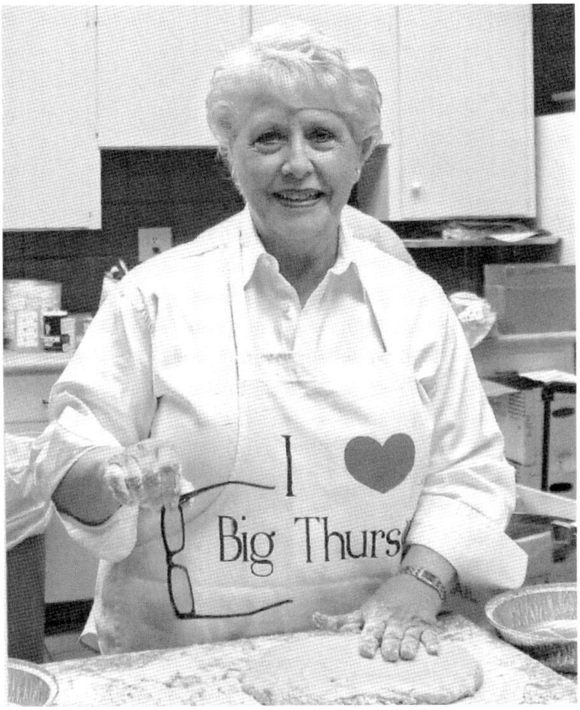

Big Thursday and Nancy Welch
Big Thursday has been a tradition in Greer since 1979 to benefit the Greer Community Ministries. Anne Helton prepared apple pies that became a yearly favorite. The next year she asked Nancy Welch, shown here, to make biscuits to sell to shoppers as they browsed the craft fair. No one thinks of Big Thursday in Greer without picturing Welch in her flour-covered apron cutting out biscuits. (Courtesy of Nancy Welch.)

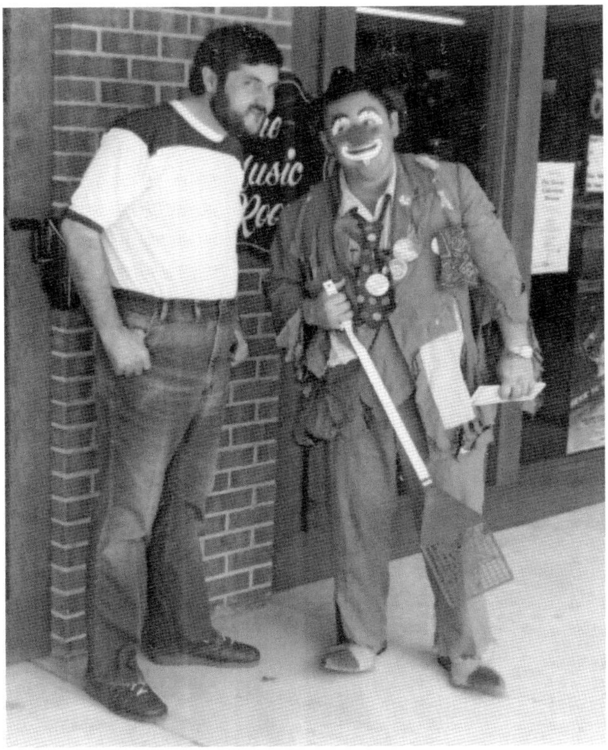

Mason Edwards and Frank Hayes
Mason Edwards poses outside the Music Room on Middleton Way with clown and humorist Frank Hayes. Edwards saw his business go from vinyl records to cassettes, and finally to CDs. He was a popular DJ at local middle and high school dances. Hayes entertained at festivals, business openings, parties, and ary gig needing a light moment. (Courtesy of Greer Heritage Museum.)

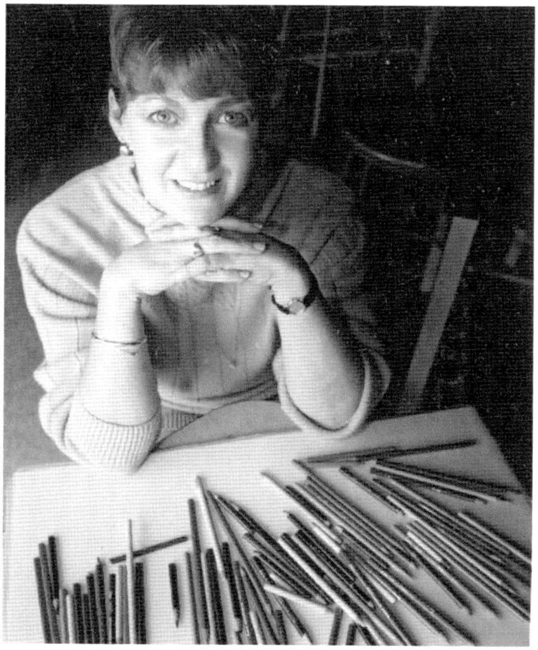

Dr. Christine J. Davis

Davis is both educator and artist. The daughter of Dr. James G. Jeanes of Lyman, she received an EdD in art education from the University of Georgia in 1992. She was a public school art teacher until retirement. Her awards and recognitions are too numerous to list. As an artist, she has captured the ordinary people of Greer using the tools laid in front of her. (Courtesy of Tom and Chris Davis.)

Aaron Tippin

Tippin was born in Florida on July 3, 1958. He was reared on a farm in Blue Ridge above Greer, and today lives on a 500-acre farm in Tennessee. He moved to Nashville in 1986 to become a writer for Acuff-Rose. In 1990, his hit song "You've Got to Stand for Something" made him a major country music star. (Courtesy Greer Heritage Museum.)

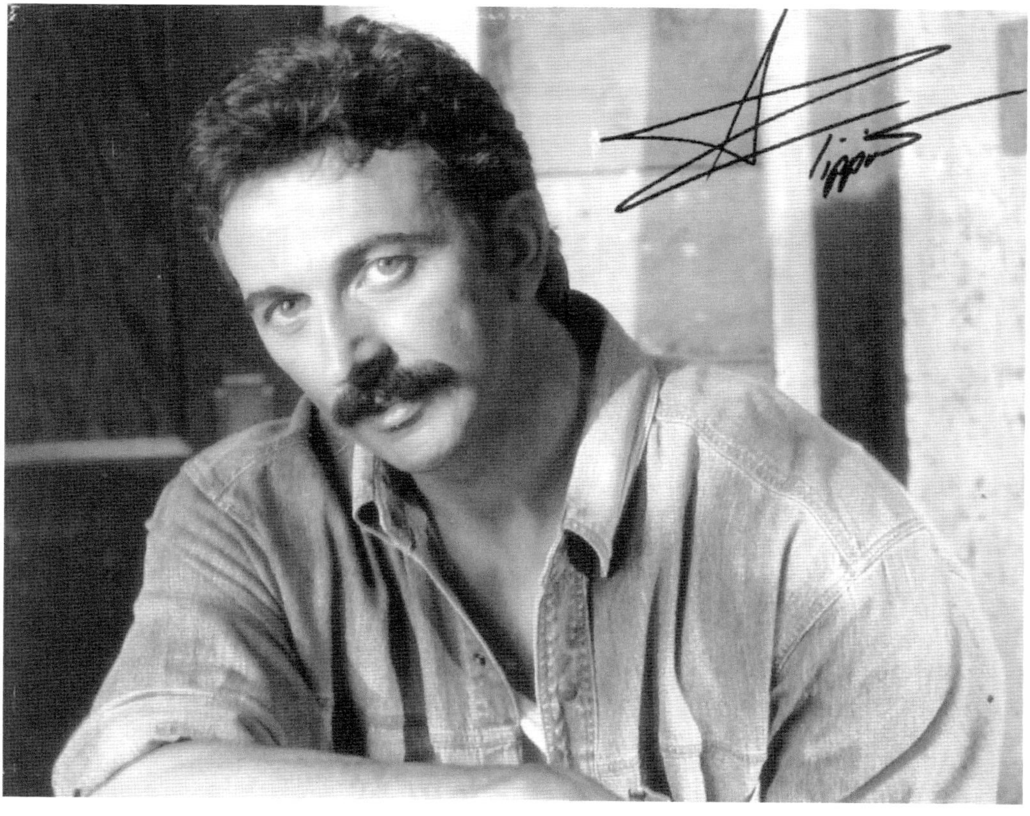

CHAPTER NINE

Families

The strength of any community is found in its families. Scots-Irish Presbyterians, and some Quaker families such as the Addingtons, followed the wagon trails from Pennsylvania and Virginia to settle in the Greer area. Early maps label the land around Greer as "good land," acreage that could sustain a family. These pioneers were the Bailey, McClimon, Brockman, Lester, Loftis, Glenn, Fisher, Forrester, Fowler, Smith, and Green families. The Fowlers named a son "America," for the promise of this new land.

One of the oldest families in the Greer area was the Hughes family. Simeon Hughes was born in 1845 and served in the South Carolina Volunteers Company C of the 22nd Regiment in the Civil War. He wrote in his diary that he joined the Confederate Army at age 17 and chose Lee's company in Virginia. After he was wounded at Fort Steadman, Virginia, he spent six weeks in a hospital. He wrote, "I met one of the best friends I ever had, a young Yankee about my age. He nursed me like a mother. Here also I met President Abe Lincoln; he shook hands and talked to us boys until he was so hoarse that he could not speak above a whisper. One only had to meet the Grand man to admire him." Later he sadly watched Lincoln's funeral procession in Washington.

In 1876, Simeon Hughes married Thurza Jane Wood, a union blessed with four children. When he died in 1924, he was hailed as one of Greer's oldest and most prominent citizens. His descendants have been doctors, educators, and business and community leaders in Greer.

Before the incorporation of Greer in 1876, there were small communities settled around churches, gristmills, cotton gins, and general stores with post offices. South of Greer was Bailey's Crossroads at Pleasant Grove where the Hughes family first settled. Abner Creek and Wood's Chapel were further south. Above Greer were O'Neal, Milford, and Ansel. To the west was Taylors.

Once Greer was incorporated, families were drawn to the little village for the advantages of better commerce and education. The African-American communities of Greentown, Maple Creek, Needmore, and Sunnyside developed alongside their white neighbors. The textile mills built villages, providing houses, schools, churches, and YMCAs. Barely subsisting on small farms, families were drawn to the promise of steady income with the mills, free schooling for their children, and houses in well-laid-out neighborhoods.

The story of the William Green Howard family is the story of many such families. They were forced to relocate, along with others, because of the establishment of the Glassy Rock Rifle and Artillery Range during World War I. They continued to live in the Glassy Mountain area, just moving on up the hollow, and sent the children to the one-room Robertson School. Green's son J.C. impressed his teacher, who encouraged him to go to high school. At age 13, he enrolled at the North Greenville Baptist Academy, whose mission was the education of mountain children. When it was time to put his name on his diploma, he admitted that he had only initials. The school gave him a proper name by signing his 1928 diploma James Calvin Howard, but he was always known to Greer as Jake.

Wanting a better life for his younger siblings, Jake encouraged the family to relocate to Greer where they opened a gas station with tourist cabins. Not a few years later, the Great Depression was felt by all families, and Jake found a way to subsidize the family income with the sale of bootleg whiskey. He still had contacts in the Dark Corner, where it was illegally manufactured by other families trying to eke out a living in hard times.

After Jake married Rometta Edwards in 1934, he worked at a textile mill and reared his family to value religion, education, and honest work. As testimony to these lessons, his twin sons went to college, one to become a teacher and one a minister.

The Durham family is another exceptional Greer family. The Reverend Joseph Carver Durham and his wife Denver Allie Bivins Durham were originally from the Reidville area. Durham received his education at Harbison Institute, a Presbyterian school for blacks in Irmo, South Carolina. After graduation, Joseph Durham taught at his alma mater for one dollar a day. Returning to the area, he farmed and taught at the one-room Mayfield Chapel School. Purchasing 30 acres near the South Tyger River, Durham planted cotton and the crops needed for livestock and 14 children. Besides his own land, he sharecropped with land owners nearby, planting both his acres and theirs to harvest a large cotton crop. On a two-acre lot in Greer, he planted produce for the Clement Brothers to sell and put his older sons to work. He continued to farm until his death in 1969.

Durham taught by example. His children learned the value of hard work. They witnessed his devout faith and knew the value of education in their lives. Six of his children graduated from college and became teachers. Others were ministers, soldiers, medical and social workers.

Hayne Preston Griffin's story began in tragedy and ended in triumph. When he was only four years old, Preston Griffin's father died. Working for the railroad, his father was killed when he went to check the trestles during a flood on the Catawba River. His pregnant mother, widowed with four children, took a job as a telephone operator in Liberty. Preston learned early the lessons of perseverance and hard work.

During World War II, he worked as comptroller for Convenience, Inc., a Greenville corporation that manufactured bandages for the US Army. This familiarity with textiles led him to establish the Mutual Home Store in 1945 as a piece goods store. There were four stores, one of which was in Greer. The success of these stores led to the establishment of a chain of furniture stores. Mutual Home Store continues to operate in Greer and four other locations.

During the 1950s, he served two consecutive terms as president of the Greer Chamber of Commerce where he was instrumental in bringing Bowers Battery and Homelite, adding different types of industries to a growing city that had been dependent upon the textile industry.

Griffin and his wife Elsie had four children who have all been successful citizens. Sons Gary and Hayne Jr., continue to run the family business. Hayne holds a doctorate in theology and is a popular Bible teacher. Daughter Margaret Burch, a musician by training, served on the Greenville County School Board representing the Greer area. She was responsible for bringing new school buildings to replace much outdated ones. Camille Graham Camp, who was the first woman in the nation to manage a male maximum security prison, is a nationally known prison consultant. In 2002, the State of South Carolina honored her by naming a women's prison for her.

The Hughes, Howard, Durham, and Griffin families represent the story of many Greer families living the American dream with each generation making life better for the next. For many Greer families, combining faith, love, education, and a strong work ethic has been a prescription for success.

Callie and Alvin Berry

Callie (left) and Alvin, shown in a formal children's portrait taken about 1914, were the daughter and son of Claude O. and Etta Gibson Berry. Callie married and moved to Taylors. Alvin entered business in Greer, becoming a successful real estate broker and auctioneer. (Courtesy of Carl Gibson.)

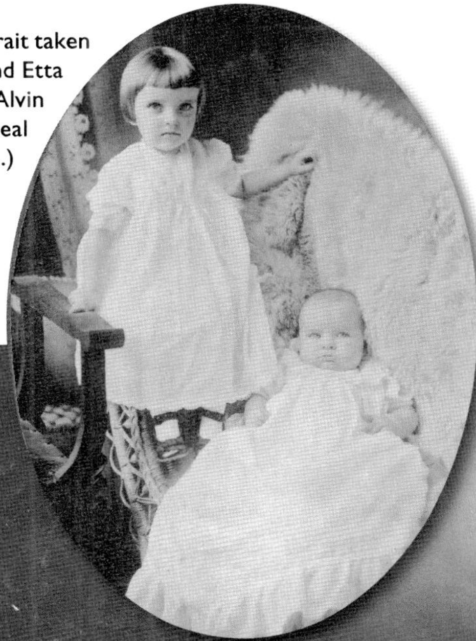

Frank and Wilton Gibson

Frank Nolan Gibson is standing beside his baby brother Wilton J. Gibson. They were the sons of Jason and Bessie Gibson. (Courtesy of Carl Gibson.)

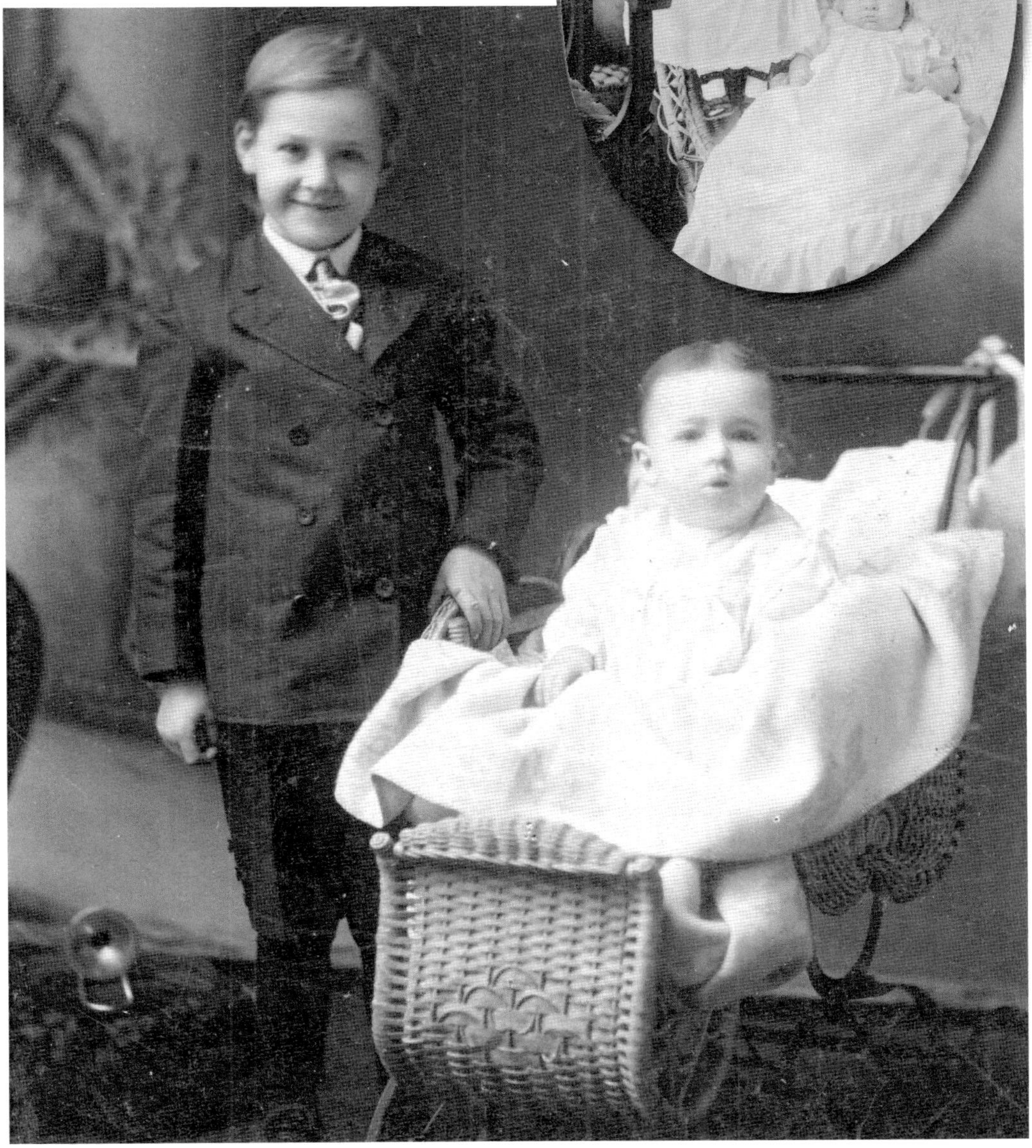

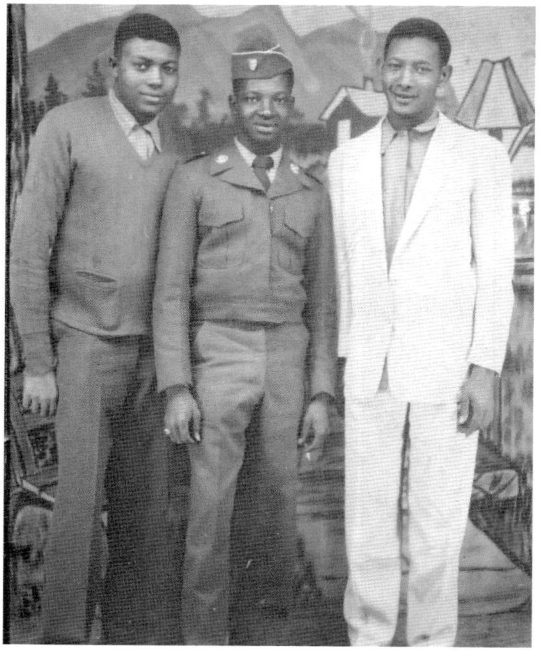

James Hill and Friends

Hill (shown at left) poses with future brothers-in-law Charles Durham and Paul Durham (right) in 1953. James, who grew up in the Pelham area, had a successful career after high school as a brick mason. He can proudly point to many buildings in Greer that are testimony to his skill. The Durham family owned a 30-acre farm near the South Tyger River. (Courtesy of Margaret and James Hill.)

The Children of John A. Robinson

John A. Robinson's children are shown in this 1929 photograph. Left to right are Eleanor, Donald Stewart, Richard Edmund, and William A. Robinson. They grew up in the family home on South Main Street where the police station is today. (Courtesy of Don Robinson.)

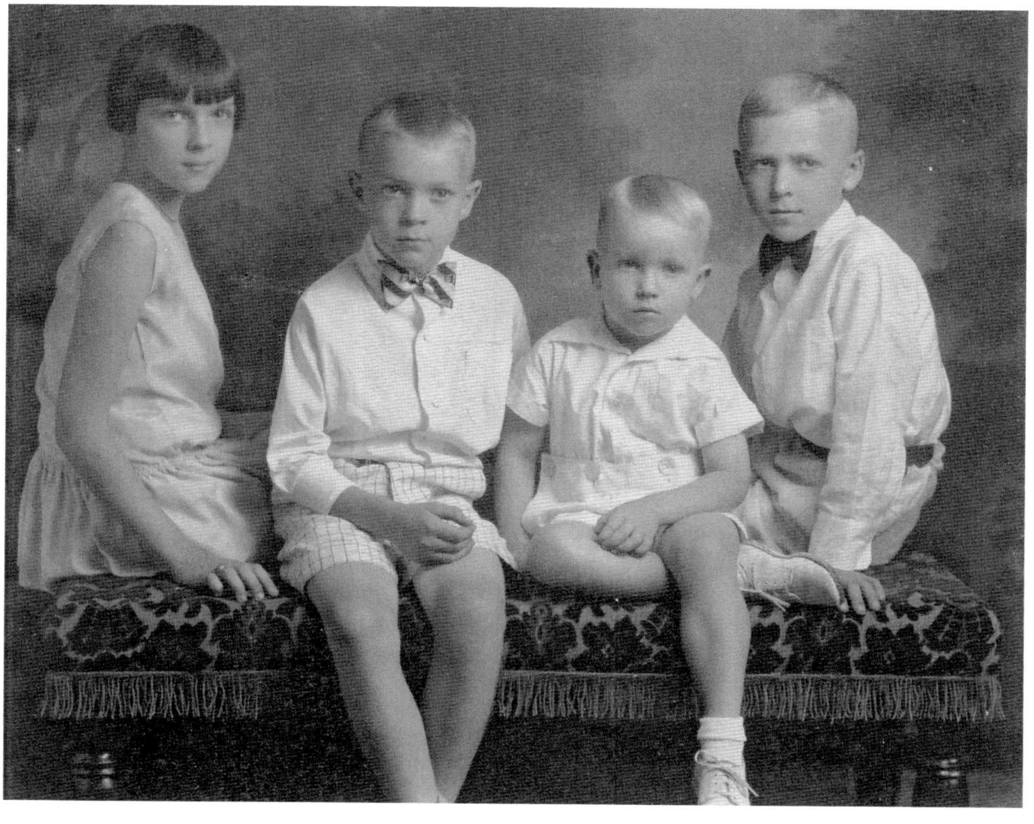

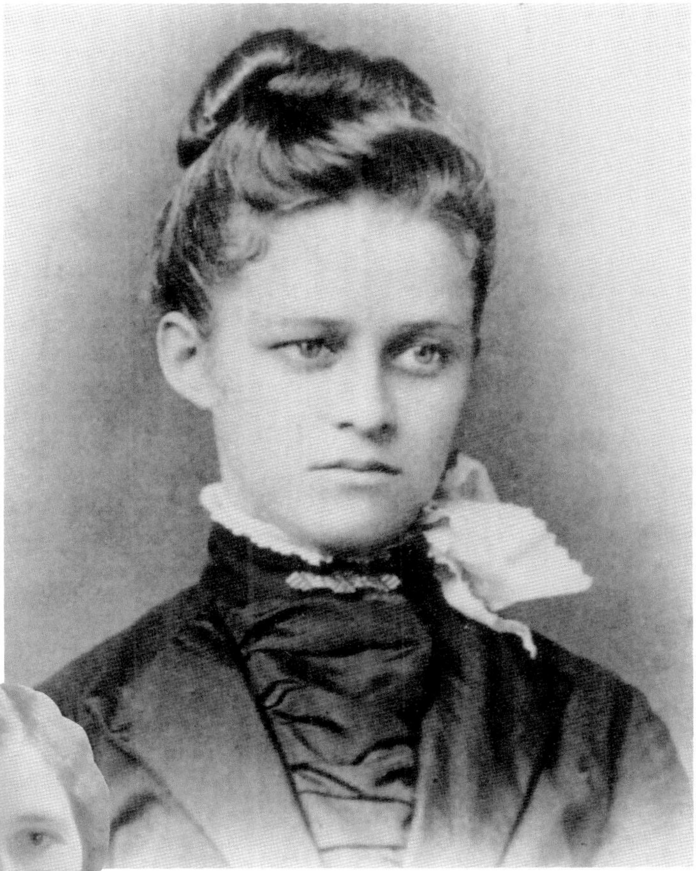

Frenchie Beeco Taylor
Taylor was James P. Taylor's second wife. His first wife Jessie Ann Moon died soon after the birth of their first child. Five more sons were born of this union to give Taylor six sons. They lived and grew peaches in the Fairview community. (Courtesy of Karolyn and Richard Taylor.)

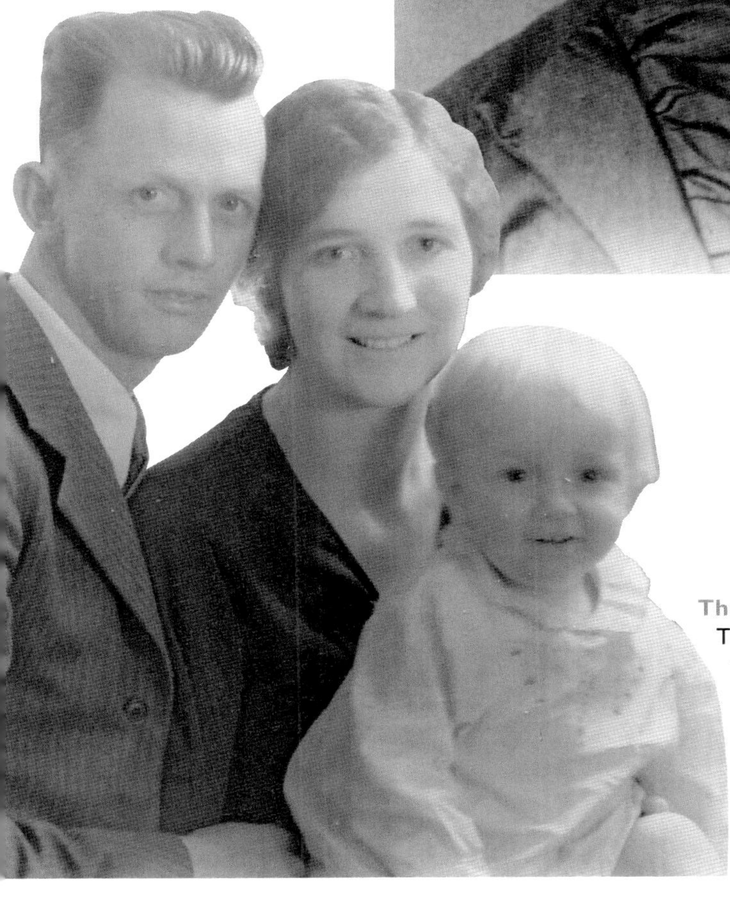

The Taylor Family
This formal portrait of the Taylor family shows Earle, Thelma, and Richard as a baby. Earle continued to grow peaches in the orchards that his father had established. Richard would be the last generation to run the Taylor Orchards. (Courtesy of Karolyn and Richard Taylor.)

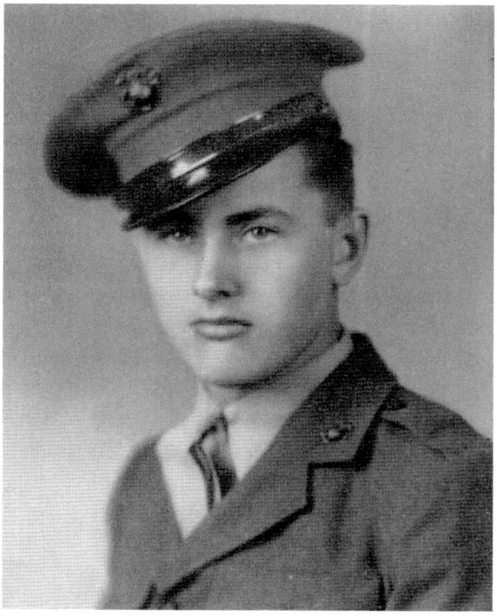

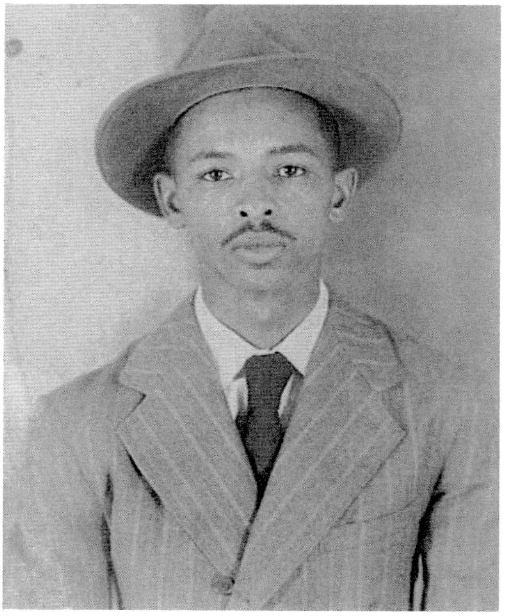

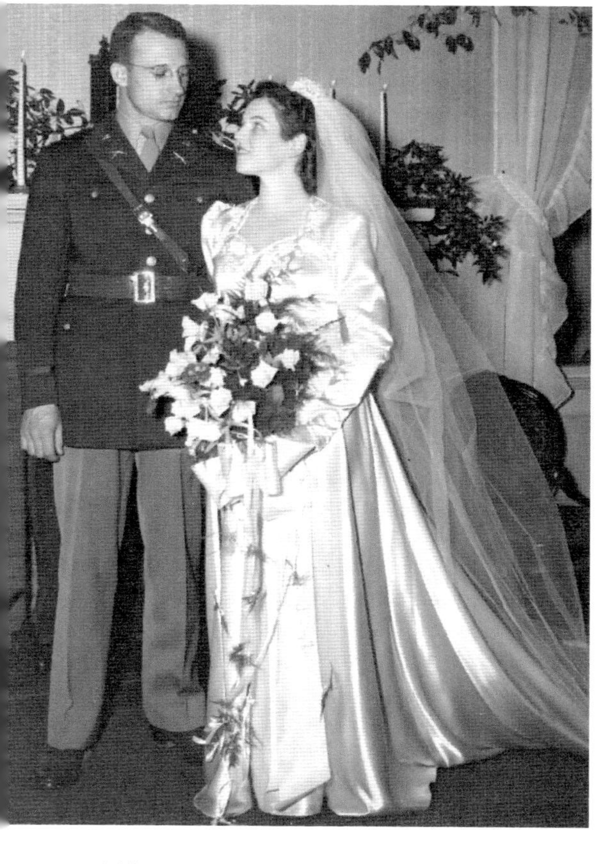

Fred Carman (ABOVE LEFT)
This formal portrait was made upon Carman's completion of basic training. He served with the Marines in the South Pacific where he was wounded in action against the Japanese during the Battle for Okinawa during the spring of 1945. (Courtesy of Jody Carman.)

Wycliffe Durham (ABOVE)
Following in his father's footsteps, Durham attended Harbison Institute, a Presbyterian college for black students in Irmo, South Carolina. This is his 1937 graduation picture. After college, he taught agriculture and became a school principal. (Courtesy of Margaret Durham Hill.)

Clyde and Anne Dobson 1943
Clyde and Anne Dobson were married December 21, 1943, while he was on leave from the US Army. Anne Heath was working with the YWCA when she was invited to speak at Memorial Methodist Church in Greer. Clyde's brother Lawrence and his wife Emily offered to keep Miss Heath during her visit. Thus began a long partnership until Clyde died in 2010. (Courtesy of Anne Dobson.)

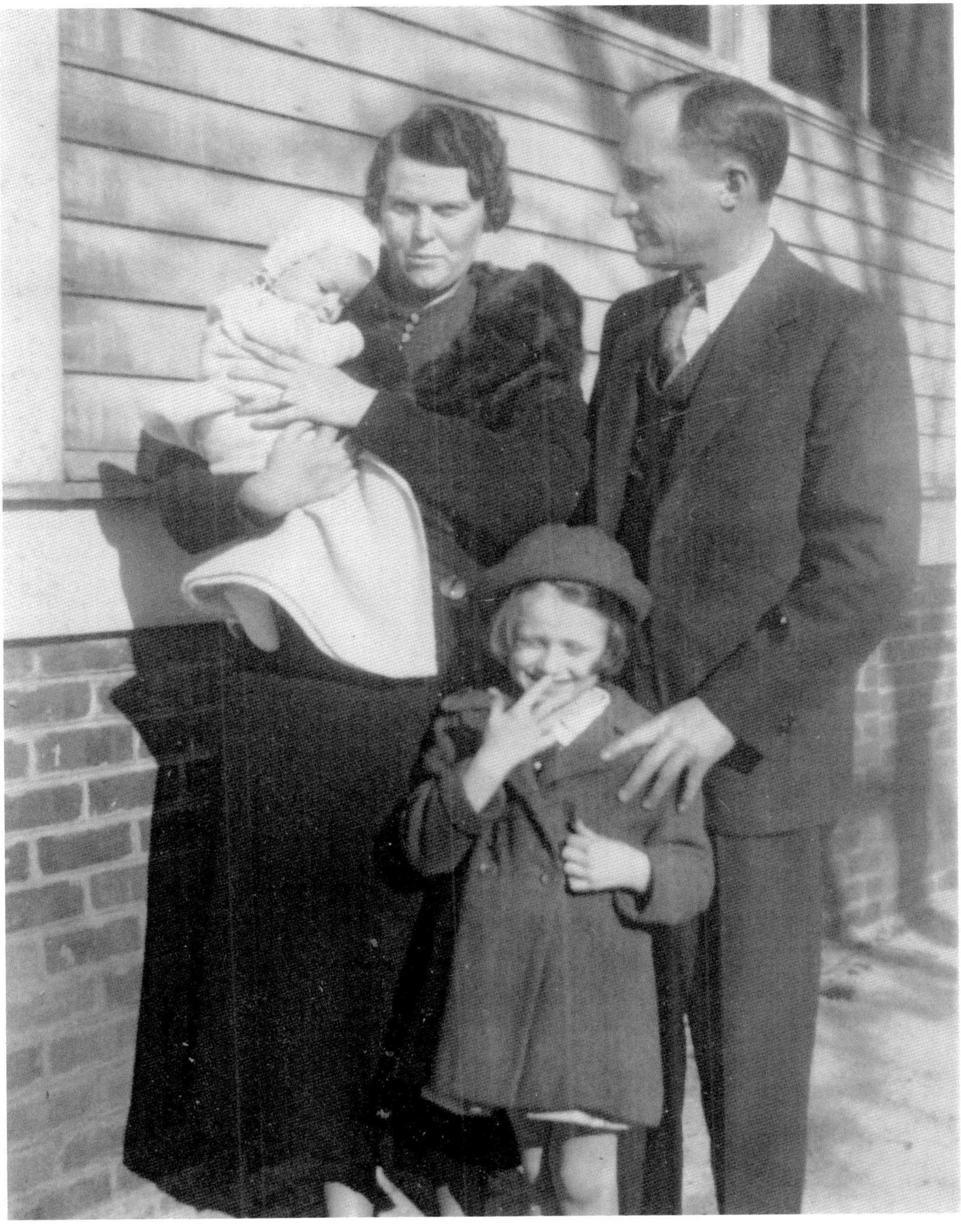

The Kendrick Family

Minnie and Charlie Kendrick are shown here with their daughters, baby Karolyn in her mother's arms and Margaret standing. Charles Kendrick was associated with the Greer Oil Mill along the railroad tracks. Cotton seed was bought by the mill to process into oil. (Courtesy of Karolyn and Richard Taylor.)

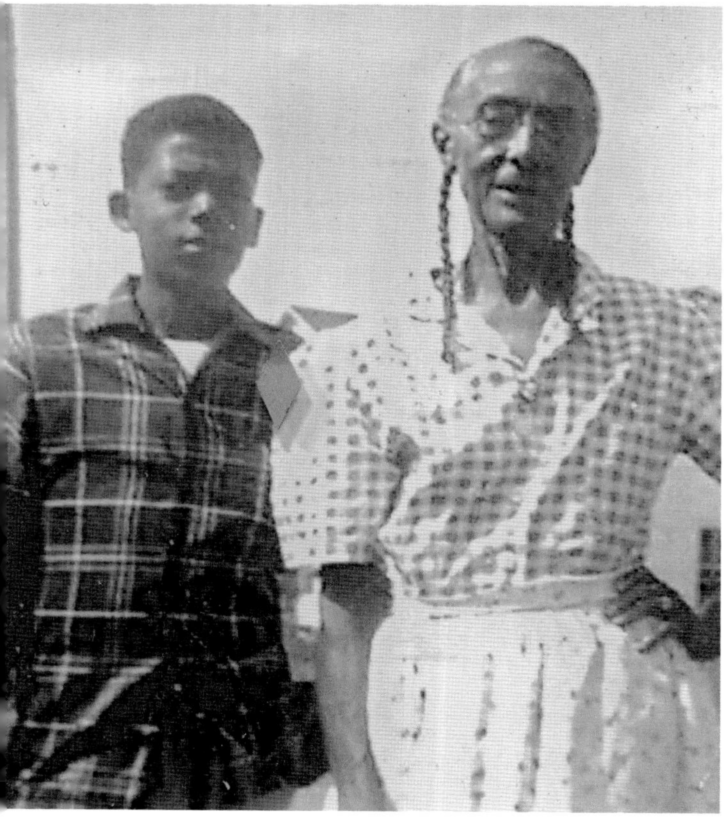

Stella Austin Cox

Cox (1872–1971) had 12 children. She and her grandson Billy Broadus pose in this 1955 picture taken in Sunnyside community. Billy's father James Broadus owned the El Morrocco Café until it burned. The Sunnyside community, one of Greer's early black communities, has produced teachers, ministers, sports figures, businessmen and women, and citizens who have contributed positively to life in Greer. (Courtesy of Nellie Williams.)

The Howard Family

William Green Howard and his wife Cora, who had nine children, are standing to the left behind twins Bobby and Billy Howard. Next to the twins are their sisters Sylvia and Wygenia. Their mother Rometta beside them holds little brother Dan and father Jake is behind her. The family operated a gas station, tourist cabins, and a taxi service based at the Sanitary Café near the depot to pick up travelers. (Courtesy of Bobby Howard.)

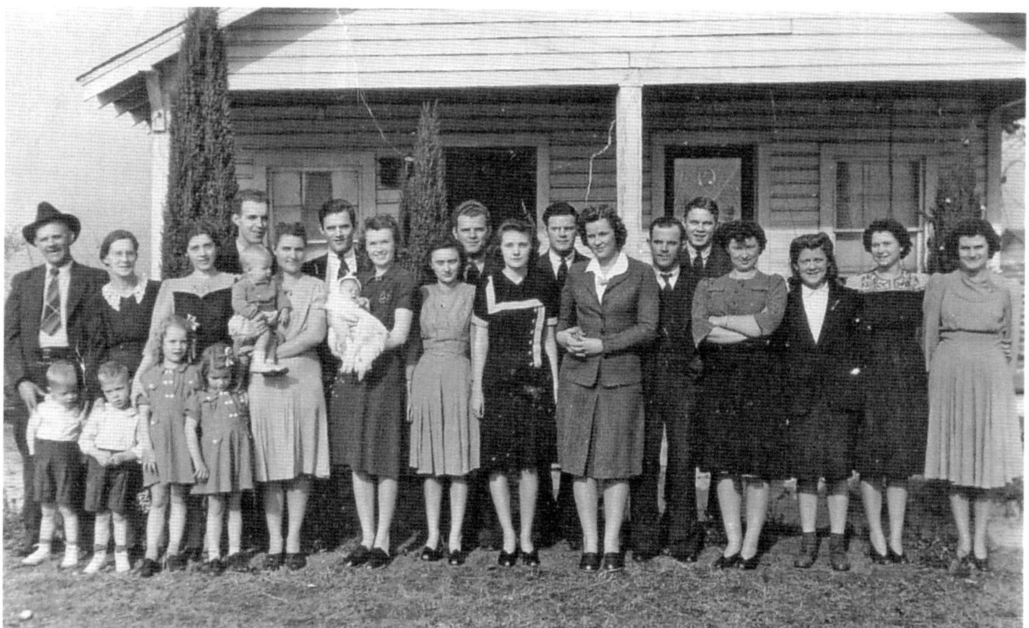

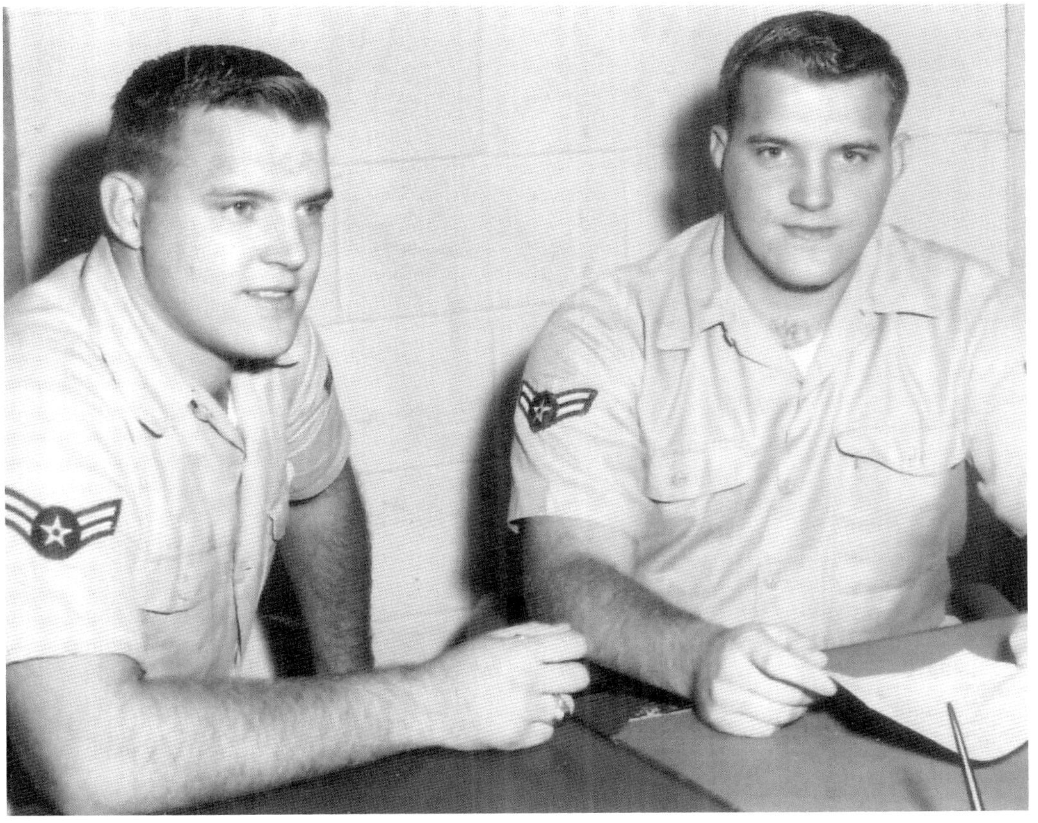

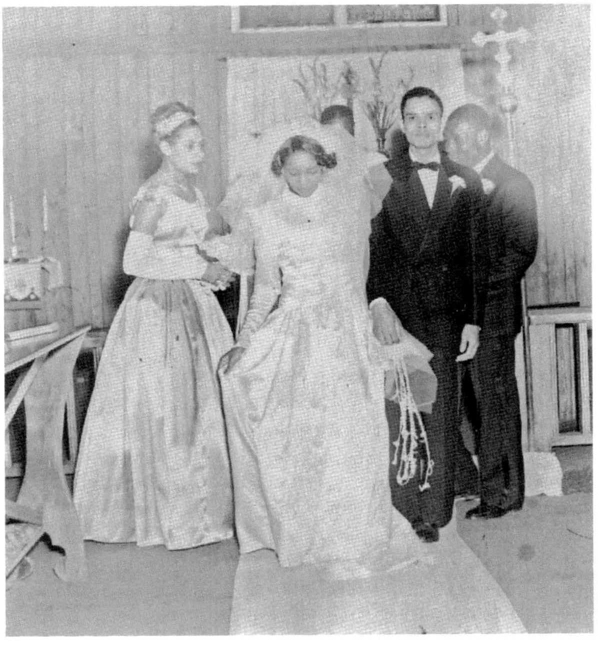

Billy and Bobby Howard
Twins Billy and Bobby Howard did things together. They played on the 1956 State Champion Greer High School football team, and then later joined the US Air Force together. Bobby (left) is retired after a successful teaching career at the Swofford Career Center, and Billy, who is a minister, received his doctor of divinity degree. They are the sons of Jake and Rometta Edwards Howard. (Courtesy of Bobby Howard.)

Benjamin and Massalena Bradford
Massalena Durham married Benjamin Bradford in Charleston, South Carolina. Her attendant to her left is her new sister-in-law Charlotte Bradford. His best man is not identified. (Courtesy of Margaret Durham Hill.)

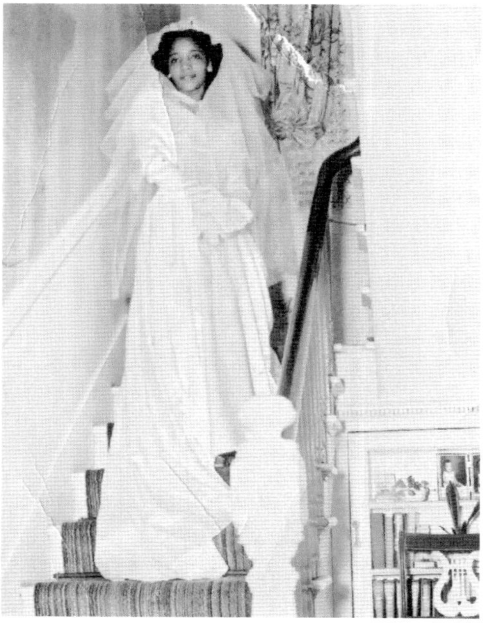

Massalena Durham
Durham was a beautiful bride on her wedding day in 1945 when she married Benjamin Bradford. She was the daughter of the Reverend Joseph Carver Durham and his wife Denver Allie Bivins Durham. Joseph Durham was a minister, teacher, and farmer who reared 14 children. Massalena graduated from Gammon Theological Seminary in Atlanta, Georgia. (Courtesy of Margaret Durham Hill.)

The James Stokes Family
The Stokes family proudly poses for their picture in 1911. Shown left to right are Cora, mother Rebecca Babb Stokes holding baby Louie James, father James Alexander Stokes, and Etta. They farmed along Jordan Road. (Courtesy of Elaine Stokes Bishop.)

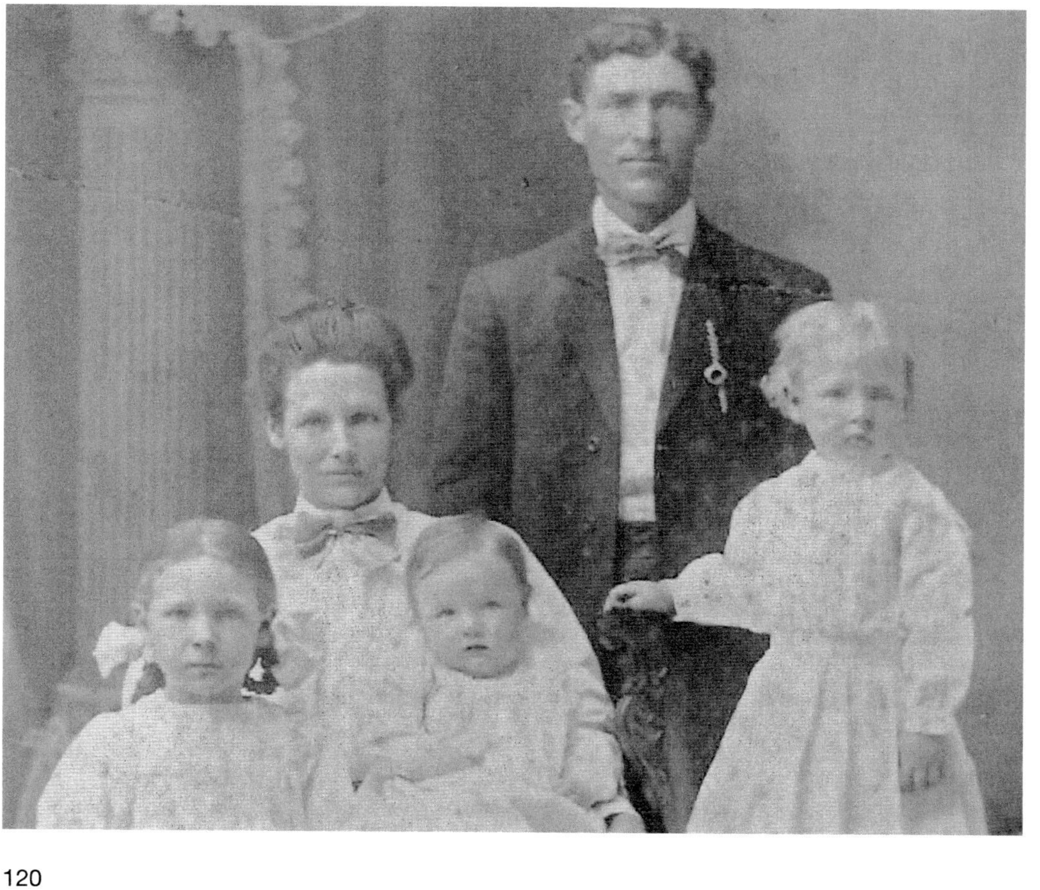

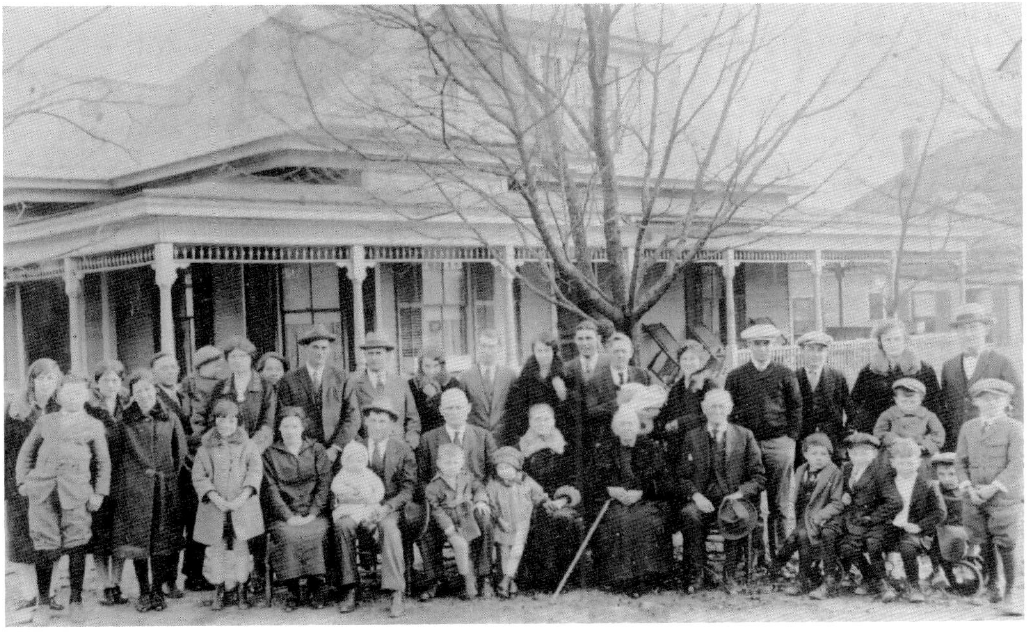

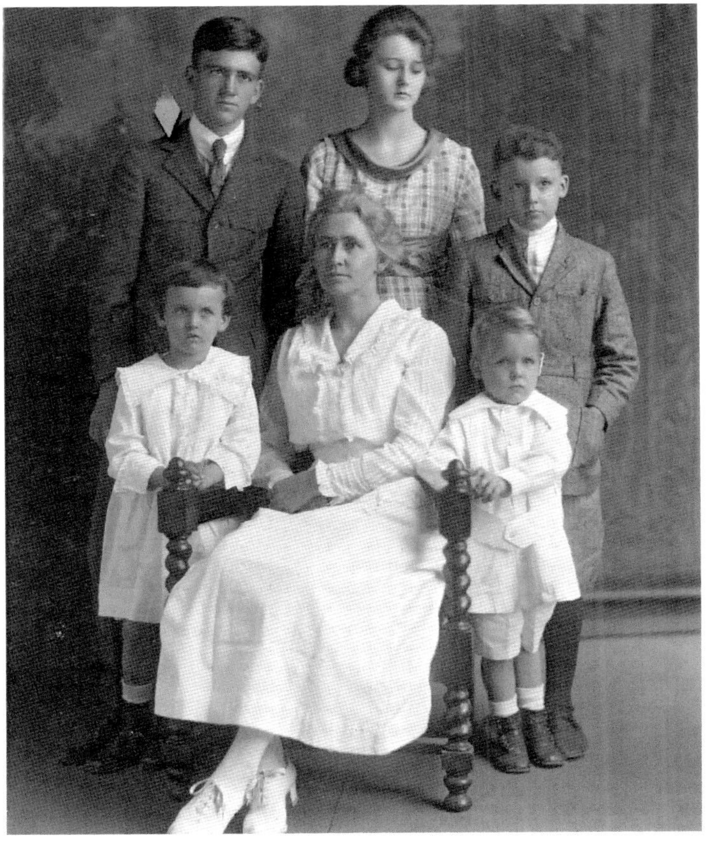

The Stokes Family Reunion 1911
The Stokes family gathered at the home place on Line Street on December 25, 1911, for a family reunion. Henry Stokes (seated sixth from left) had a general store downtown. An existing ledger shows business from 1908 until 1911. His daughter Mary married Robert Turner (back row third from left holding Robert Jr.). (Courtesy of Elaine Stokes Bishop.)

The Davenport Family
In this formal portrait, Clare Davenport is surrounded by her children. Pictured from left to right are (front row) Martha, Clare, and Dan (father of George and Denby Davenport); (back row) Pete, Constance, and Malcolm. (Courtesy of Denby Davenport.)

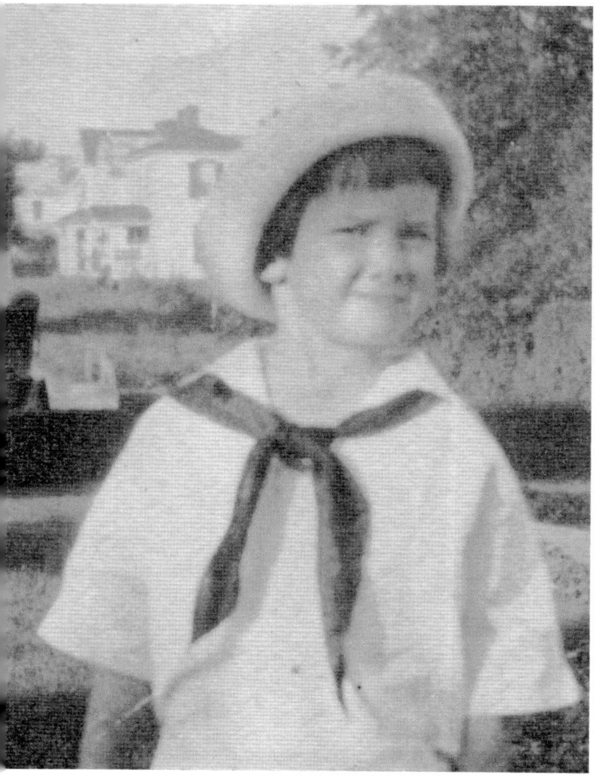

Allen Bennett
Little did Allen Bennett know when he posed in his sailor suit that he would serve in World War II as a naval surgeon aboard the destroyer USS *Cooper*. He was born in Greer on December 31, 1913. After he graduated from VMI, he studied medicine at the University of Virginia and served a surgical residency at Doctor's Hospital in Washington, DC. (Courtesy of Allen Cullum.)

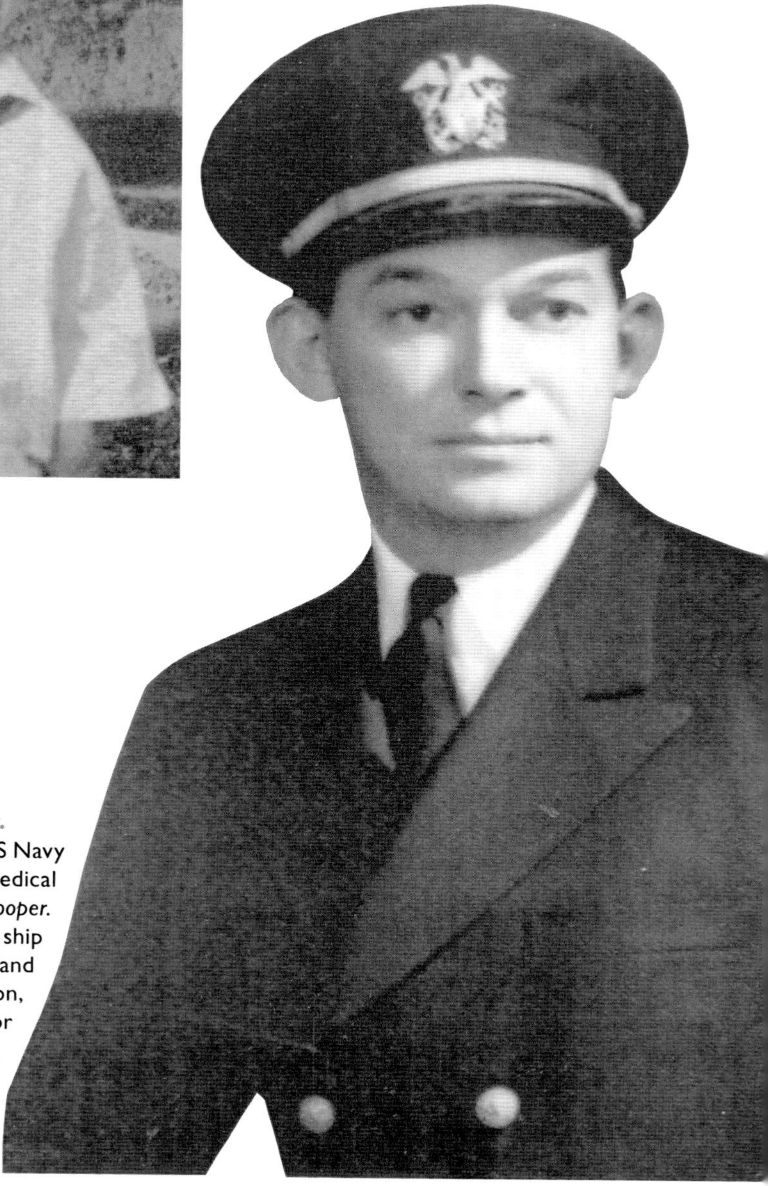

Dr. Belton Allen Bennett Jr.
In 1943, Bennett entered the US Navy and was assigned as chief medical officer aboard the destroyer *Cooper*. On December 3, 1944, his ship was torpedoed in Ormoc Bay and he was killed. To honor his son, B.A. Bennett donated land for a hospital in Greer. On May 1, 1952, Allen Bennett Hospital was dedicated in memory of Dr. Bennett. (Courtesy of Allen Cullum.)

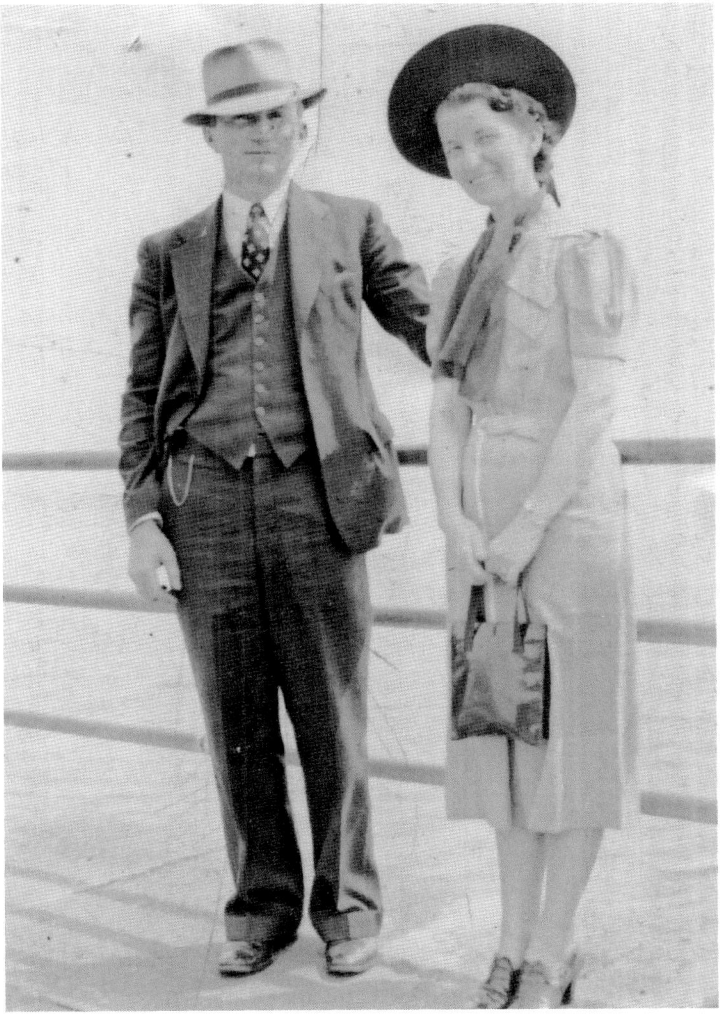

Palmer and Constance Dillard 1939
Newlyweds Palmer and Constance Dillard pose for their picture just after they married on May 14, 1939. Constance was a schoolteacher and Palmer was a peach orchardist. Dillard planted his first orchard of Elberta peach trees in 1923. (Courtesy of Ann Dillard Withrow.)

The Hughes Family
Dr, James Langston Hughes and his wife Helen whom he married in 1934 sit in the midst of their children and grandchildren. Their six children are Dr. Rick Hughes, Edith Hughes Horner, Miriam Hughes Owens, Dr. Jim Hughes, Alan Hughes, and Tommy Hughes. (Courtesy of the Hughes family.)

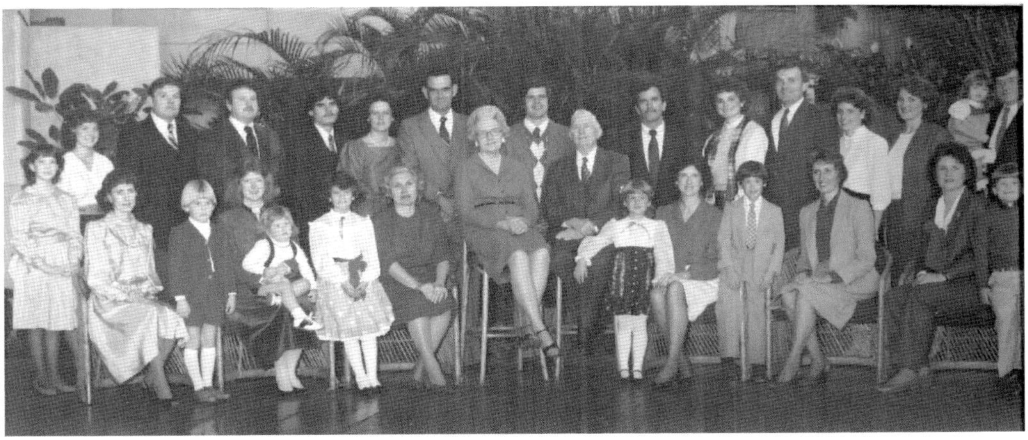

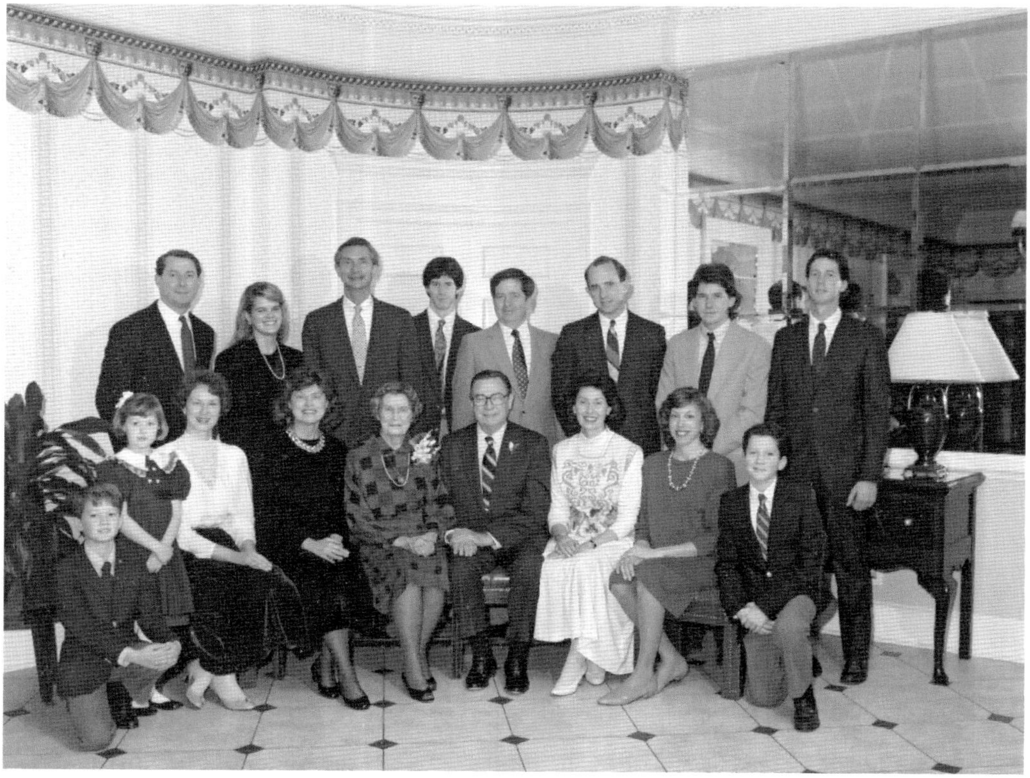

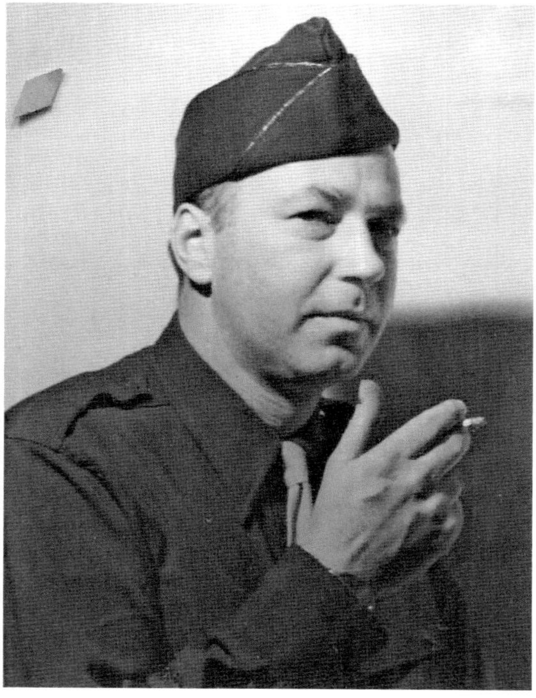

The Griffin Family

The Griffin Family in 1989 are (front row left to right) Hayne P. Griffin III, Elizabeth Griffin, Virginia Griffin, Camille Graham Camp, Elsie Griffin, Hayne Preston Griffin, Margaret Griffin Burch, Ruth Harrill Griffin, and John David Burch; (back row left to right) Hayne Griffin, Jr., Camelia Graham, George Camp, Preston Burch, Leland Burch, Gary Griffin, Joey Burch, and Eddie Burch. (Courtesy of Margaret & Leland Burch.)

Winfield R. Walkley

Walkley (1909–1954) of New York worked for the Treasury Relief Art Project that employed artists during the Great Depression. He was commissioned to create a mural for the Greer Post Office. His 1940 mural, "Cotton and Peach Growing," can be seen in Greer's museum today. During World War II, he served in the Office of War Information as an artist-offset technician. (Courtesy of Milda Walkley and Susan Topper.)

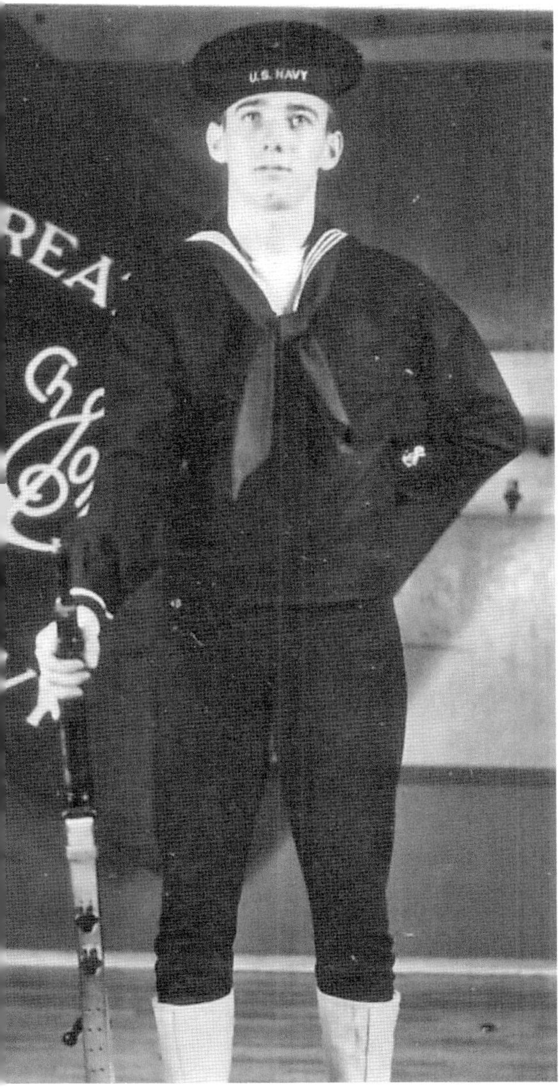

William H. "Bill" Jordan 1943

Jordan played in the first Greer High School Band. In 1943, he joined the US Navy and became a member of the Blue Jacket Choir. This picture was made at Great Lakes Naval Training Center. After a long career first as a music teacher and then as a minister of music, he retired to Greer. (Courtesy of William Jordan.)

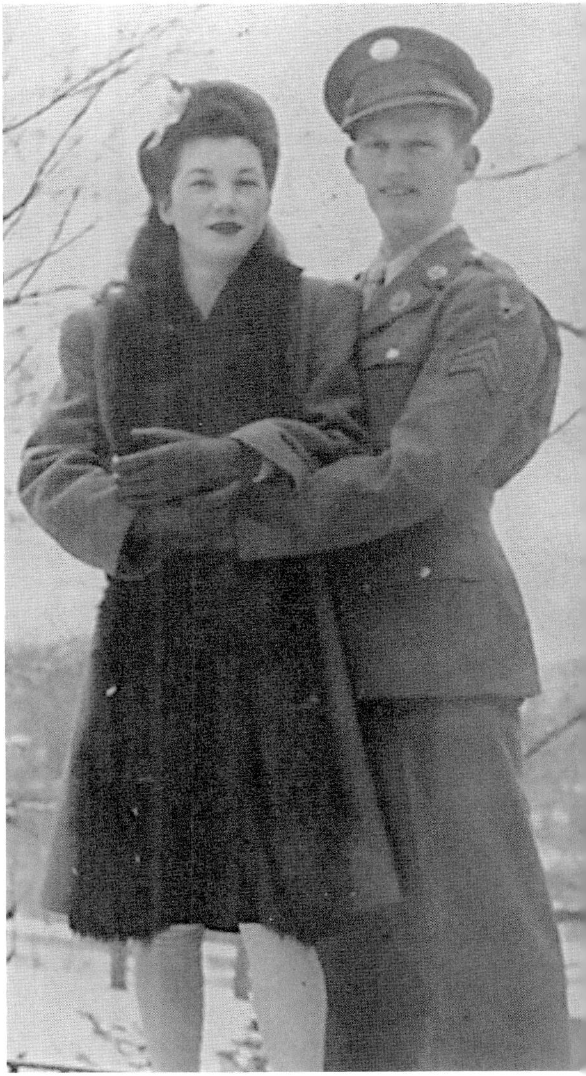

Nathan and Audrey Jordan

Nathan Jordan, a salesman for Standard Candy Company, moved his family to Greer in 1934 from Georgia. The Jordan family, who lived on North Main Street, sent three sons to World War II—Nathan, William, and Richard. Staff Sergeant Nathan Jr. poses here with his sister Audrey Mary on his last visit home to Greer. He died in 1944 on a battlefield in France. (Courtesy of William Jordan.)

INDEX